JOHN CLARE

and

OTHER STUDIES

JOHN MIDDLETON MURRY

JOHN CLARE
and
OTHER STUDIES

PETER NEVILL LIMITED
London *New York*

KRAUS REPRINT CO.
New York
1968

PETER NEVILL LIMITED
50 Old Brompton Road
London   SW7   and
122 East 55th Street, New
York 22   N Y

L.C. Catalog Card Number A51-8983.

KRAUS REPRINT CO.
A U.S. Division of Kraus-Thomson Organization Limited

Printed in U.S.A.

CONTENTS

PREFACE

With this volume begins the republication of a series of critical essays I wrote between twenty and thirty years ago. In their original form they passed through several editions. Then, owing to the paper shortage, they could not be kept in print, and the copyright automatically reverted to me. Owing to the kindly initiative of Messrs. Peter Nevill Ltd., I am now in a position to republish them, differently arranged and under different titles.

The only ones of those collected into the present volume which have undergone any substantial alteration are on *The Creation of Falstaff*, *Coriolanus* and *The Mortal Moon*. From the others I have merely made a few deletions.

Thelnetham,

June 5, 1949.

THE POETRY OF JOHN CLARE

In 1820 Messrs. Taylor & Hessey published two books whose immediate renown was in singular contrast with their after-fame. *Poems Descriptive of Rural Life and Scenery*, by John Clare, a Northamptonshire Peasant, ran into four editions within a year; the five hundred copies of the single edition of *Lamia, Isabella, and other Poems,* by John Keats, were not exhausted till the 'forties. Clare's popularity dwindled gradually into complete neglect; he had been all but forgotten by the time that Monckton Milnes assumed the practical task of impressing upon the world the conviction of the poets that Keats was among the greatest. Quickly the labours of piety were accomplished; within a few years Keats's poetical remains were gathered together, until nothing substantial remained to be added. Clare went on writing indefatigably in the exile of an asylum for nearly thirty years after he had been forgotten, and not till 1920 did Mr. Edmund Blunden set himself to the task of rescuing all that is valuable in his work.[1]

It is not merely because the year and the publishers were the same that we are drawn to think of Keats and Clare together. The association of the great name and the small one has a curious congruity. Keats and Clare both suffered a vast shipwreck of their life's esteem, the one sudden and intolerably tragic, the other lingering and not without a sunset-haze of vaguely remembered happiness. There were elements common to their characters—they were both parvenus in the ranks of men of letters, and they shared a resolution and an independence which became almost intolerant; Keats had an unusual, and Clare a unique knowledge of country sights and sounds; the most perfect poem of each is an *Ode to Autumn.*

We are inclined to lay stress on the points of resemblance in order that the cardinal point of difference may more plainly appear; for the eagerness with which we welcome this collection of Clare's poetry is likely to be so genuine and so justified as to disturb our sense of proportion. Into a generation of poets who

[1] *John Clare Poems*: Chiefly from M.S. selected and edited by Edmund Blunden and Alan Porter.

7

flirt with nature suddenly descends a true nature-poet, one whose intimate and self-forgetful knowledge of the ways of birds and beasts and flowers rises like the scent of a hay-field from every page. Surely the only danger is that the enthusiasm of our recognition may be excessive; the relief overpowering with which we greet a poet who not only professes, but proves by the very words of his profession, that his dream of delight is

> To note on hedgerow baulks, in moisture sprent,
> The jetty snail creep from the mossy thorn,
> With earnest heed and tremulous intent,
> Frail brother of the morn,
> That from the tiny bents and misted leaves
> Withdraws his timid horn,
> And fearful vision weaves.

We have indeed almost to be on our guard against the sweet, cool shock of such a verse; the emotional quality is so assured and individual, the language so simple and inevitable, the posture of mind so unassuming and winning, that one is tempted for a moment to believe that while Wordsworth was engaged in putting the poetry of nature wrong by linking it to a doubtful metaphysic, John Clare was engaged in putting it right.

And so in a sense it was. As a poet of nature Clare was truer, more thoroughly subdued to that in which he worked than Wordsworth. Wordsworth called upon the poet to keep his eye upon the object; but his eye was hardly so penetrating and keen as Clare's. Yet Wordsworth was a great poet, and Keats, with whom Clare's kinship was really closer, was a great poet, and Clare was not; and it is important in the case of a poet whose gifts and qualities are so enchanting as Clare's are to bear in mind from the outset the vital difference between them. Wordsworth belongs to another sphere than Clare in virtue of the range of his imaginative apprehension: Keats in virtue not only of his imagination, but also of his art. In one respect Clare was a finer artist than Wordsworth, he had a truer ear and a more exquisite instinct for the visualizing word; but he had nothing of the principle of inward growth which gives to Wordsworth's most careless work a place within the unity of a great scheme. Wordsworth's incessant effort to comprehend

8

experience would itself have been incomprehensible to Clare; Keats's consuming passion to make his poetry adequate not merely in content but also in the very mechanism of expression to an emotional experience more overwhelming even than Wordsworth's would have seemed to him like a problem of metaphysics to a ploughboy.

Clare was indeed a singer born. His nature was strangely simple, and his capacity for intense emotion appears at first sight to have been almost completely restricted to a response to nature. The intensity with which he adored the country that he knew is without a parallel in English literature; of him it seems hardly a metaphor to say he was an actual part of his countryside. Away from it he pined; he became queer and irresponsible. With his plants and birds and bees and fields he was among his own people. The spiked thistle, the firetail, the hare, the white-nosed and the grand-father bee were his friends. Yet he hardly humanized them; he seems rather to have lived on the same level of existence as they, and to have known them as they know each other. We feel that it is only by an effort that he manages to make himself conscious of his emotion towards them or of his own motive in singing of it. In those rare moments he conceives of the voice of Nature as something eternal, outlasting all generations of men, whispering to them to sing also. Thus, while he sits under the huge old elm which is the shepherd's tree, listening to 'the laugh of summer leaves above',

> The wind of that eternal ditty sings,
> Humming of future things that burn the mind
> To leave some fragment of itself behind.

That is the most imaginative statement Clare ever made of his own poetic purpose. He, the poet, is one more of Nature's voices; and the same thought or the same instinct underlies the most exquisite of his earlier poems, *Song's Eternity*, a precious discovery of his present editors:

> Mighty songs that miss decay,
>   What are they?
> Crowds and cities pass away
>   Like a day.

9

Books are out and books are read;
   What are they?
Years will lay them with the dead—
   Sigh, sigh;
Trifles unto nothing wed,
   They die.

Dreamers, mark the honey bee,
   Mark the tree
Where the bluecap *tootle-tee*
   Sings a glee
Sung to Adam and to Eve—
   Here they be.
When floods covered every bough
   Noah's ark
Heard that ballad singing now;
   Hark, hark,

Tootle tootle tootle tee.
   Can it be
Pride and fame must shadows be?
   Come and see—
Every season owns her own;
   Bird and bee
Sing creation's music on;
   Nature's glee
Is in every mood and tone
   Eternity.

In many ways that is the most perfect of Clare's poems; it has
a poetic unity of a kind that he attained but seldom, for in it
are naturally combined the highest apprehension of which Clare
was capable and the essential melody of his pre-eminent gift of
song. It is at once an assertion and an emotional proof of the
enduringness of the voice of Nature. Clare does not, like the
modern poet who has chosen the same theme, adduce the
times and the seasons and thereby challenge the evolutionary
theory; his history is the history of myth. Not the Neanderthal
man but Adam and Eve heard the bluecap's same immortal
song; for it is not the fact, but the sense of song's eternity that

10

the poet has to give us. Clare does it triumphantly. Moreover, in this poem, which we believe must henceforward take its place by right in every anthology of English poetry, Clare achieved that final perfection of form which was so often to elude him.The bird-note begins, rises, dies away: and the poem is finished.

Clare's music was a natural music; as with Shelley's skylark, his art was unpremeditated and his strains profuse. He was perhaps never to find a form which fitted his genius so intimately as that of *Song's Eternity*. His language was to become more coherent and more vivid; but the inward harmony that is essential to a great poem was too often to escape him. He was like a child so intoxicated with his wonderful gift for whistling and with his tune that he whistled it over and over again. The note is so pure, the tune so full of delight that we can never be tired; we listen to it as we listen to the drowsy enchantment of the monotony of sounds on a summer's afternoon, for it is as authentic and as sweet as they. The eternity of song was in Clare's blood; and when he recurs to the theme of enduring nature in simple stanzas,

> Some sing the pomps of chivalry
> As legends of the ancient time,
> Where gold and pearls and mystery
> Are shadows painted for sublime;
>
> But passions of sublimity
> Belong to plain and simpler things,
> And David underneath a tree
> Sought when a shepherd Salem's springs,
>
> Where moss did into cushions spring,
> Forming a seat of velvet hue,
> A small unnoticed trifling thing
> To all but heaven's hailing dew.
>
> And David's crown hath passed away,
> Yet poesy breathes his shepherd skill,
> His palace lost and to this day
> A little moss is blossoming still,

we feel that here, too, is a music that need never end.

Clare's difficulty as a poet, in fact, can and ought to be put baldly; he did not know when to stop. Why, indeed, should he stop? He was either a voice, one of the unending voices of

Nature, or he was an eye, an unwearied eye watching the infinite process of Nature; perhaps never a poet consciously striving by means of art to arouse in men's minds an emotion like his own. All the art he had was that which he gained from his recollection of other poets' tunes; the structure of their harmony eluded him, he remembered only the melodies. Take, for instance, his extremely beautiful *Autumn*: the melody comes directly from Collins's famous *Ode*; yet how greatly Clare enriches it, as though with a material golden stain of autumn! The last leaf seems to be falling at our feet, the last bee zooming in our ears.

> Heart-sickening for the silence that is thine,
> Not broken inharmoniously as now
>   That lone and vagrant bee
>   Booms faint with weary chime.
> Now filtering winds thin winnow through the woods
> In tremulous noise that bids at every breath
>   Some sickly cankered leaf
>   Let go its hold, and die.

Not only these, but any one of a dozen other stanzas in the poem have a richer mellowness, reveal a finer sensitiveness than any in Collins's lovely *Ode*. For all that the melody derives from Collins, we are borne away from him to the neighbourhood of Keats's great poem. But Collins had a classical, almost Miltonic, sense of form; what he lacked in the richness of direct perception he supplied by his careful concentration of emotional effect: so that, despite the more splendid beauty of the elements of Clare's poem, we dare not say it is really as fine as Collins's *Ode*. Collins gathers up all his more exiguous perceptions into a single stimulus to emotion: Clare lets them fall one by one, careless of his amazing jewels. Set his *Autumn* against Keat's three strophes, where the imagination has come to crystallize perceptions not less rich in themselves than Clare's into a single symbol—the very spirit of Autumn.

> Who hath not seen thee oft amid thy store?
>   Sometimes whoever seeks abroad may find
> Thee sitting careless on a granary floor
>   Thy hair soft lifted by the winnowing wind;
> Or on a half-reaped furrow sound asleep
>   Drowsed with the fume of poppies, while thy hook

12

Spares the next swathe and all its twined flowers;
And sometimes like a gleaner thou dost keep
  Steady thy laden head across a brook
  Or by a cyder-press, with patient look,
Thou watchest the last oozings hours by hours.

Clare could not do that; for Keats had Collins's art and Clare's richness of perception, and he had also that incomparable imaginative power which alone can create the perfect symbol of an overwhelming and intricate emotion.

Yet we need to invoke Keats to explain Clare, and to understand fully why his wealth of perception was refined into so few perfect poems. Collins himself is not sufficient for the purpose; one cannot well invoke the success of a poorer to explain the failure of a richer nature. Keats, the great poetic artist, however, subsumes Clare. Careless critics, confusing the life of every day with the life of the poetic mind, rebuke Keats for his lack of discipline. Yet where in English poetry shall we find a power of poetic discipline greater than his, a more determined and inevitable compulsion of the whole of a poet's emotional experience into the single symbol, the one organic and inevitable form? In him were combined miraculously the humanity that can reject no element of true experience and the artistic integrity to which less than a complete mastery and transformation of experience is intolerable. When, therefore, we invoke Keats to explain Clare, when we feel the need to merge Clare into Keats in thought in order that we may discover his own poetic fulfilment, by completing the great pattern of which he is a fragment, we are passing a judgment upon the value and quality of Clare's own work of which the implications are unescapable. It is a fragment, but it is a fragment of the Parthenon pediment, of intrinsic value, unique, and beyond price.

Clare's qualities were authentic and without alloy. It was the power to refine and shape his metal that was denied him; his workshop is littered not with dross but with veritable gold—of melody, of an intensity of perception (truly, his 'mind was burned'), and, more rarely, of flashes of that passion of the pure imagination which is the mysterious source of the magic of poetry. Let our partial quotation of *Song's Eternity* suffice to prove the quality of his spontaneous melody. For the intensity of perception we may choose at random any page in this book.

13

Is not a picture such as this cast upon 'that inward eye'?

> Where squats the hare to terrors wide awake
> Like some brown clod the harrows failed to break.

Such things are scattered throughout Clare; they range from the quiet vision of the actual, focused by a single word, such as

> The old pond with its water-weed
> And danger-daring willow tree,
> Who leans, an ancient invalid,
> O'er spots where deepest waters be,

to the authentic fancy of

> Here morning in the ploughman's songs is met
> Ere yet one footstep shows in all the sky,
> And twilight in the East, a doubt as yet,
> Shows not her sleeve of gray to know her by.

How perfect is the image, as perfect to its context and emotion as the 'sovran eye' of Shakespeare's sun! And what of the intense compression of a phrase like 'ploughed lands thin travelled by half-hungry sheep', precise not merely to a fact, but to an emotion?

This unmistakable core of pure emotion lies close to the surface throughout Clare. His precision is the precision of a lover; he watches nature as a man might watch his mistress's eyes; his breath is bated, and we seem to hear the very thumping of his heart, and there are moments when the emotion seems to rise in a sudden fountain and change the thing he sees into a jewel. 'Frail brother of the morn' to a jetty snail is the tender cry of a passionate lover; there is a delicateness in the emotion expressed which not even Wordsworth could attain when he called upon the Lesser Celandine. It is love of this kind that gives true significance to the poetry of nature, for only by its alchemy can the thing seen become the symbol of the thing felt: washed by the magic tide of an overwhelming emotion, the object shines with a pure and lucid radiance, transformed from a cause to a symbol of delight, and thus no longer delighting the senses and the emotions alone, but the mind. This mysterious faculty is not indeed the highest kind of poetic imagination, in which the intellect plays a greater part in the creation of the symbol; this emotional creation leaps from particular to par-

14

ticular, it lacks that endorsement from a centre of disciplined experience which is the mark of the poetic imagination at its highest: but it is purely poetic and truly creative.

In this authentic kind Clare was all but a master, and it may even be suspected that his unique gift would have suffered if he had possessed that element of technical control which would have made him a master indeed. For when we come to define as narrowly as we can the distinctive, compelling quality of his emotion, we find that in addition to tenderness we need the word impulsive. Clare's most beautiful poetry is a gesture of impulsive tenderness. It has a curious suddenness, almost a catch in the voice.

> The very darkness smiles to wear
> The stars that show us God is there.

We find, too, a still more authentic mark of the tenderness of impulsive love in his way of seeing his birds and beasts as ever so little absurd. 'Absurd' has a peculiar and delightful meaning in the converse of lovers; Clare's firetail is 'absurd' in precisely the same sense.

> Of everything that stirs she dreameth wrong,
> And pipes her 'tweet-tut' fears the whole day long.

And so, too, are his bees—the 'grandfather bee', the wild bees who 'with their legs stroke slumber from their eyes', 'the little bees with coal-black faces, gathering sweets from little flowers like stars'; even the riddle of the quail appears to be rather a delicate and loveable waywardness in the bird than a mere ignorance in the man.

> Among the stranger birds they feed,
> Their summer flight is short and low:
> There's very few know where they breed
> And scarcely any where they go.

A tenderness of this exquisite and impulsive kind might have been damaged as much as strengthened by a firmer technical control; a shiver of constraint might have crept into the gesture itself and chilled it; and perhaps we may touch the essential nature of Clare's emotion most closely in the mysterious and haunting Asylum poem, discovered by the present editors, and by them *Secret Love*.

15

I hid my love when young till I
Couldn't bear the buzzing of a fly;
I hid my love to my despite
Till I could not bear to look at light:
I dare not gaze upon her face
But left her memory in each place;
Where'er I saw a wild flower lie
I kissed and bade my love good-bye.

I met her in the greenest dells
Where dewdrops pearl the wood blue bells.
The lost breeze kissed her bright blue eye.
The bee kissed and went singing by;
A sunbeam found a passage there,
A gold chain round her neck so fair;
As secret as the wild bee's song
She lay there all the summer long.

I hid my love in field and town
Till e'en the breeze would knock me down.
The bees seemed singing ballads o'er,
The fly's bass turned a lion's roar;
And even silence found a tongue
To haunt me all the summer long;
The riddle nature could not prove
Was nothing else but secret love.

Clare is invoking the memory of Mary Joyce, the girl lover
whom he did not marry, and who, though long since dead,
lived for him as his true wife when he was immured in the
asylum. But the fact of this strange passion is less remarkable
than its precise quality; it is an intolerable tenderness, an unbearable surge of emotion eager to burst forth and lavish itself
upon an object. Whether it was his passion for Mary Joyce
which first awakened him to an awareness of the troublous
depths of emotion within we cannot tell, for this poem is in
itself no evidence of fact. But it bears witness unmistakable
to the quality of the emotion which underlay all that is characteristic and unforgettable in his poetry.

When we have touched the unique emotional core which
consists throughout the work of a true poet, we have come
perhaps as near as we can to his secret. We stand as it were

16

at the very source of his creation. In the great poetic artist we may follow out the intricacies and ramifications of the intellectual structure by which he makes the expression of his central emotion complete, and the emotion itself permanent. In Clare the work is unnecessary. The emotion is hardly mediated at all. The poetic creation is instinctive and impulsive; the love is poured out, and the bird, the beast, the flower is made glorious. It is the very process which Stendahl described as *la cristallisation de l'amour*.

We may therefore most truly describe Clare as the love poet of nature; and we need not pause to explore the causes why nature and not a human being was not turned to crystal by the magical process of his love. Those who care to know may find the story woven in among the narrative of Mr. Blunden's sympathetic introduction; they can discover for themselves the reason why Clare appears in the world of grown men and women as a stranger and a changeling; why the woman of his dreams is disembodied; why, when he calls to her in his *Invitation to Eternity*, the present is 'marred with reason'—

> The land of shadows wilt thou trace,
> Nor look nor know each other's face;
> The present marred with reason gone,
> And past and present both as one?
>
> Say, maiden, can thy life be led
> To join the living and the dead?
> Then trace thy footsteps on with me:
> We are wed to one eternity.

In eternity perhaps a woman, but in the actual Nature was Clare's mistress; her he served and cherished with a tenderness and faithful knowledge unique in the poetry of nature. Like a true lover he stammered in long speeches, but he spoke to her the divinest and most intimate things. Assuredly his lines were cast so that he had no need of woman even in eternity, and perhaps the truest words he ever wrote of himself are those of the poem by which he is most generally known:

> I long for scenes where man has never trod;
>   A place where woman never smiled nor wept;
> There to abide with my creator, God,

17

And sleep as I in childhood sweetly slept:
Untroubling and untroubled where I lie;
The grass below—above the vaulted sky.

[JANUARY, 1921]

THE CASE OF JOHN CLARE

Not many poets justify and repay editorial piety more bountifully than John Clare. Though comparatively few of his poems achieve the beauty of form which is the evidence of completely mastered and related perceptions, scarce one of them is without a strange intrinsic beauty of the perception itself. Clare's sensibility was of the finest and most delicate, and his emotional reponse to nature almost inhumanly sweet and pure. His weakness lay in his power of poetic thought. Inevitably, in reading the precious additions made by Mr. Blunden to his previous collection of Clare's poetry, we are reminded once more, as we were reminded at the time of the first collection, of Wordsworth. Even more than then the comparison of Clare with Wordsworth seems necessary if we are to gain that precise sensation of Clare's individuality, without which it is scarcely possible to know a poet fully. And not only does Wordsworth appear necessary to a criticism of Clare, but Clare to a criticism of Wordsworth. The reference is reciprocal: it is also quite unavoidable. We doubt whether anyone could read, without thinking immediately of Wordsworth, Clare's beautiful poem in this volume on *The Primrose Bank*:

> With its little brimming eye
> And its crimp and curdled leaf
> Who can pass its beauties by?

For here evidently was someone to whom a primrose by the river's brim was in a sense, just a primrose: but it was wholly a primrose, not 'something more' indeed, but altogether itself. 'Its little brimming eye,' 'its crimp and curdled leaf,' are phrases which almost make us hold our breath in order not to disturb the exquisite perfection of their truth. And this truth is of such a kind that it is complete: there is nothing more to be said, and perhaps nothing more to be thought. At least it is hard to imagine that the poet to whose vision a primrose thus appeared, who could express what he saw with an ease and naturalness such that the expression strikes as part of the very act of seeing.

[1]*Madrigals and Chronicles*: Being newly found Poems written by John Clare, edited with a Preface and Commentary by Edmund Blunden.

in whose eyes (it is obvious) 'Solomon in all his glory was not arrayed like one of these,' should ever have thought, or ever have had the impulse to think, about what he saw. The particularity of the created universe was sufficient for him; he saw each several thing in itself as sovereign and beautiful. What more did he need, what more can we ask?

Clare's faculty of sheer vision is unique in English poetry. not only is it far purer than Wordsworth's, it is purer even than Shakespeare's. Or, it might be wiser to say, Shakespeare passed so quickly beyond this stage of pure vision that only traces of it remain. And yet we feel there is an intrinsic impossibility that vision of this kind, so effortless and unparading, should ever pass beyond itself; we feel it must demand so complete an engagement and submission of the whole man that it leaves no margin for other faculties. Clare's vision, we might say paradoxically, is too perfect. Shakespeare had as much of it as a man can have if he is to develop into a full maturity; Wordsworth had some of it. Wordsworth's vision came to him in flashes, therefore it seemed to him an abnormal and extraordinary visitation which needed to be related by thought and meditation to ordinary experience. We may put it in this way: if Wordsworth had seen a primrose as Clare saw it—and he did occasionally see things thus—he would have felt that he was seeing 'into the heart of things,' whereas Clare—who seems always to have seen in this way—felt that he was merely seeing things. It is dangerous to be made after so unusual a pattern, and Clare was locked up.

The penalty was monstrous, an indescribable refinement of torture for this child-man whose very life was seeing things. But it was a cruel approximation made by half knowledge to the truth that Clare was not really a man. Those thoughts, for which his seeing left no room to grow, are necessary to the condition of manhood, and therefore necessary also to the writing of the finest poetry. Wordsworth, in his preface to the second *Lyrical Ballads*, was essentially right.

All good poetry is the spontaneous overflow of powerful feelings: and though this be true, poems to which any value can be attached were never produced on any variety of subjects but by a man who, being possessed of more than

usual organic sensibility, has also thought long and deeply.
Never were the primary conditions of poetry, as Wordsworth
defined them, more exactly satisfied than by Clare. He was
possessed of infinitely more than 'usual organic sensibility,' and
all his poetry is 'the spontaneous overflow of powerful feelings.'
Wordsworth's general definition is a precise description of Clare's
work: the epithets, 'organic' of his sensibility and 'spontaneous'
of his emotion, fit Clare more happily than any other poet who
comes to mind. And the reason is that the poetic natures of
Clare and Wordsworth were closely allied. The difference
between them is that Clare could not, while Wordsworth could,
think long and deeply.

This inability of Clare's was a defect of his quality; and it
was because Wordsworth's sensibility was not so pure or so
uninterrupted as Clare's that he had the opportunity and the
need for thought. But even for him thought was something
almost unnatural, so that he was extremely conscious of himself
thinking and of himself as a thinker. His thought is not always
spontaneous as Shakespeare's is always spontaneous and
as Keats's thought promised to be spontaneous; we are
often aware of it as an element that is not really fused with his
perception, but super-imposed upon it, and Wordsworth's poetry
then takes on that slightly didactic, slightly distasteful tone of
which Keats (who belonged to the Shakespearian order) was so
acutely conscious when he wrote about Wordsworth:

We hate poetry that has a palpable design upon us, and if
we do not agree, seems to put its hand into its breeches
pocket. Poetry should be great and unobtrusive, a thing
which enters into one's soul, and does not startle or amaze it
with itself, but with its subject. How beautiful are the retired
flowers! How they would lose their beauty were they to throng
to the highway, crying out, 'Admire me, I am a violet! Dote
upon me, I am a primrose!'

In this criticism of Wordsworth by a still finer poetic mind than
his own, the ground is, as it were, once more cleared for a just
approach to Clare. Again the very words are apt to him. His
poetry is 'unobtrusive.' 'How beautiful are the retired flowers!'
is true of him perhaps more than any other poet. His poetry has

21

no 'palpable design upon us'; it has no design upon us at all.

The cause of Clare's so curiously fitting into these utterances of his great poetic contemporaries, is, first, that he was in the essential as authentic a poet as they and, secondly, that he was allied to Wordsworth by the nature of his 'organic sensibility' and to Keats by his wonderful spontaneity. Wordsworth would have denied poetic 'greatness' to Clare because of his lack of thought, but Keats would have denied poetic 'greatness' to much of Wordsworth's work because of its lack of spontaneity and unobtrusiveness. These criticisms, in their ascending order, are just and profound, and they establish the real precedence of these three true poets. Moreover, this conclusion follows: in order that Clare should have been as great a poet as he was a true one, the quality of his thought would have needed to be equal to the quality of his perception, equally spontaneous, equally organic. Then he would have been, in Keats's phrase, both 'great and unobtrusive,' and a very great poet indeed. As it is, he is unobtrusive and true, not a great poet, but assuredly not a little one—a child, on whom the rarest and most divine gift of vision had so abundantly descended that he could not become a man.

The quality in Clare which most enthrals us, the general quality of which the quintessence is manifest in the beauty of his seeing, is one which we can only describe as a kind of *naïveté*. If we use a similitude, we might say it was an abiding sense of a quite simple fraternity with all the creatures of the world save self-conscious man. Man, the thinker, the calculator, the schemer, falls outside this universe of simple comprehension, and is the inhabitant of an alien world. He will not enter. he has no wedding garment. And the reality of Clare's vision and its power over our hearts is such that there are moments when our conviction that this is a limitation of Clare's understanding suddenly abandons us and we have a secret fear that his may be the true and unattainable wisdom. 'Except ye become as little children . . .' That fear does not remain with us; we know that the word is not thus literally to be understood. Our childhood must come to us as the achievement of our manhood. We cannot divest ourselves of our birthright. But Clare's *naïveté* reinforces the admonition of the word, that unless we can achieve, out of all our wisdom and despair, a comprehension as pure as was his vision, we shall have lost the day.

For in Clare's vision is indubitable truth, not comprehensive, not final, but because it strikes our hearts as truth, and is truth, it is prophetic of the final and comprehensive truth.   It is melody, not harmony:

> Yes, night is happy night,
> The sky is full of stars,
> Like worlds in peace they lie
> Enjoying one delight.

But true melody, as this is, is separated from false harmony by a whole universe of error.   If it has not been troubled by thought, it has also not been corrupted by the temptation to turn stones into bread.   The spontaneous feeling of

> [He] felt that lovely mood
> As a birthright God had given
> To muse in the green wood
> And meet the smiles of heaven,

though it does not itself achieve it, would at least never be satisfied by thought that was not as spontaneous as itself; it would have no room for the speculations of mere intellectual pride. And Clare's nascent thoughts, as far as they go, are as true as his feelings; indeed they *are* feelings:

> I thought o'er all life's sweetest things
> Made dreary as a broken charm,
> Wood-ridings where the thrush still sings
> And love went leaning on my arm.

Experience, the organic knowledge from which organic thought is born, was for Clare the dreary breaking of a charm.   The phrase is beautifully, agonisingly true.   Up to the extreme verge of his capacity Clare never betrayed himself.   On the one side his world of his vision, on the other side broken charms and mystery; he did not, he could not, try to reconcile them.   When he was shut out by destiny and the hand of man from his own world, he lived within the memory of it.   In *Mary*, a poem to his

23

child-love, the memory is heart-breaking even to us:

> Mary, or sweet spirit of thee,
>   As the bright sun shines to-morrow
> Thy dark eyes these flowers shall see
>   Gathered by me in sorrow,
> In the still hour when my mind was free
> To walk alone—yet wish I walked with thee.

Something terrible has been done to this child-man that he is forced to wander in an alien world alone. It was intolerable to him, and it is intolerable to us who hear the voice of his suffering. Yet, though the charm was broken and he was outcast from his world, he was loyal to it. He did not betray his knowledge. The evidence of his triumphant loyalty is in the last, and the greatest of the poems in this book. It is obscure, because Clare was struggling with an order of thought to which he was not born, but in spite of the obscurity, its purity and truth and justice are manifest. He had indeed 'kept his spirit with the free.'

> I lost the love of Heaven above,
>   I spurned the lust of Earth below,
> I felt the sweets of fancied love
>   And Hell itself my only foe.
>
> I lost Earth's joys, but felt the glow
>   Of Heaven's flame abound in me
> Till loveliness and I did grow
>   The bard of Immortality.
>
> I loved, but woman fell away;
>   I hid me from her faded flame.
> I snatched the sun's eternal ray
>   And wrote till Earth was but a name.
>
> In every language upon earth,
>   On every shore, o'er every sea,
> I gave my name immortal birth
>   And kept my spirit with the free.

                                        [1924]

24

THE MADNESS OF CHRISTOPHER
SMART

MR. EDMUND BLUNDEN, faithful to his self-imposed task of rescuing his poet predecessors from oblivion, has followed up his edition of the poetry of John Clare with a new edition of Christopher Smart's *Song to David*. Not that Kit Smart is quite so forgotten as Clare was: he is one of the little flies immortalised in the pellucid and enduring amber of Boswell's *Johnson.*

BURNEY: How does poor Smart do, Sir; is he likely to recover?

JOHNSON: It seems as if his mind had ceased to struggle with the disease; for he grows fat upon it.

BURNEY: Perhaps, Sir, that may be from want of exercise.

JOHNSON: No, Sir; he has partly as much exercise as he used to have, for he digs in the garden. Indeed, before his confinement, he used for exercise to walk to the ale house; but he was *carried* back again. I did not think he ought to be shut up. His infirmities were not noxious to society. He insisted on people praying with him; and I'd as lief pray with Kit Smart as any one else. Another charge was, that he did not love clean linen; and I have no passion for it.

While he was shut up in the asylum, Kit Smart wrote the *Song to David* and the *Hymns and Spiritual Songs*. No doubt in the 1760's, in the full prime of the Age of Reason, those poems were an additional and conclusive evidence of Smart's insanity. The same rationality which clapped Smart in the madhouse imposed the Stamp Act on the American Colonies. Nowadays, pretending to a wisdom after the event, we should call this reason a want of imagination. But whether we English have any more imagination now is a question to which an honest answer might be disturbing.

From this angle the history of English poetry in the eighteenth century is a singularly depressing story. The real poets were all 'mad.' Chatterton, Savage, Collins, Smart, Cowper, were suicides or lunatics, or both. Even the equable Gray was on the verge of melancholia. At the end of the sombre procession comes John Clare, 'the asylum poet,' whom the doctor certified for the madhouse because he showed an unconquerable inclin- ation to write verses. And at the end of the period, when a few holes in the leaden pall of 'rationality' had been made by the lightnings of the French Revolution, some of the great ones had narrow escapes. Blake was suspect; Coleridge was safely lodged in Gilman's house: and what would have happened to Keats and Shelley, had they not died before society had begun to take serious notice of them. who can say? Words- worth opted for sanity and his poetry fled.

It is not a comfortable retrospect. In the old, old days before modern 'civilisation' had begun its levelling, there was more room for the poets. They were mad, but their madness was 'divine.' The gods, nay, the very principle of the divine, visited them. But in the Age of Reason, they were simply mad. No more divinity about their delusions: no more reverence for the great unspeakable power which manifested through them. Our modern civilisation is wonderful, tremendous, terrifying; but it has no room for these things. It does not want, and it will not have, the prophet and the seer. The poet, the authentic poet, is no less: he is the *vates sacer* now, as ever, for the truth he knows is eternal. But there is no room for it in the philosophy of modern civilisation, and modern civilisation will one day pay the penalty for trying to shut out what is older and more enduring than itself.

Such are the thoughts one has in reading Christopher Smart again. Most people who know anything about poetry know the *Song to David*: there is a good solid chunk of it in the *Oxford Book of English Verse*; but a whole is better than a part, and the most astonishing thing about the *Song to David* is that it is a whole. For its uniqueness—and there is *nothing* like it in the great range of English poetry—chiefly consists in the unexpected combination of unity, of swift and firm design, of vivid *ordon- nance* (to use Coleridge's word) with an impassioned and ecstatic sublimity which one would have thought rebellious by nature to such discipline. Not to know the *Song to David* as a whole is in a very real sense not to know it at all.

But the *Song to David* is not new : what will be new to most people is the strange quality of Smart's *Hymns and Spiritual*

26

Songs, some of which Mr. Blunden has rescued, together with a good deal of merely trivial verse. These *Hymns and Spiritual Songs for the Fasts and Festivals of the Church of England* were printed together with his versions of the Psalms and the second edition of the *Song to David* in 1765. I imagine from the internal evidence that Smart wrote the versions of the Psalms first, then being uplifted by the splendour of the Psalmist's imagination and controlled by his knowledge of the Psalmist's art, uttered the *Song to David*, and finally, relaxed into a mood of calm and simple serenity, composed the *Hymns and Spiritual Songs*.

However this may be, there are marvellous things in them, and these things are marvellous in a way quite different from that of the *Song to David*. Consider, for example, the last two verses of *The Nativity*.

> Spinks and ouzels sing sublimely,
>   ' We too have a Saviour born; '
> Whiter blossoms burst untimely
>   On the blest Mosaic Thorn.

> God all-bounteous, all-creative,
>   Whom no ills from good dissuade,
> Is incarnate, *and a native*
>   *Of the very world he made.*

There is a simple miracle in that last line and a half ; and one need not be a professing Christian to feel that it is the miracle of the Nativity itself. Or take lines from *St. Philip and St. James*.

> And the lily smiles supremely
>   Mentioned by the Lord on earth . . .

This is the true, the strange Christian *naïveté* : the sense or the knowledge that all living creatures are brothers of men, children of God, and can only be understood in virtue of the one love which unites them all. By this spirit the primæval innocence of Eden (of which Rubens had a Pisgah-sight in his great picture) is restored, and for the moment that we share it we are no longer fallen away from our first perfection. It is the great Christian *naïveté* of St. Francis. It was to be manifested again, half a century later, in the poetry of John Clare, for the fitful yet unmistakable gleam plays over all Clare's work.

> The very darkness smiles to wear
> The stars that show us God is there.

It is a perception, a knowledge, a mode of understanding, which Christ Himself brought into the world. ' Solomon in all his glory was not arrayed like one of these.' ' Are not two sparrows sold for a farthing? ' Before Christ, no one of whom memory remains to us had spoken words like these : before Him, this sense of communion in life between all living creatures did not exist. There is no record of it in the words of the wise before Him: the beautiful descriptions of nature in the ancient poets— and in spite of the common report, there *are* beautiful descriptions of nature in the ancient poets—are of another kind. They have not this immediacy of contact : the blood bond of brothers is not there. And, to speak truth, it is not in many poets of the Christian era : it is not, I believe, in Shakespeare, or in Dante, or in Milton, or even in Wordsworth. Wordsworth is too deliberate ; there is a grave and deep philosophy in his attitude. But this *naïveté* is spontaneous, like the kiss one may sometimes surprise between two little children who believe themselves unwatched. I have seen such a kiss between two tiny staggerers in the Luxembourg Gardens. It is innocent, it is rapturous, and it is wise.

I find the gleam of it everywhere in Smart's *Hymns and Spiritual Songs*, as I find it everywhere in Clare. I can decribe it only as a glimpse of simple and incredible purity. No one can hold a mystery all the time; perhaps few can perceive it when it is pointed out to them: the pointing-out stands in the way. But it seems not only to hover, but to rest in the last three verses of *St. Philip and St. James*.

> Hark! aloud the blackbird whistles,
> With surrounding fragrance blest,
> And the goldfinch in the thistles
> Makes provision for her nest.
>
> Even the hornet hives for honey,
> Bluecap builds his stately dome,

> And the rocks supply the coney
> With a fortress and a home.

> But the servants of the Saviour,
> Which with gospel-peace are shod,
> Have no bed but what the paviour
> Makes them in the porch of God.

That, to me, is Franciscan poetry *in excelsis*.

And suddenly, when I think that Christopher Smart and John Clare, who had perhaps more of this strange and peculiar gift of *naiveté* than any other of our poets, were both shut up in asylums, I wonder whether St. Francis, yes, and Christ himself, would not be safeguarded in the same way; and I turn out of my pocket-book a cutting of *The Times* report of the Harnett lunacy case, which has lately shocked English public opinion. 'All that Mr. Harnett had'—of the evidence on which he was certified as a lunatic—'was the statement of Dr. Gray (the assistant medical-officer at the asylum) that "You have too much Jesus about you." It is a dangerous thing to have.

We take our Dr. Johnson too much from Boswell. We cannot help it. If we are to see the great man at all, we must see him through Boswell's eyes. But we should be on our guard against feeling him through Boswell's mind. We need not echo the thundering paradox of Macaulay, in order to agree with him that Boswell was too small to *understand* his hero. Boswell was smug and satisfied in the Age of Reason: Johnson had had terrifying glimpses of what lay beyond. If Johnson had written only the single phrase, 'the hunger of the imagination which preys upon life,' we should know that he knew there were more things in heaven and earth than were dreamed of in Boswell's philosophy. We must never forget that Johnson was religious in an age of irreligion; and the knowledge which he compressed by force of will within the rigid framework of his rationality shows nowhere more clearly than in the implications of his later remarks on Kit Smart:

> Madness frequently discovers itself by unnecessary deviation
> from the usual modes of the world. My poor friend Smart
> showed the disturbance of his mind by falling upon his knees,

and saying his prayers in the street, or in any other unusual place. Now, although, rationally speaking, it is greater madness not to pray at all, than to pray as Smart did, I am afraid there are so many who do not pray, that their understanding is not called in question.

[APRIL, 1924]

30

SHAKESPEARE AND LOVE

In a very interesting essay the late Professor Herford discussed Shakespeare's attitude to love and marriage, and insisted upon what he called the profound 'normality' of the poet's conception of love. He points out that love is but seldom the substantial theme of Shakespeare's greater tragedies and that Shakespeare conceives it as a condition which, so far from inevitably containing the seed of its own disruption, is so naturally strong that it needs the invasion of an alien power to be prevented from the bliss of perfect fulfilment. If we may translate Shakespeare's idea of love into terms he would certainly not himself have used, we may say, following out Professor Herford's view, that Shakespeare instinctively thought of love as a beneficent power in the human world, which could be thwarted from its true purpose only by forces foreign to itself. Professor Herford concluded:

'Shakespeare certainly did not, so far as we can judge, regard sexual love (like some moderns) as either the clue to human life or as in any way related to the structure of the universe. But if instead of these abstract questions, we ask whether any poet has united in a like degree veracious appreciation of love in its existing conditions with apprehension of all its ideal possibilities, we shall not dispute Shakespeare's place among the foremost of the poets of love.'

That is, in substance, a very just conclusion, and yet, we think, it will strike a reader of Shakespeare as a little cold. It would, perhaps, scarcely have occurred to him that Shakespeare's place among the foremost of the poets of love should be disputed; and it is not unlikely that his natural impulse would be to call Shakespeare the greatest love-poet of them all. For the love of many other great poets, 'the love which moves the sun and the other stars,' is a wonderful and mighty power, but it is hardly love. It bears the name only by a sublime analogy; it is no native of the earth.

But in Shakespeare love is not remote and celestial; it is warm and human, and generation after generation of men and women to whom the intellectual love of a Dante, a Spinoza, or a Shelley would be an unintelligible fantasy have recognized it as a reflection of something they had felt or might hope to feel. If we take that which ninety-nine out of a hundred of all sorts and conditions of men feel or dream or understand at the word love, as the rough ore of the mysterious element, and if we refine this to the utmost of our power, casting nothing away that truly belongs to it, then of the recognizable universal love which remains Shakespeare is the pre-eminent poet. Nor is this love less ideal because it has nothing of the abstract-metaphysical in its composition, unless we are to hand over the word 'ideal' wholly to the mercies of the philosophers. Shakespeare's conception of love is ideal in the most humane sense of the word, an enchanting and attainable perfection of the real.

Tradition, the popular voice, the judgment of the critics are at one in regarding Shakespeare as the poet of the earthly felicity of love. For this he was 'sweet' and 'gentle' in his own day, as he is in ours. The evidence of the plays is beyond all doubt. It is not a question of scattered lines or single characters, but of the general sentiment pervading all his plays: it cannot be escaped; it is the very air we breathe in them. Yet in this there is something strange, something miraculous almost; for whatever may be our estimate of the precise value of the Sonnets as autobiography, it is impossible for any one but a briefed advocate to assert that they do not substantially contain the record of the poet's own disaster in love. That earthly felicity of love between man and woman which runs, with but a single moment of interruption, like a thread of gold through the work of Shakespeare the dramatist, would seem to be the one aspect of love of which knowledge was denied to Shakespeare the sonnetteer. He seems to have tasted only the despairs, the degradations and the bitternesses, even though it was he also who declared his faith in the loyalty of a true lover's heart.

> Love is not love
> Which alters when it alteration finds
> Nor bends with the remover to remove.

If we seek a simple explanation of the fact, we shall say, well knowing that we trespass against Signor Croce's canons of criticism, that the sonnets of tormented love belong to the moment when the golden thread in the plays is suddenly and unexpectedly snapped. We shall hold that the Sonnets represent an episode in Shakespeare's experience which caused a momentary but a complete overclouding of the reflection in the mirror of the plays. The episode passes and the reflection becomes calm and serene once more. The Sonnets give us, as it were, a year of Shakespeare's attitude to love; the plays give us a lifetime. In other words, even in this single matter of love, it is a mistaken effort to measure the plays by the sonnets; what we have to do is to measure the Sonnets by the plays. If we do this the sonnets of disastrous love seem to fall naturally into place in that period of profound disturbance which is expressed in *Hamlet,* in *Measure for Measure,* in *Troilus and Cressida,* and in *All's Well that Ends Well.* No doubt this disturbance had its manifest reactions in realms of Shakespeare's faith other than his faith in love; it may have been the proximate cause of his greatest tragedies. But for these we need not assume an origin in personal catastrophe. Moreover, in the great tragic period Shakespeare's faith in love has manifestly begun to reassert itself. We have only to imagine *Antony and Cleopatra* written in the mood of *Troilus and Cressida* to understand what Shakespeare actually chose to do with a theme that would have lent itself magnificently to all the bitterness of an outraged heart.

If we put aside the plays of this period of disturbance, which ordinary readers and literary critics alike have felt to be discordant with Shakespeare's work as a whole, we discover pervading the rest an attitude to love which all cynics and most critics have conspired to describe as romantic. It is true that it appears to flower divinely in what we call the romantic comedies; but that does not mean that the love portrayed in them is romantic in essence. Classification of this kind is superficial and confusing. A poet uses the most convenient plot as a foundation on which to build up the expression of his emotional attitude. The mere accident that the plot contains improbable coincidences and enchanted islands cannot affect the substance of the attitude expressed by its means. The romantic comedy of one poet may be a trivial indulgence of the fancy, while that of another is the flashing of a warm light into the verity of the human soul. We have only to compare Shakespeare's comedy on the one hand with Beaumont and Fletcher's, and on the other with Ben Jonson's, to discover how far asunder they are in their poetic truth. The segregation of Shakespeare's comedies is misleading unless it is considered merely as the distinction of an aspect within the whole work of Shakespeare. The most immature of his comedies is nearer in spirit to the most perfect of his tragedies than it is to the comedies of Jonson or Fletcher, whatever merits of their own these may possess.

To call the love of Shakespeare's romantic comedies itself romantic is meaningless, or it is the expression of a private and personal conviction concerning the nature of love. It may mean that in the opinion of the judge love is not in fact so happy, nor so secure, nor so deeply irradiated with the heart's delight as Shakespeare represented it; but it can mean nothing more. And we cannot tell whether Shakespeare himself believed that love actually was as he chose to represent it. But we can say that he did believe either that it was so, or that it ought to be so; and that he found it natural to create men and women who are alive with a reality no other created characters possess, who love in the way he chose to make them love, with a tenderness and a gaiety, an open-eyed confidence in themselves and the future, a shyness and a humour, a marvellous equality in affection, which have made them for a whole world of mankind the embodiment of their experience if they were happy in love, or of their dreams if they were disappointed. And this love, which is as solid and as ethereal, as earthly and as magical as a rose in full bloom, is in all his early comedies; it is essentially the same in *A Midsummer Night's Dream* as in *Much Ado about Nothing*. We can hardly say more than that the light changes from moonlight to full sunshine as we pass from Lysander and Hermia, through Orsino and Viola, to Benedick and Beatrice, and that when we reach *As You Like It* the midday brightness is faintly mellowed with afternoon. Nor is it possible to say that the love of the *Merchant of Venice* or of

Romeo and Juliet is of another kind, though the one is calm and the other tempestuous. It is only the tempest of circumstance which wrecks the love of Romeo and Juliet. There is a peculiar ecstasy in their surrender to the enchantment which bursts out like a flame at the clash of contact between the enemy houses; but in their love no seed of disruption or decay is visible, much less of disaster. Theirs is a love of which all human foresight could prophesy its

> Outliving beauty's outward with a mind
> That doth renew swifter than blood decays.

They are the victims not of their passion but of crass casualty; they are the fools of fortune, not themselves. *Romeo and Juliet*, as Professor Herford truly says, 'appears not to be the tragedy of love, but love's triumphal hymn.'

The love which shines so gloriously through this period of Shakespeare's work is as mysterious and natural as birth. It is a thing that happens; to ask why it happens is to wait till doomsday for an answer; and if these lovers ask each other, they can only make up jesting replies. When Phebe applies Marlowe's line to her own sudden love of Rosalind-Ganymede, she speaks for them all, men and women alike.

> Dead Shepherd, now I find thy saw of might:
> 'Who ever loved, that loved not at first sight?'

For the most part they know themselves what has happened; and even where, as with Benedick and Beatrice, we seem to know it before they do, it is only because of their shyness of themselves and each other, which will not suffer their heads to confess the truth of their hearts.The moment that Benedick and Beatrice open fire on one another we know that they are caught. It is only love that makes a man and a woman single on each other for such teasing.

> *Beatrice.* I wonder that you will still be talking, Signior Benedick; nobody marks you.
> *Benedick.* What! My dear Lady Disdain, are you yet living?

Benedick might have called her the dear lady of his heart and had done with it, for he gave himself as completely away in that address as he could ever have done in the sonnet they found in his pocket at church, in which no doubt he rhymed, as he feared to rhyme, 'ladies' and 'babies.' Yet, though *Much Ado About Nothing* has precisely the same radiant substance as the rest of the love-comedies—love at first sight —it stands apart from them because the drama itself consists in the delicate working out of the psychology of this heavenly condition. It is not entangled with alien accidents, and owes nothing to the enchantment of disguise; it deals, with an absolute perfection of art, with the process by which the message of unhesitating love steals from the heart to the mind. For this cause it is at once the simplest and the subtlest of all Shakespeare's comedies of love. For once Shakespeare chose to communicate the reality of love to us realistically: we can imagine the essence of the play—for what does Don John matter?—being played in real life at this very moment in the garden of any kindly country house; the process is as old as the hills and as new as the morning.

But generally Shakespeare preferred to let one of his lovers or both know at once what had happened to them. The recognition is as quick as the love of Celia and Oliver.

Your brother and my sister no sooner met but they looked; no sooner looked but they loved; no sooner loved but they sighed; no sooner sighed but they asked one another the reason; no sooner knew the reason but they sought the remedy.

The condition is presented to us a thing elemental, inscrutable, which either is or is not. But if it is, Shakespeare can prove to us immediately that it is the true metal. He does not profess to show how it happens, he does something far more difficult; he convinces us that it has happened. He makes his lovers say the simplest and divinest things; they seem to drop sunbeams from their lips. In reality love is too often tongue-tied: Shakespeare gives it speech that seems as natural and magical as love itself. When Orlando says of Rosalind that she is 'just as high as his heart', when Rosalind says that 'men have died from time to time, and worms have eaten them, but not for love', when Beatrice

36

answers the Prince's 'Out of question you were born in a merry hour',

> 'No, sure, my Lord, my mother cried, but then there was a star danced, and under that I was born.'

we recognize the speech of love as surely as the old prophets recognized the voice of the Lord. This is how lovers would speak if they could. What wonder that they should have recognized their spokesman, and with a single voice elected him the poet laureate of love?

So natural is this flowering that we cannot imagine any end to it but the perfect happiness of marriage. These lovers are too open-eyed to be victims of the sad illusion; their felicity is destined to outlive beauty's outward. They seem to be poised in a balance of perfect equality; yet if we have to pronounce which way the scale imperceptibly inclines we must say it is to the woman's side. The Duke says to Cesario:

> For, boy, however we do praise ourselves,
> Our fancies are more giddy and unfirm,
> More longing, wavering, sooner lost and worn
> Than women's are.

Certainly the Duke himself changed his affection quickly from Olivia to Viola; but then we may truly urge that he was in love with Cesario all the while. Claudio suspected Hero suddenly and condemned her violently. But these, after all, are only the subordinate necessities of the romantic fable; they do not determine the quality of the belief with which Shakespeare charged it.

The happiness of the love in the mature comedies passes undisturbed into the married security of *Henry IV* and *Julius Caesar*. Kate and Hotspur are the proof that marriage, which is the inevitable end of Shakespeare's lovers, born not merely under a lucky but a dancing star, does not mean the end of love-making.

> I' faith I'll break thy little finger, Harry .   .   ,
> An if thou wilt not tell me all things true.

They are married, and as much in love as when first they met. There is no room for such gaiety between Brutus and Portia.

37

Brutus is caught in a conspiracy, and is venturing his life in an enterprise which Portia feels must bring disaster. Only the anxiety and devotion can appear, but it is equal. Portia knows that her husband cannot resist her appeal to 'the great vow which did incorporate and make them one.'

> Dwell I but in the suburbs
> Of your good pleasure? If it be no more,
> Portia is Brutus' harlot, not his wife.

And even in the relation of Mistress Quickly and Doll Tear-sheet to Falstaff we catch the undertone of a fidelity not altogether unworthy to be compared to this. Both these women loved the genial old ruffian, who in his way loved them; and there are moments when nothing in Shakespeare seems to reveal more clearly his faith in the loyalty of love than the words he makes the cockney landlady say of Falstaff's death:

Nym. They say he cried out of sack.

Host. Ay, that a' did.

Bard. And of women.

Host. Nay, that a' did not.

Boy. Yes, that a' did; and said they were devils incarnate.

Host. A' never could abide carnation; 'twas a colour he never liked.

Boy. A' said once, the devil would have him about women.

Host. A' did in some sort, indeed, handle women; but then he was rheumatic, and talked of the whore of Babylon.

Then comes an abrupt and startling change. Suddenly the steady, shining stream of Shakespeare's presentation of love as happiness and loyalty is disturbed and muddied. The moment coincides with a sudden check in the confident advance of Shakespeare as a poet and a dramatist. We are confronted with what we may roughly call 'the Hamlet period', which includes that strange *sosie* of *Hamlet, Measure for Measure, Troilus and Cressida*, and *All's Well that Ends Well*. In all these plays there are sustained passages of poetry of form and content incomparable, in which

38

Shakespeare definitely passes beyond the highest point that poetry had reached before him, or has reached after him. It was no even temporary weakening of his purely poetic powers that assailed him; but we have a sudden sense of loss of all direction, an invasion of bitterness, of cynicism, and of a conscious helplessness. We feel we are in contact with a wounded and bewildered spirit that can see life steadily and whole no more. Shakespeare managed to project this bewilderment out of himself most completedy and almost to master it in the realm of art in *Hamlet*. He concentrated it all in a character, divided in his deepest being against himself, but yet one; nevertheless the play is bewildering; not, we believe, because there may be remnants of an old play in it—Shakespeare had re-written old plays before without leaving us in any doubt of his dramatic intention—but simply because the attitude to life which every great poet must convey had suffered a chaotic disturbance. We feel the same indecision in *All's Well*. Here also we are told that the unsatisfactory nature of the whole composed of such brilliant parts is due to its being a revision of an earlier *Love's Labour Won*. Again we must reply that Shakespeare knew how to rewrite plays; he had spent his life at the business. What we seek to know is the reason why he suddenly began to fail in a task he had performed for years with brilliant success, and was to perform again more marvellously still.

When we find precisely the same fundamental indecision, the same deep hesitation of a mind that can by nature never be more than half-cynical, in the two other plays of this period, against which the defect of rehashing has not yet been urged; when we find that those four plays are as closely united to each other as they are separate from the whole of the rest of Shakespeare's work, we may fairly neglect the hypothetical 'Ur-Hamlets' and earliest versions and stick to what we have. Of these four plays we may say that we do not clearly understand Shakespeare's dramatic purpose or the direction of his sentiment in any of them. Whether the cause of this clouding actually lay, as we ourselves sometimes incline to believe, in the love-catastrophe reorded in the

Sonnets, is a minor matter; but the fact is that the disturbance is most clearly to be distinguished in his treatment of
love. The main intention of *Hamlet* is on the whole fairly
clear. But who has ever spoken convincingly on the significance of Hamlet's love for Ophelia? It remains mysterious to
us. The final effect of *Troilus and Cressida* is a feeling that
again Shakespeare could not really face his own subject. For
a moment he handles the love of Troilus and Cressida firmly,
then he appears to let it drop as though it were unbearable
and to turn away to deride the Homeric heroes and the idea
of chivalry. In a play which contains, in Ulysses' speeches
and Troilus' love addresses, some of Shakespeare's finest
poetry, we are struck at the last chiefly by its strange inferiority
to Chaucer's wonderful poem. Shakespeare could have
handled the love theme with the mastery of his great predecessor; but something prevented him, and the consequence
of his hesitation is that essays are now written to prove that
he meant only a satire on hero-worship. Seeing that Shakespeare put his finest declaration of the idea of love into the
play, we may assume that this master of love would have worked
out the tragedy of love if he could have borne to do so.

Measure for Measure is that one of Shakespeare's plays
which Coleridge could never bring himself to like. The treatment of love in it is as near to pure cynicism as Shakespeare
could get. Claudio, who really loves, and is loved by Julietta,
is sentenced to death for anticipating the marriage he intends.
Isabel, who will not sacrifice her chastity to save her brother,
ends by acting like a woman of the town, but one utterly
devoid of the humanity which glows in Doll Tearsheet or
Bianca. Believing her brother dead, she pleads for Angelo,
the reverend justice who has killed him and would have
ravished her, in these terms:

> Look, if it please you, on this man condemn'd,
> As if my brother lived: I partly think
> A due sincerity govern'd his deeds,
> Till he did look on me; since it is so,
> Let him not die. My brother had but justice,
> In that he did the thing for which he died:

40

For Angelo,
His act did not o'ertake his bad intent,
And must be buried but as an intent
That perish'd by the way: thoughts are no subjects;
Intents but merely thoughts.

This is the reverse of *spretae injuria formae,* with a vengeance.
Dr. Johnson's note on it is properly cynical, but it is too
good-humoured. The lines contain a fierce and bitter caricature of love, and we must believe that Shakespeare meant
it. Then there is the trick, significantly repeated in *All's
Well,* by which Angelo possessed the faithful Mariana in the
belief that she was Isabel. And over the whole play hangs
the sinister cloud of preoccupation with death, suddenly
crystallized into the sardonic figure of Barnardine. Whatever
may be the dramatic purpose of this singular 'comedy', the
condition of mind from which it sprang is manifest. Life is
hateful and contemptible; and as for love, your bawd is your
only honest man.

In *All's Well that Ends Well*—supremely cynical title—
Shakespeare seems deliberately to take revenge on his own
idealism of love. He deliberately makes Bertram detestable
and shows that the bragging coward, Parolles, is the better
man. Then he makes Helena fall in love, passionately,
tenderly, delicately with the unpleasant young nobleman,
builds her up as surely as Beatrice or Rosalind, puts into her
mouth the divinely hesitating reply to Bertram's purely brutal
'What would you have?'

Something and scarce so much: nothing, indeed.
I would not tell you what I would, my lord:—
Faith, yes;
Strangers and foes do sunder and not kiss.

Yet after all this she plays the Mariana trick. One wonders
what can be the conception of the poet in the minds of those
who imagine that he had written a romantic comedy with a
happy ending. The self-torturing mood of the play, the bitter
mood of 'I'll show you a happy ending', is only too apparent.
But Shakespeare, it seems, could never succeed in projecting

41

an attitude of embitterment completely: his hand weakened, his idealization of love and humanity interfered. That is one reason why the fascination of the plays of this strange period is out of all proportion to the sureness of their achievement as works of dramatic art.

We may speculate that the true poetic realization of this period, whose stress we imagine we can measure by Othello's words—'when I love thee not Chaos is come again'—is to be found in the great tragedies. The shattering personal experience there found its place in a vision of life as a whole. There is no bitterness any more; and in the microcosm of his vision of life which is his attitude to love it is apparent that Shakespeare has regained his belief. The love of Othello and Desdemona is in itself unclouded. No human mind could resist the villainy of Iago. Their perfect happiness is overwhelmed by no defect of their love, and Othello's very act of murder is, as Coleridge said, an act of sacrifice to love; it is the tragedy of an ideal shattered by an alien power. Had there been no Iago their love would have endured to death. So, too, with the miniature of this great picture of married happiness, which we have in *Coriolanus*. Virgilia's reticent devotion to her proud and passionate husband is matched by his gentleness in her presence. Her 'gracious silence' wields a charm over him which Shakespeare makes us feel completely in the few dozen lines he gives to her. In *Macbeth* also, though the bond holds between natures far darker than these, it holds unbreakable. Lady Macbeth may be her husband's evil genius, but she is united to him more deeply by their love than their crime. And of *Antony and Cleopatra*, with even more force than of *Romeo and Juliet*, it may be said that it is a triumph rather than a tragedy of love. At the last the mutual devotion is complete. Cleopatra in her death-scene remains what she has been, capricious as she is passionate; but her surrender is entire. 'Husband, I come. Now to that name my courage prove my title.' It is a love which may not promise the golden happiness on which Shakespeare so fondly dwelt, but it is one which transfigures the lovers and lifts them to heights of feeling and sacrifice of which neither they nor we had dreamed.

42

Shakespeare's final period is one of return to the love of his youth. During the great tragedies love had been on the whole—save in *Antony and Cleopatra*—a subordinate issue. He had other things to convey—the conclusion of his brooding on his experience of that life of which love is a mighty part, but only a part. Yet we may discover how great a part it was to him by his return to the theme in all his three last plays, *The Winter's Tale, Cymbeline,* and *The Tempest.* We feel that it was only the love scenes of the first two of these that deeply interested him. In those scenes his touch is perfectly firm, his mastery evident, while in the rest it is hesitating and perfunctory. But something ethereal is added to the love of the earlier comedies and something earthly taken away. The light is no longer golden but silver. Lovers are no more witty together; they are almost enfolded in a dream of tenderness. After the wild storm of the tragedies, culminating in *King Lear,* we hear the poet proclaiming through Florizel and Perdita, Imogen and Posthumus, Ferdinand and Miranda, that love is the only light to follow. The message sounds with a magical clearness in the silver note of *The Tempest.* The wise magician throws away his book: he has seen his vision of human life.

> The cloud-capp'd towers, the gorgeous palaces,
> The solemn temples, the great globe itself,
> Yea, all which it inherit, shall dissolve
> And, like this insubstantial pageant faded,
> Leave not a wrack behind. We are such stuff
> As dreams are made on, and our little life
> Is rounded with a sleep.

Yet with his wisdom and his pain of heart, Prospero gives way to the faith and the freedom of love; and his creator looks at the world not through his eyes only, but through Miranda's also.

> O wonder !
> How many goodly creatures are there here!
> How bounteous mankind is! O brave new world,
> That has such people in't!

So 'the world's great age begins anew'. The magic of Shakespeare's last enchantment is that he makes us for a moment believe that the eyes of love alone can see the miracle; and perhaps it is the ultimate truth of life that indeed they do.

[SEPTEMBER, 1921]

SHAKESPEARE'S DEDICATION

At some time in the middle fifteen-eighties Shakespeare came to London in search of a livelihood, and more: in search of the means to re-establish the fortunes of his family. We may guess that he arrived in London by 1586, we may make more or less plausible conjectures concerning the manner of his occupation after his arrival; but the one thing we *know* is that in 1593 he had written a beautiful, and within its limits, a masterly poem, *Venus and Adonis,* and that he was dedicating it to a young nobleman, the Earl of Southampton, in language which, though it may sound unduly humble to us who regard Shakespeare as one of the wonders of the world, would sound with dignity and independence surprising to an Elizabethan ear.

Compare the language in which Shakespeare addressed the young Earl of Southampton with that of a dedication made at the same time to the same young nobleman by a writer who lacked neither courage nor genius—Thomas Nashe. Nashe's language is fulsome; to-day it is comic in its exaggeration, but then it was natural. 'Incomprehensible', says Nashe to Southampton, 'is the height of your spirit, both in heroical resolution and matters of conceit. Unreprievably perisheth that book whatsoever to waste paper, which on the diamond rock of your judgment disasterly chanceth to be shipwrackt. . . .' But thus Shakespeare:

'Right Honourable, I know not how I shall offend in dedicating my unpolisht lines to your Lordship, nor how the worlde will censure mee for choosing so strong a proppe to support so weake a burthen, onelye if your Honour seem but pleased, I account my selfe highly praised, and vowe to take advantage of all idle hours, till I have honoured you with some graver labour. But if the first heire of my invention prove deformed, I shall be sorie it had so noble a god-father: and never after eare so barren a land, for feare it yeeld me still so bad a harvest. I leave it to your Honourable survey, and your Honor to your heart's content which I wish may alwaies answere your owne

45

wish, and the world's hopefull expectation.

> 'Your Honor's in all dutie,
>
> 'William Shakespeare.'

Surely, this dedication is, in its kind, a lovely thing. We may say that Shakespeare had the knack of making all things lovely, and that it is merely a trick of the golden pen by which the marriage of deference and dignity is accomplished. I have no great belief in the effect of a trick of the pen; I think that even in so seeming slight matter as the grace of this dedication, more than a trick was required: some motion of the heart as well. And we may note that Shakespeare, in promising some graver labour if *Venus and Adonis* be well received, is careful to promise only what he can perform. He will take advantage of all *idle* hours. He is a journeyman of the theatre who can give no more than his spare time to the composition of poems for his patron. That he will give; and that, so far as we can tell, ne did give: In another year, the graver labour was accomplished: *The Rape of Lucrece*. The dedication is brief, and the tone is changed.

'The love I dedicate to your Lordship is without end: whereot this Pamphlet without beginning is but a superfluous Moity. The warrant I have of your Honourable disposition, not the worth of my untutord Lines makes it assured of acceptance. What I have done is yours, what I have to doe is yours, being part in all I have, devoted yours. Were my worth greater, my duety would show greater, meane time, as it is, it is bound to your Lordship; To whom I wish long life still lengthened with all happinesse.

> 'Your Lordship's in all duety.
>
> 'William Shakespeare.'

This time it is not lines that are dedicated, but love; and the careful devotion of 'all idle hours' gives way to the large surrender: 'What I have done is yours, what I have to do is yours, being part in all I have, devoted yours.' A dedication is, indeed, far removed from a confession. Yet it is hard, and for me impossible, to believe that the words of the second dedication coming from the writer of the first have not their intimate meaning. There was a progress in dedication.

It happens that this word 'dedicate' was one of Shakespeare's favourite words. He obtained from it, in his poetry, some of his most beautiful effects. Of these one or two, at least, will come unaided to the memory of the reader: the others will be glanced at in this essay one by one. For the history of this lovely word in Shakespeare seems to me of some significance.

Before the dedication of *Venus and Adonis* to the Earl of Southampton in 1593, the words 'dedicate' and 'dedication' are nowhere to be found in his plays. Probably, none of these plays was altogether his play, and he meant what he said when he called *Venus and Adonis* 'the first heir of his invention'. It was the child of his invention, whereas the earlier plays had been invented before he put his hand to them. But in them his handiwork is plentiful; yet the word 'dedicate', which he was to use so exquisitely, is not in it. For young Clifford's speech at the end of the second part of *Henry VI* (v. ii. 31), which contains the word, is manifestly an addition made to the play in or about 1598. There is nearly ten years' difference between the rhythm and diction of lines 31—53 and those of the surrounding verses.

The word 'dedicate' enters Shakespeare's vocabulary in 1593, and the occasion is his actual dedication of his first book; it next appears a year later, in 1594, when he dedicates his second book to the same man. Southampton had been pleased with *Venus and Adonis*, and Shakespeare had fulfilled his promsie to take advantage of all idle hours. But now he dedicated not merely his new poem, not merely his love, but all himself—'all I am, devoted yours'.

Was he serious? It is impossible for me to read the Sonnets as courtly exercises in compliment. I am one of those who must believe that 'with this key Shakespeare unlocked his heart'. The change of tone between the two actual dedications of *Venus* and *Lucrece* only confirms me in the supposition I find necessary. And the beautiful sonnet—the only one—in which the word occurs (No. 82) gives still more colour to this belief that Shakespeare took his act of dedication seriously:

> I grant thou wert not married to my Muse,
> And therefore may'st without attaint o'erlook

The dedicated words that poets use
Of their fair subject, blessing every book.
Thou art as fair in knowledge as in hue,
Finding thy worth a limit past my praise,
And therefore art enforced to seek anew
Some fresher stamp of the time-bettering days.
And do so, love; yet when they have devised
What strained touches rhetoric can lend,
Thou truly fair were truly sympathiz'd
In true plain words by thy true-telling friend;
   And their gross painting might be better used
   Where cheeks need blood; in thee it is abused.

Shakespeare is speaking here not of sonnets, but of dedications; and the signs are that he is hurt. In his dedications he has spoken the truth, and truth in Southampton's case is all the grace that is needed. He is disappointed that his young patron is beguiled by 'the strained touches rhetoric can lend'. Of these we have seen a good example in Nashe's hyperbole of flattery.

'I grant thou wert not married to my Muse', says Shakespeare; but the undertone of implication is that Shakespeare had indulged himself with the belief that he was. And that fits exactly with the situation which the two successive dedications themselves suggest. Shakespeare the man of twenty-nine had fallen in love with the young nobleman of nineteen. A ridiculous thing to do, perhaps. That is a matter of opinion. More important for our present purposes, and for a realization of Shakespeare's nature, is to recognize the fact that such things have happened, do happen, and, so far as we can tell, always will happen.

The evidence, as I read it, is that Shakespeare's dedications had been very serious indeed. When he said to the young Earl that all he was, was devoted his, he meant it. We may say that he was cheating himself, and that he was investing the relation of patron and poet with the glamour of illusion. The real point, if that be our judgment, is that Shakespeare was the kind of man who needed to invest with the glamour of real devotion the equivocal, and often merely sordid, relationship between patron and poet. He believed not merely what he wanted, but what he needed, to believe   He loved his young patron, and the act of dedicating his poems to him was an act, not of the calculating mind, but of the heart and soul.

The simple facts are in harmony with this supposition. Never again to the end of his life did Shakespeare dedicate a volume to any man.   What he had done, for Southampton, he had done once for all.   Whatever happened between them, this act of his should stand alone.   Again, we may say, pure accident; it simply happened that Shakespeare wrote no more poems, and wrote no more dedications.   It is possible.   I am merely concerned to point out that the terms of the dedications themselves, the tone of the sonnet which speaks of the dedications, and the fact that Shakespeare dedicated no more, fall into natural and unforced harmony with the story whose outlines we gather from the sequence of the Sonnets themselves.

Not only are these simple facts thus in natural harmony, but the more delicate evidences to which we have already alluded. Before the actual dedication of *Venus and Adonis*, the word 'dedicate' is nowhere to be found in Shakespeare's plays.   In the actual dedications and in the sonnet which speaks of them, the word is used simply: Shakespeare dedicates his book: then he dedicates his love; then all that he is.   There is progressive dedication.   The new word takes on a depth of intimate meaning.

With a suddenness almost startling 'dedicate' becomes a precious word in Shakespeare's language.   A little while before it did not exist, now it is elected to convey the tenderest and most exquisite meanings.   We have only to listen.   It describes the birth of love in Romeo.

> But he, his own affection's counsellor,
> Is to himself—I will not say how true—
> But to himself so secret and so close,
> So far from sounding or discovery,
> As is the bud bit by the envious worm,
> Ere he can spread his sweet leaves in the air
> Or *dedicate* his beauty to the sun.   (I. i. 158.)

Or, in *Twelfth Night*, it springs from Shakespeare's mind to describe the disappointed Antonio's devotion to Sebastian.

49

> A witchcraft drew me hither:
> That most ungrateful boy there by your side,
> From the rude sea's enraged and foamy mouth
> Did I redeem; a wreck past hope he was:
> His life I gave him and did thereto add
> My love, without retention or restraint,
> *All in his dedication.* (v. i. 86.)

We cannot escape the echo: 'What I have done is yours: yhat I have to do is yours; being part in all I have, devoted yours.' Or, in a lighter vein, it is used by Benedick in *Much Ado* to describe Claudio's infatuation for Hero, while he is blind to his own for Beatrice.

> I do much wonder that one man seeing how much another man is a fool when he *dedicates his behaviours to love* will, after he hath laughed at such follies in others, become the argument of his own scorn by falling in love. (II. iii. 9.)

'Dedication' and love appear to be part of a single thought, or a single experience. A natural collocation, it may be said. Natural or not, it was unknown to Shakespeare's language before he dedicated to Southampton. And who can tell whether it is not largely by the magic of Shakespeare's language that the collation seems so natural to us to-day?

Or again the image from the description of Romeo in love as the bud bit by the envious worm ere he 'can dedicate his beauty to the sun' appears, magically changed, in the picture of Henry V on the morning before Agincourt.

> For forth he goes and visits all his host,
> Bids them good-morrow with a modest smile,
> And calls them brothers, friends, and countrymen.
> Upon his royal face there is no note
> How dread an army hath enrounded him;
> Now doth he *dedicate one jot of colour*
> Unto the weary and all-watched night. (iv, chor. 37.)

There beauty and valour are one. In young Clifford's thrilling speech at the end of 2 *Henry VI*, it is to valour alone that dedication is made; but what dedication is, is plainly and passionately declared.

> O war, thou son of Hell,

Whom angry heavens do make their minister,
Throw in the frozen bosoms of our part
Hot coals of vengeance! Let no soldier fly.
He that is *truly dedicate to war*
Hath no selflove, nor he that loves himself
Hath not essentially, but by circumstance,
The name of valour. (v. ii. 37.)

Dedication is utter self-surrender, to love, to valour, or, in Isabella's lovely words to Angelo in *Measure for Measure*, to God.

Isab. Hark how I'll bribe you: good my lord, turn back.
Ang. How! bribe me?
Isab. Ay, with such gifts that heaven shall share with you.
Not with fond shekels of the tested gold,
Or stones whose rates are either rich or poor
As fancy values them; but with true prayers
That shall be up at heaven and enter there
Ere sun-rise, prayers from preserved souls,
From fasting maids *whose minds are dedicate*
To nothing temporal. (II. ii. 154.)

Already we have chronicled every occasion on which the word 'dedicate' is used by Shakespeare from the time of his dedication of *Venus and Adonis* until *Measure for Measure*. We have omitted none. Can it be mere accident that we have compiled a tiny anthology of perfect felicities? Or does not the experience rather confirm our surmise that the word itself was precious?

Can it be mere accident again that the word which has been used to express such exquisite or heroic self-devotions suddenly takes on a sinister meaning It is now Cressida's word, at the moment when Troilus is aching to believe that his integrity and truth to her (his 'dedication', in fact)

Might be affronted by the match and weight
Of such a winnow'd purity in love.

(III. ii. 174.)

It is Troilus, alas, who is dedicated; but it is Cressida who speaks the word.

Pan. What, blushing still? Have you not done talking yet?
Cres. Well, uncle what folly I commit, I *dedicate* to you.

(III. ii. 109.)

Or it describes the fearful disillusion of Timon, bitten by the rankling tooth of man's ingratitude.

1 *Serv.* So noble a master fall'n. All gone! and not
    One friend to take his fortune by the arm,
    And go along with him.
2 *Serv.*   As we do turn our backs
    From our companion thrown into his grave,
    So his familiars to his buried fortunes
    Slink all away, leave their false vows with him,
    Like empty purses picked; and his poor self,
    A dedicated beggar to the air,
    With his disease of all-shunned poverty,
    Walks, like contempt, alone. (IV. ii. 13.)

The poetry is superb; the use of the word magnificent. But the human emotion how changed We cannot but remember the former dedication to the air, of which the rose-bud in *Romeo* was cheated. We remember too the false vows of Cressida. It may be mere accident that somewhere in the background of 'dedication' seems to hover a suggestion of treachery. And the same suggestion creeps out again in the use of the word in *Cymbeline*, where it forms part of Iachimo's loathsome suggestion to Imogen, and his treachery to Posthumus.

Imo.   Revenged!
    How should I be revenged? If this be true—
    As I have such a heart that both mine ears
    Must not in haste abuse—if it be true,
    How should I be revenged?
Iach.   Should he make me
    Live, like Diana's priest, between cold sheets,
    Whiles he is vaulting variable ramps,
    In your respite, upon your purse? Revenge it.
    I dedicate myself to your sweet pleasure (I. vi. 136.)

The word, it seems, could suffer no greater defilement than this. Yet perhaps in *Macbeth* it does, in the scene where Malcolm

52

makes trial of Macduff. Macduff is being bitterly disillusioned while Malcolm tells of his vices. 'There's no bottom, none, in my voluptuousness', says Malcolm. With weary cynicism Macduff replies:

> Boundless intemperance
>
> In nature is a tyranny; it hath been
> The untimely emptying of the happy throne,
> And fall of many kings. But fear not yet
> To take upon you what is yours: you may
> Convey your pleasures in a spacious plenty,
> And yet seem cold, the time you may so hoodwink.
> We have willing dames enough; there cannot be
> That vulture in you, to devour so many
> *As will to greatness dedicate themselves,*
> Finding it so inclined. (IV. iii. 75.)

The use here touches an absolute of revulsion. The word is trampled on in the cold and ghastly joke of such 'a dedication to greatness'. The transvaluation of values is complete.

After that, the mere suggestion of yielding oneself up to a desperate and forlorn adventure is even comfortable. Thus the word is used, in a passage of pure poetic beauty in the *Winter's Tale,* when Camillo warns Florizel against

> *A wild dedication of yourselves*
> *To unpath'd waters,* undream'd shores, most certain
> To miseries enough: no hope to help you,
> But as you shake off one to take another;
> Nothing so certain as your anchors, who
> Do their best office if they can but stay you
> Where you'll be loath to be. (IV. iv. 579.)

The final use of the word, in *The Tempest,* is in Prospero's story to Miranda.

> I, thus neglecting worldly ends, *all dedicated*
> *To closeness and the bettering of my mind*
> With that, which, but by being so retired,
> O'erprized all popular rate, in my false brother
> Awaked an evil nature. (I. ii. 89.)

Dedication and treachery seem still to be close companions.

53

But now the dedication itself is pure again; the word itself is no longer contaminated, as it was by Cressida and Iachimo and in *Macbeth*. It is simply that the dedicated soul is simple and by the fact of its dedication laid open to treachery. That is 'the mystery of iniquity', and not even in *The Tempest* could Shakespeare solve it. He recognized it simply as a condition of an order of existence from which men must free themselves.

We have followed precisely the history of the word 'dedication' in Shakespeare; we have examined every occasion of its use, save one. Is it mere fancy that impels us to believe that its story is not fortuitous? Till 1593 the word is unknown in Shakespeare; it appears then, quite simply, in two actual dedications, to the same young nobleman to whom the sonnets were written. These were the only dedications—or shall we say the only dedication?—which Shakespeare ever made. Hard upon this the word enters on a period of delicate metaphorical life, during which it is inseparably connected with true and complete devotion. 'Dedication' holds the beauty of devotion: it is a beauty of language to describe a beauty of soul.

Abruptly there is a change in its human quality. It is given over to cynicism, and made the accomplice of treachery. Dedication is no longer to love, but to lust; no longer of love, but of lust. Or the dedicated man, like Timon, betrayed by his friends, or, like Prospero, by his brother; or the outcast and desperate man in dedicated to the air, or to the wild waters. Can it be all pure accident that the lovely suggestion of the word is now altogether lost? Is it simply that in plays of 'the tragic period' even a word must suffer a little tragedy of its own? The answer will not suffice. Iachimo need not have 'dedicated' himself to Imogen, nor Macduff have caricatured the high associations of the word. The degradation here, at least, was deliberate, even though it was unconscious. Shakespeare is turning the barb in the wound.

What was the wound? How was it caused, and by whom was it caused? Perhaps the answer may be sought in the one remaining use of the word which we have so far forborne to chronicle. It is in *Timon,* and it comes at the very opening of of that strange play. The poet, with the painter, and the jeweller, and the merchant, is standing in the great man's ante-room. Suddenly, the poet begins reciting to himself some lines which the painter indistinctly overhears.

Pain. You are rapt, sir, in some work, some dedication
To the great lord.
Poet. A thing slipp'd idly from me

Our poesy is as a gum which oozes
From whence 'tis nourish'd: the fire i' the flint
Shows not till it be struck; our gentle flame
Provokes itself, and like the current flies
Each bound it chafes. What have you there

Pain. A picture, sir. When comes your book forth?
Poet. Upon the heels of my presentment, sir. (I. i. 19.)

The situation is clear. The poet has dedicated his book, and it waits only for formal presentation to the great lord to be made public. The presentation is accomplished two lines later in the scene.

Poet. Vouchsafe my labour, and long live your lordship!
Tim. I thank you; you shall hear from me anon:
Go not away. (I. i, 153.)

So the poet awaits his reward from Timon's Treasurer. While he is waiting, he accosts Apemantus.

Poet. How now, philosopher!
Apem. Thou liest.
Poet. Art not one?
Apem. Yes.
Poet. Then I lie not.
Apem. Art not a poet?
Poet. Yes.
Apem. Then thou liest: look in thy last work, where thou hast feigned him a worthy fellow.
Poet. That's not feigned; he is so. (I. i. 221.)

The poet is obviously sincere. His long previous talk with the painter shows him convinced of Timon's 'good and gracious nature'. It is not Timon who is unworthy, but 'the glib and slippery creatures' whom his wealth attracts to seeming service.

Not merely the poet's own expressed opinion, but the whole theme and conduct of the play make it impossible that Timon should have been in his mind, when the thing slipped idly from him. The thing itself is memorable, because it sticks out clear from the course and sense of the scene.

Poet. [*Reciting to himself.*] When we for recompense have
praised the vile,

It stains the glory in that happy verse
Which aptly sings the good. (I. i. 15.)

Either it is totally irrelevant, or the connexion is that the thought of his dedication to the good Timon, whom he has aptly sung in happy verse, reminds the poet of a former dedication, wherein he praised the vile for recompense. By this past soil his sincere praise is now stained.

So, at the turning-point of the history of the word 'dedication' in Shakespeare's poetry, we find that it abruptly descends from the heaven of metaphor to the earth of sordid experience. Only here, at the beginning of *Timon*, since it first entered Shakespeare's vocabulary, does the word return to its direct and most familiar use on the lips of a writer: the dedication of a book. There is nothing divine, nothing beautiful, nothing ideal about it. At this moment 'dedication' is prostitution: 'when we for recompense have praised the vile', and a prostitution that leaves behind it an enduring stain. And as we have seen, if there is one predominant strain in the later meaning of 'dedication' in Shakespeare's poetry, it is precisely this of prostitution. On the lips of Cressida. of Macduff, and Iachimo that is, in the earthliest sense, its meaning.

Cymbeline is among the very latest plays of Shakespeare. *Timon, Troilus,* and *Macbeth* we cannot date precisely. They belong roughly together, and the accepted date for them is anything between 1606 and 1609. Did anything happen between those dates which might have made the word 'dedication' suddenly turn to ashes in Shakespeare's mouth?

Something did happen then, and so far as we can tell at this distance of time, it was the one thing which must have had precisely this effect. In 1609 Shakespeare's intimate sonnets were published to the world. To Shakespeare, whose plays reveal him as beyond all men of his time (or of ours) sensitive in this matter of love, the publication must have been a fearful violation. And, ultimately, Southampton must have been responsible for it. Whether it was in deliberate malice, or indifferent contempt, or mere carelessness, that he allowed these sonnets to fall into the hands of an unscrupulous publisher, would have made no difference to the effect on Shakespeare of this publication. Malice in such an issue would be no worse than carelessness, although in fact carelessness is hardly conceivable.

What Shakespeare's relations with Southampton had been for a dozen years before the catastrophe of publication, we can only guess. The passionate infatuation had certainly cooled, and probably there was real estrangement. The young nobleman, as he passed from youth to manhood, learned that his attachment to a poet and a strolling player was a thing to be forgotten. Shakespeare would have acquiesced in the necessity, and consoled himself with the thought that in each remained a memory of what had been. But when, perhaps many months before their actual publication, he learned that his sonnets had been handed over to the gutter-press of those days, then the last veil of possible illusion was torn away. All that had been was cankered.

The sudden revulsion from the past was fearful; there came a moment of brutal injustice to himself, when it seemed to him not merely that Southampton was vile: but he himself was viler still. He had deliberately deceived his own soul; he had pretended love where he had sought reward; he had not dedicated, but prostituted himself. The self-revelation, though false, was appalling.

[March. 1929]

57

MARCEL PROUST

The most apparent phases in the evolution of literature are marked by a twofold change, a change in the intelligence and a change in the sensibility that find expression in it. The writers of a new period seem both to know and to feel more than the writers of the period before them ; and these separate developments are bound together in the mesh of a continual interaction. They feel more because they know more. A man who has absorbed into his consciousness the aimless principle of Natural Selection develops a new nerve of sensibility which perceives, isolates, and emphasises a quality of aimlessness in all experience. Similarly, a man who has assimilated the Freudian psychology will respond with a new awareness to every manifestation of the sex impluse in the life before his eyes. Every atom of new knowledge that is really apprehended and digested by the mind serves, if not positively to enlarge, at least to re-arrange the mechanism of the sensibility. In life we look for that which we know and feel that for which we are prepared. The logicians assure us that it is impossible to know or feel anything besides.

But these epoch-making changes in the intelligence and the sensibility, though they mark the historical advance of one period upon another, and serve to distinguish phases of the general consciousness in the literature into which it is projected, do not necessarily mark advance in the quality of the literature itself. The changed sensibility will respond to many elements in experience which have hitherto passed unnoticed; it will emphasise, and may easily over-emphasise them. It will be induced to fasten upon a new truth of fact—as, for example, the ubiquity of the sex impulse under the strangest disguises—and to neglect old truths of fact which are not less true because they are familiar—as, for example, that the disguises which the sex-impulse is compelled to assume are essential to civilisation. So that when we leave the historical or evolutionary aspect of literature for literature itself, the significance of a change in the general intelligence and sensibility

58

becomes dependent upon the degree of comprehensiveness that has been reached after the change. An extension of the sensibility has in itself no literary value ; and, even when the creative alchemy of art has intervened, the expression of a new emotion will be far less significant than the expression of a comprehensive attitude to life, into which the new perceptions have been absorbed.

The final purpose of literature remains 'to see life steadily and see it whole;' but the definition is insufficient because it may equally be applied to the scientist or the philosopher. The writer sees and re-creates the quality of life as a whole, the quality of experience being precisely the element which is ignored by philosophy and science. Only in so far as the extension of the sensibility which comes with an advance in knowledge is made to heighten the perception of the quality of experience as a whole can it have a positive literary value. By the aid of the new psychology we may be able to detect the working of the sex impulse in an incident of life where we did not previously suspect it ; but this power is useless to the writer unless it enables him to seize more completely the unique quality of the incident, to compass its particularity, as it were, on another side, and so make his grasp of it firmer. If he imagines that this new aspect is the whole of the incident, he is merely indulging in the simplification of science. An extension of the sensibility has positive literary value only when it is a means towards the fuller penetration of the material of literature, which is the quality of our experience. We may perceive this quality in a new relation ; but this new relation does not supersede the old familiar ones, it only helps to complete them. When a young man of eighteen suddenly develops a passion for exquisite clothes and beautiful ties, to say it is a manifestation of the sex impulse is true; it may indeed be for the biologist a complete truth, but for the writer it is a fragmentary and untransmuted fact. Unless he combines it with a hundred other perceptions—of the boy's desire to be beautiful, to be unobtrusive, to be independent, to be ideal— so that it endorses and intensifies them, he is an inferior man of science instead of (as he often imagines) a superior writer.

But if the new faculty of perception is brought into harmony with the old ones, if the new relation in which the quality of experience is perceived does complete and not merely supersede the familiar relations, it changes them all ; and when this new complex of perceptions is expressed in a work of literature, the work will be unfamiliar, however great may be its comprehensiveness and truth. Only as we persevere with it and accustom ourselves to the mechanism of the sensibility expressed in it. will its strangeness begin to disappear.

Whatever may have been our final judgment on the strange novel of M. Marcel Proust, *Du Côté de chez Swann,* which appeared in the year before the war—and the book at least had this obviously in common with a great work of literature, that it lent itself to judgment on many different planes—the persistent element in all our changing opinions was that it marked the arrival of a new sensibility. We were being made aware in new ways, induced to perceive existence in new relations. We seemed to be drawn by a strong and novel enchantment to follow the writer down the long and misty avenues of his consciousness to the discovery of a forgotten childhood. And it was not as though his compelling us to enter into and share the process of his self-exploration was accidental ; it was most deliberate. Whatever might be his underlying purpose M. Proust was not in the least like an artist who should leave all the tentative lines of his discarded sketches upon the paper.

The book opened with a description of the hypothetical writer (who might be more or less than M. Proust himself, but whom we shall for brevity's sake identify with him) asleep and waking in the night. In the effort to identify the room in which he is, he passes through a series of memories awakened by the sensation of that effort, and he proceeds to describe what is for him the archetype of that sensation, namely, his anxiety when a child at going to bed without his mother's kiss. From this central point he explores the past and discovers the figure of Swann, a friend of the family, whose presence at dinner it was which prevented him from having at all, or having fully, the kiss without which sleep was impossible. He explores all the avenues of memory until they are exhausted, and he has given us a picture, vague in some places and astonishingly precise in others, of a childish universe in which Swann is the mysterious hero, and his mother and grandmother the guardian angels. That picture, like the vision of the robber Golo which came from the magic-lantern given him to keep his night terrors away, disappears abruptly, and the grown man appears again. He is in his home in Paris, dipping a *madeleine* into a cup of tea. Again the sensation, as he puts the cake into his mouth, is mysteriously familiar. He tries to empty his mind of everything else and to leave his consciousness free for the memory concealed in the sensation to emerge. It returns from the past; it is the taste of the sop of *madeleine* which his aunt used to give him. He remembers the moments; he remembers the room; and gradually he begins to recreate another aspect of the past—his aunt Léonie's house at Combray, Françoise the faithful servant, and, above all, his walks ' du côté de chez Swann,' on that side of the town where the road skirted Swann's park. The other side, the other hemisphere of his world, is ' du côté de Guermantes,' where the road, never followed to its august destination, leads eventually to the chateau of the Duc de Guermantes, the great notable of the countryside and one of the greatest aristocrats in all France. Most of the boy's walking is done on Swann's side, however, though most of his dreaming concerns the other. Nevertheless, 'chez Swann' is hardly more accessible than the mysterious Guermantes; for Swann has made a scandalous marriage, since which the boy's parents have never visited nor allowed him to visit the house. Only one day, when Swann and his family are supposed to be away, he and his father and grandfather take the short cut which runs through Swann's park; and the boy sees a freckled girl—Swann's daughter—who pokes out her tongue at him. He also hears her name called out: ' Gilberte! '

Again there is an abrupt change in the narrative. The story of Swann's love for the mistress he has married, Odette de Crécy, is told at length. At first it seems to have no relation to the consciousness of the narrator; it must have taken place before he was even born. But, although the history of Swann

61

and Odette cannot have been obtained by any exploration of the mental *Hinterland* such as yielded the first part of the story, it becomes apparent that the behaviour of Swann's mind during his love affair is governed by the same laws that operated in the writer's rediscovery of his childhood. While Swann's passion for Odette grows, hers for him cools ; but in the midst of his agony his knowledge and memory of their love seems to have dissolved. *Sentit et excruciatur*; but what he has lost he cannot tell until one night he goes to a musical evening in the Faubourg St. Germain. If we had to choose a single episode from M. Proust's enormous book as a sample of the whole, it would be twenty odd pages describing this evening. In a sense they are too good to be truly representative; but every quality that can be found in them will be found in a more or less concentrated form througout the work. But whereas in the rest of the book they are often, as it were, held in solution, here they are solidified into cystals. That complete projection of the sensibility which distinguishes great literature is here beautifully accomplished. Since it is impossible to continue the description of M. Proust's book at length, we may try to give an account of this episode.

Swann, the darling of the most exclusive Parisian society, preoccupied with his love for Odette, has given up frequenting it. When he enters Mme. de Ste. Euverte's house on this evening, what was once familiar has become strange to him. He finds himself in an alien universe. Each one of the multitude of lackeys on the stairs, each one, from the first who 'semblait témoigner du mépris pour sa personne, et des égards pour son chapeau,' appears to him mysterious. At last, with an accumulated sense of strangeness, he enters the salon. He sees a number of once familiar friends, like himself, wearing monocles. But to-night their monocles, instead of passing unnoticed, are peculiar: General de Froberville's seem like 'a wound that it was glorious to receive, but indecent to display;' the Marquis de Forestelle's 'a superfluous cartilage whose presence was inexplicable and material precious;' while M. de Palancy's 'grosse tête de carpe aux yeux ronds . . . avait l'air de transporter seulement avec lui un fragment accidentel et peut-être purement symbolique de son aquarium.' By these curious and striking images we are made to feel how utterly foreign to Swann is become his once habitual environment. He stands near by a fashionable lady, Mme. de Franquetot, and her country cousin, Mme. de Cambremer, and watches their strange contortions to mark their interest in the music. Then the feelings of Mm. de Gallardon, a connection of the Guermantes, are described. Then the young Princesse de Laumes, soon to be the Duchesse de Guermantes, enters. Mme. de Gallardon makes a not too successful attempt to enter into conversation with her and is snubbed. M. de Froberville tries to be intro- duced to Mme. de Cambremer's daughter-in-law. The Princesse de Laumes shows her contempt for the princes of the Empire, and catches sight of Swann. He refuses her invitation to Guermantes, introduces Froberville to young Mme. de Cam- bremer, and longs to escape from this place 'où Odette ne viendrait jamais, où personne, où rien ne la connaissait, d'où elle était entièrement absente.'

Suddenly the pianist begins a sonata, and Swann hears a little musical phrase to which he and Odette had listened together in the salon where they used continually to meet.

Et avant que Swann eût eu le temps de comprendre, et de se dire: 'C'est la petite phrase de la sonate de Vinteuil, n'écoutons pas!' tous ses souvenirs du temps où Odette était éprise de lui, et qu'il avait réussi jusqu'à ce jour de maintenir invisibles dans les profondeurs de son être, trompés par ce brusque rayon du temps d'amour qu'ils crurent revenu, s'étaient réveillés, et à tire d'aile étaient remontés lui chanter éperdûment, sans pitié pour son infortune présente, les refrains oubliés du bonheur.

All the particularity of his love returns with a stab; in a moment of time he relives every incident of it.

Et Swann aperçut, immobile en face de ce bonheur revécu, un malheureux qui fit pitié parce qu'il ne le reconnut pas tout de suite, si bien qu'il dut baisser les yeux pour qu'on ne vît pas qu'ils étaient pleins de larmes. C'était lui-même.

Quand il l'eut compris, sa pitié cessa, mais il était jaloux de l'autre lui-même qu'elle avait aimé, il fut jaloux de ceux dont il s'était dit souvent sans trop souffrir, 'elle les aime peut-être,' maintenant qu'il avait échangé l'idée vague d'aimer, dans laquelle il n'y a pas d'amour, contre les pétales du chrysanthème et l' 'en tête' de la Maison d'or qui, eux, en étaient pleins. Puis sa souffrance devenant trop vive, il passa sa main sur son front, laissa tomber son monocle, en essuya le verre. Et sans doute s'il s'était vu à ce moment-là il eut ajouté à la collection de ceux qu'il avait distingués le monocle qu'il déplaçait comme une pensée importune et sur la face embuée duquel, avec un mouchoir, il cherchait à effacer les soucis.

After the episode which culminates in this incident, the narrative returns, apparently for good, to the growing consciousness of the boy. His childish love for Swann's daughter, his visit to the Brittany sea-side at Balbec where he meets another love, Albertine, and one of the less fashionable but authentic Guermantes, Mm. de Villeparisis and her nephew, Robert de Saint-Loup, who becomes his intimate friend; the death of his grandmother; his entry into the central shrine of the Guermantes by dining with the Duchess herself, his encounter with another Guermantes, M. de Charlus—these incidents are the bare skeleton of the three following volumes. But they are treated with such wealth of psychological detail that a summary of incidents, however lengthy, could only be misleading.

We may leave aside provisionally the problem of M .Proust's deeper intention, confining ourselves to the suggestion that his literary purpose has perhaps changed or developed in the course of his narrative; for if, as it seems, his main object is to record the growth of a modern consciousness, the brilliant episode of Swann's love affair which can never have been present to that consciousness, is, in spite of its value in itself, an alien element. Moreover, the long and masterly description of the dinner-party at the Duchesse de Guermantes also exists independently rathei than in relation to the young man's consciousness. He was, in fact, present at the dinner-party, but we do not feel his presence there; we do not perceive the company through his mind. And this objection will hold good still, even if we regard the scheme of the narrative so far as built upon succsssive contrasts between the dream and the reality of Swann and the dream and the reality of Guermantes. M. Proust seems at times to waver undecided between the psychological history of a modern mentality and an anatomy of modern society.

Nevertheless, it is better to admit that on a canvas so large a strict subordination of every part to the literary purpose of the whole is not to be expected. We are conscious that a single sensibility pervades all the parts, even though the power of projecting it so completely as in the episodes of the musical evening and the death of the grandmother is intermittent. And this sensibility is our chief concern. The underlying motive which animates, or law which governs it, is that which appears so plainly in the first volume—the dependence of memory and mental life as a whole upon association. Without the taste of *madeleine*, the boy's past at Combray, without the *petite phrase*, Swann's knowledge of the realities of his love for Odette, would have been sunk in the dark backward and abysm of time. This psychological fact at once governs the conduct of the narrative itself in so far as it is presented in terms of a single consciousness, and determines the conduct of the various characters who appear in it. More than this, the act of penetrating through some present circumstance, to a fragment of past experience which it seems to hold strangely concealed behind it, is represented as a consummation of personality. To enter into complete possession of the past by means of such present circumstances is to possess oneself wholly; they are, M. Proust says, the door that opens upon *la vraie vie*. This conviction of the writer can be interpreted in two ways, according as we regard the whole narrative as the history of the consciousness of a writer, or as the development of an extreme but none the less typical modern mind. In one of the few indications of his own plan, M. Proust seems to declare that his aim is to describe the evolution of a literary sensibility.

Si en descendant l'escalier je ravivais les soirs de Doncières, quand nous fûmes arrivés dans la rue brusquement, la nuit presque complète où le brouillard semblait avoir étient les reverbères, qu'on ne distinguait, bien faibles, que de tout prés, me ramena à je ne sais quelle arrivée le soir à Combray, quand la ville n'était encore éclairée que de loin en loin, et qu'on y tâtonnait dans une obscurité humide, tiède et sainte de crèche, à peine étoilée çà et là d'un lumignon qui ne brillait plus qu'un cierge. Entre cette année d'ailleurs incertaine de Combray et les soirs à Rivebelle revus tout à l'heure au-dessus des rideaux, quelles différences! J'éprouvais à les percevoir un enthousiasme qui aurait pu être fécond si j'étais resté seul et m'aurait évité ainsi le détour de bien des années inutiles par lequelles j'allais encore passer avant que se déclarât *la vocation invisible dont cette ouvrage est l'histoire.*

On the other hand, the description of his vain endeavour to seize the significance of three strange-familiar trees seen while driving in Mme. de Villeparisis' carriage at Balbec suggests a larger scope to this activity of the mind.

Ce plaisir (the delight of penetrating their significance) dont l'objet n'était que pressenti, que j'avais à créer moi-même, je ne l'éprouvais que de rares fois, mais à chacune d'elles il me semblait que les choses qui s'étaient passées dans l'intervalle n'avaient guére d'importance et qu'en m'attachant à sa seule réalité je pourrais enfin commencer une vraie vie. . . . Je vis les arbes s'éloigner en agitant leurs bras déses-pérés, semblant me dire: Ce que tu n'apprends pas de nous aujourd'hui tu ne le sauras jamais. Si tu nous laisses retomber au fond de ce chemin d'où nous cherchions nous hisser jusq'à toi, toute une partie de toi-même que nous t'apportions tombera pour jamais au néant. En effet, si dans la suite je retrouvai le genre de plaisir et d'inquiétude que je venais de sentir encore une fois, et si un soir trop tard, mais pour toujours—je m'attachai à lui, de ces arbres eux-mêmes en revanche je ne sus jamais ce qu'ils avaient voulu m'apporter ni où je les avais vus. Et quand la voiture ayant bifurqué, je leur tournai le dos et cessai de les voir . . . j'étais triste comme si je venais de perdre un ami, de mourir à moi-même, de renier un mort ou de méconnaitre un Dieu.

Perhaps we may find in the reference to the final and enduring penetration of the hidden reality a hint of the conclusion of the book considered as the history of an 'invisible vocation.' It suggests that at the end we may find the writer deliberately, and with all the resources of his will, concentrating upon that very sensation of reminiscence, the malaise at night in bed, with which *A la Recherche du Temps Perdu* opens. Such a doubling of the consciousness upon itself would make a fittingly subtle finale to the subtlest of all modern psychological fictions, and present us at the last with a book which would be in essentials the story of its own creation. But for the moment it is suffic- ient to regard the writer's conviction of the supreme importance of these acts of penetration as dictated by the knowledge of his own vocation, as a declaration that the *vraie vie* is that to which the intuition of the writer has access, and rather as a deliberate placing of the literary consciousness at the summit of the mental hierarchy than an assertion that complete possess- ion of the self by this means is the highest mortal end, the most perfect ascêsis, for all human beings.

What M. Proust undoubtedly does, however, is to represent this process of association as dominant in the mental lives of all men who can be said to live at all. A writer's exclusive preoccupation with it is only completer realisation of a tendency which distinguishes the higher grades of consciousness. It determines, for instance, Swann's attitude to Odette, and his decision to marry her really rests upon it. In more general terms, M. Proust regards the life of man as a perpetual effort to penetrate an unknown—the mind of the woman he loves the friend he admires, the society with which he is acquainted. This desire is, indeed, the very condition of love. 'Que nous croyions qu'un être participe à une vie inconnue où son amour nous ferait pénétrer, c'est de tout ce qu'exige l'amour pour naître, ce à quoi il tient le plus.' But this desire to penetrate the unknown of others is never satisfied. We live in perpetual illusion; the imagined friend, the imagined lover, the imagined society, the imagined reality, are never real. Suddenly, by a devious way, we hear of something said or done which cannot enter into our picture: we are shocked and pained, then we rebuild another picture, no less illusory, and imagine that this

67

at least is true. This recurrent theme of perpetual disillusion, of impotent encounter with the unknown, may be called the philosophical background of the book, and from this angle we might regard it as a philosophical justification of the art of writing, presented through the history of a consciousness. For as the growing man turns away from the continual disillusion which is the only result of his attempt to penetrate the reality beyond himself, he more clearly sees that the only reality he can hope to master is his own experience. Thus to enter into complete possession of the past by the method of which *Du Côté de chez Swann* is an example is presented not only as the goal to which an 'invisible vocation' was calling a particular person, but in fact also as the highest end of man, *la vraie vie* indeed. In so far as literature is based upon that method of evoking the past through an associated symbol (and it certainly is one very important element in literary creation) it is, according to this underlying philosophy, the supreme activity of life.

This concealed motive it is which differentiates M. Proust's book from all that have gone before. The metaphysician might call it the history of a solipsist. But such a definition would be as misleading as all other attempts to find a philosophical definition for a particular work of literature. For, though M. Proust is in a sense applying a theory to experience, he is doing so by the strikingly novel method of describing the process by which the theory was gradually and inevitably formed in the consciousness which applies it. If, therefore, M. Proust's book ends, as we believe it will end, in its own beginning, it will have a unity—in spite of the apparent discrepancy of certain of the parts—of a kind which has never been achieved in a work of literature before: it will be the first book which has been the psychological history of its own creation and a philosophical justification of its own necessity.[1] It will belong in this respect to a new order of literature. And that is what we already vaguely feel as we read it. It is something more than a book in an unfamiliar language, more than a fiction of greater psychological subtlety than we are accustomed to. For better

[1] This essay was written in 1921. There is now, alas, no hope either of proving or confuting the prophecy.

or worse, it marks the emergence of a new kind, the arrival of a new sensibility.

That is its uncommon significance. To find an approximate parallel in the history of modern literature we should probably have to go back to Rousseau. There we should discover the paradox of a man not primarily a literary artist whose work revolutionised the literature of the next hundred years. M. Proust likewise is not primarily a literary artist. Nothing could be more significant than the length of the process of his finding his 'invisible vocation.' Like Rousseau, he is ultimately compelled to writing as a satisfaction for his sensibility. The chief point of difference is that where Rousseau was compelled to express his sensibility upon alien themes, M. Proust has been in the privileged position of one who could afford to wait for the truly inevitable occasion. Still, the only work of literature with which *à la Recherche du Temps Perdu* could profitably be compared is the *Confessions* of Jean-Jacques. There is a real likeness between the driving impulses at work in these books, and a careful comparison might enable us to determine the more important differences between the new sensibility of the eighteenth, and the new sensibility of the twentieth century. At all events, a century of science has passed between. M. Proust is not preoccupied with finding God, but with finding *la vraie vie,* though a previous quotation shows that where Rousseau always did, he sometimes does identify them. But more apparently still, a century of scientific psychology, of astronomical physics, of the biology of Natural Selection, has intervened. The last shreds of anthropocentrism have been worn away. Where Rousseau felt his own isolation and was tormented by the discrepancy between his dream and the reality, and could not reconcile himself to his isolation or his torment, M. Proust can. He accepts these conditions, he formulates them as an actual law of human existence; and the acceptance has been incorporated into the very mechanism of his sensibility. He discerns in the world that which he feels in himself; he is a Rousseau to whom some of the hidden causes of his perplexity have been made plain.

And the detailed knowledge of a century of applied science

is at his fingers' ends to help him refine and express his sensibility. How many times does he use the simile of a camera to make more apparent the working of two planes of consciousness! 'Ce qu'on prend en présence de l'être aimé n'est un cliché négatif, on le developpe plus tard.' By that means he expresses in a sentence a truth which lies behind a whole section of the fifth volume, 'Les Intermittences du Cœur,' where for the first time realising the loss of his beloved grandmother, months after her death, the young man learns that the uniqueness of our most precious experience eludes us till the opportunity of it is lost for ever. Again, when the boy, occupied with the anxiety of obtaining his mother's kiss, waits nervously at the dinner table—'comme un malade, grâce à un anésthésique, assiste avec pleine lucidité à l'operation qu'on pratique sur lui, mais sans rien sentir, je pouvais me réciter des vers que j'aimais ou observer les efforts que mon grand'père faisait pour parler à Swann du duc d'Audiffret-Pasquier, sans que les premiers me fissent éprouver aucune émotion, les seconds aucune gaîté.' And on the same occasion, having to take the kiss in public, he had not even the time or the freedom of mind necessary 'pour porter à ce que je faisais cette attention des maniaques qui s'efforcent de ne pas penser à autre chose pendant qu'ils ferment une porte, pour pouvoir, quand l'incertitude maladive leur revient, lui opposer victorieusement le souvenir du moment où ils l'ont fermée.' And for a final example we may choose the part played by the Duchesse de Guermantes' tree, which needs to be fertilised by an insect, in the explication of the psychology of the closing pages of *Du Côté de Guermantes*, and the writer's declaration: 'Mes réflexions, avaient suivi une pente que je décrirai plus tard et j'avais déjà tiré de la ruse apparente de fleurs une conséquence sur toute une partie inconsciente de l'œuvre littéraire.' Such are some of the typical contributions of the science of the nineteenth century towards the expression of a sensibility shaped by its larger knowledge.

But in endeavouring to analyse the singular impression which M. Proust's work makes upon us and to isolate the elements which produce the effect of novelty, in trying to investigate and assess its deeply-rooted originality, we are in danger of neglecting the more obvious qualities of a book which exhibits at least as many beauties as it conceals. It needs no second reading to appreciate the subtlety of psychological observation, the ironic detachment of the writer's vision of high Parisian society. If the dinner-party at the Guermantes is a masterpiece in not wholly unfamiliar genre, in the description of the musical evening at Mme de St. Euverte's the same lucid irony is perceptibly lifted to a higher plane and made to subserve a complex emotional effect. And though the biting wit which flashes home again and again through the narrative of *Du Côté de Guermantes* is of the very highest order in its kind, though the semi-satirical portrait of the *bien pensant* ambassador, M. de Norpois, at the beginning of *A l'Ombre des Jeunes filles* is perfect, they yield in impressiveness to the certainty of the single touch with which, in the description of the grandmother's illness, M. Proust sounds the note of the tragedy of death. When the grandmother has had a paralytic stroke in the Champs Elysées, and the boy suddenly sees 'son chapeau, son visage, son manteau dérangés pur la main de l'ange invisible avec lequel elle avait lutté,' we feel we are in the presence of a great writer indeed. And besides the command of tragic simplicity and wit, M. Proust has also the gift of humour. To appreciate this picture of life in the kitchen it is necessary to know that it was an established convention that the servants should not be disturbed at their lunch.

Déjà depuis un quart d'heure, ma mère qui n'usait probablement pas des mêmes mesures que Françoise pour apprécier la longueur du déjeûner de celle-ci, disait:

'Mais qu'est-ce qu'ils peuvent bien faire. voilà plus de deux heures qu'ils sont à table.'

Et elle sonnait timidement trois ou quatre fois. Françoise, son valet de pied, le maître d'hôtel entendaient les coups de sonnette comme un appel et sans songer à venir, mais pourtant comme les premiers sons des instruments qui s'accordent quand un concert va bientôt recommencer et qu'on sent qu'il n'y aura plus que quelques minutes d'entr'acte. Aussi quand les coups commençant à se répéter et à devenir plus insistants, nos domestiques se mettaient à y prendre garde et estimant qu'ils n'avaient plus beaucoup de temps devant eux et que la reprise du travail était proche, à un tintement de sonnette un peu plus sonore que les autres, ils poussaient un soupir et prenant leur parti, le valet de pied descendait fumer une cigarette devant la porte, Françoise, après quelques réflexions sur nous, telles que 'ils ont surement la bougeotte,' montait ranger ses affaires dans son sixième, et le maître d'hôtel ayant été chercher du papier à lettres dans ma chambre expédiait rapidement sa correspondance privée.

But it is not these qualities, rare and valuable as they are, which make *A la Recherche du Temps Perdu* one of the most significant of contemporary works of literature. They are precious qualities, but they are in a sense superficial, and they might be outweighed by the undoubted obscurity, the awkward complication of language, in large portions of the book. It is something much more than a dark narrative with frequent gleams of beauty; it is a book with at least one of the qualities of permanence, an animating soul. It is maintained by a high and subtle purpose, informed by a view of life as a whole, and because this secret fire glows steadily within it, we feel the radiance through the most forbidding pages long before we are able to detect its source. One consequence of this is that though M. Proust's language is sometimes alembicated to a point of grotesqueness, he has style; we might more exactly apply to him a phrase which he himself has aptly used of a great predecessor, Stendhal, and say that his work has *la grande ossature du style,* a thing of infinitely more importance than limpidity or beauty in the detail of expression. M. Proust's style, in this larger meaning, is as new and original as is the sensibility to which it owes its being.

[JULY, 1921]

THE POETS' POET

When Charles Lamb gave Edmund Spenser the title he has borne ever since, of "the poet's poet", he was not merely recording the simple fact that most of the English poets since Spenser's time had been deeply read in his work; he was also asserting that there was a very good reason why Spenser has always been beloved of his similars.

But since what was simple fact in Charles Lamb's day is simple fact no longer, we may refresh our memories. When Wordsworth heard, with his mind's ear, old Triton blow his wreathèd horn, the sound came to him through Spenser; when Keats sat down to write a new 'romance' and began—

> Fair Isabel, poor simple Isabel . . .

he was, whether he remembered it or not, singing over again a tune he had learned from Spenser—

> To Philemon, false faytour Philemon.

Again, even the very terms of that advice of Keats to Shelley, which some have found so harsh, that 'an artist must serve Mammon . . .' were derived from Spenser; nor can they be properly understood without a memory of the Cave of Mammon similar to that upon which Keats himself, consciously or unconsciously, was drawing. 'You will forgive me,' he said to Shelley, 'for sincerely remarking that you might curb your magnanimity, . . . and load every rift of your subject with ore.' What was in his mind was the house of Mammon.

> That house's forme within was rude and strong,
> Like an huge cave hewne out of rocky clifte,
> From whose rough vaut the ragged breaches hong
> Embost with massy gold of glorious guifte
> And with rich metall loaded every rifte. . . .

Keat's mind, indeed, was saturated with Spenser, whose influence upon him was second only to the more subtle and more intimate, and in a sense less scrutable, influence of Shakespeare. From Spenser, one might say, he learned to be a poet; from Shakespeare to be a great one.

Assuredly in Lamb's day Spenser was the poets' poet, as he

had been Milton's poet, and probably at one time Shakespeare's also. But to-day things are different. True, Charles Doughty could proclaim "Edmund my lodestar" but Doughty was writing an epic of England, in twenty-four books, and who can pay attention to-day to an epic in twenty-four books? Obviously, the same sort of people who can read *The Faerie Queene*—antediluvians manifest. For Spenser is, for the practical purposes of modern poetry, sadly out of fashion. And this is not because he is ancient simply; for one of the most accomplished of our modern poets can recommend his contemporary poets to seek in Dante their sustenance and the pattern of their skill. But Spenser belongs to the archaeology of literature.

This is strange, and worth consideration; for the tradition of English poetry is rooted in Spenser. And it is a very real question whether, if these roots are severed, English poetry will flourish again. Charles Doughty thought not. It is a pity that he never argued his opinion; he was content to assert it in the text of his epic from time to time, and get on with the writing. But, if he had argued it, he would have argued it, we may suppose, in this fashion. Spenser, he would have said, is the great 'maker' of English poetry; he is the man who, by his learning, his passion, his exquisite sense of form and his delicate ear, was able to establish in the English tongue all that the English language would admit of the tunes and technique accumulated during the fifteen hundred years that European poetry had been extant. This was Spenser's service, done to English poetry, once for all; for what Spenser did not transmit to his poetic successors was not transmissible. It was not, so to say, poetic 'material'; it was idiosyncrasy, the ungovernable, incalculable and inimitable personal element—that which a poet cannot learn, but can only learn how to express. This fundamental distinction, between poetic commonplace and poetic idiosyncrasy, between impersonal and personal style, is itself alien to modern criticism. Whether it calls itself a classical or romantic, modern criticism is on this essential point altogether romantic. It unquestioningly accepts the principle that 'le style, c'est l'homme même'; and almost as unquestioningly it accepts the converse of the dictum: 'l'homme même, c'est le style'. But the English romantics themselves, from whom this opinion ostensibly is derived, were not at all of this mind. They were conscious that their art was inherited; they conceived it as an acquisition, and they practised to acquire it. In their own view—surely a true one—they were not men who broke with the poetical tradition, but men who reasserted it. Since they were fine critics—indeed, their whole effort, like Spenser's own, was grounded on a deliberate critical realization—they distinguished without difficulty, between the personal and the impersonal elements in the style of their great predecessors. For the impersonal element, which they might reasonably hope to acquire, they went chiefly to Spenser.

The reason why their example was not followed in the nineteenth century was partly, no doubt, because their practice was not understood; partly, also, because it was the inimitable, even the accidental, elements in their achievement which chiefly fascinated their successors. How great a mass of mid-nineteenth-century poetry and art, for instance, grew out of a single casual poem by Keats which he did not think worthy to be included in his last volume: *La Belle Dame sans Merci!* But certainly more important than either of these causes was the change that was taking place in the structure of English society. Democracy was establishing itself, and with democracy the democratic art of literature—the Novel. Whatever optimists may believe poetry is not a democratic art: it has never been, and never will be unless the day shall arrive when democracy becomes itself aristocracy. It is futile to appeal to the example of the Ballads, which, however beautiful, do not at all belong to the kind of great poetry: or to the example of Shakespeare, whose *Hamlet* succeeded rather because it contained twenty-seven good pieces of stage-business than by reason of the poetry which Shakespeare could not keep out of it. The truth is that Keats himself was probably the last relatively poor man in England who was able honestly to believe that he might make a living by serving a full apprenticeship to the art of poetry. When at the beginning of *Endymion* he sat down to write to Haydon, quoting Spenser again,

The noble hart that harbours vertuous thought,

75

And is with childe of glorious great intent,
Can never rest, untill it forth have brought
Th' eternal brood of glorie excellent . . .

he really believed that by bringing forth that brood in the form of poetry he could achieve livelihood and fame. Nor was it an unreasonable illusion. His friends, some of them well-tried journalists, believed it. Yet more, his publisher believed it. Mr. Abbey, tea merchant and guardian did not. Mr. Abbey was right.

There were popular poets in Keats's time: there was Scott, there was Byron, there was Moore. Whatever qualities they had, they had not the qualities of great poets. Thinking of them in 1864, Walter Bagehot wrote:

Almost the sole result of the poetry of that time is the harm which it has done. It degraded for a time the whole character of the art. It fixed upon the minds of a whole generation, it engraved in popular memory and tradition, a vague conviction that poetry is but one of the many *amusements* for the enjoying classes, for the lighter hours of all classes. The mere notion, the bare idea, that poetry is a deep thing, a teaching thing, the most surely and wisely elevating of human things, is even now to the coarse public mind nearly unknown.

Bagehot was expecting a change; but what was true of England in 1864 is equally true of England to-day. Our poetry is slight, occasional, indisputably minor. Only by thus circumscribing its intentions does it exist at all. The 'mere notion, the bare idea' that a man should, from the beginning, devote his life to poetry, to expressing through the medium of poetry the thought that is born of a lifetime's full experience, is become almost fantastic.

The position of Spenser, the great teacher of English poets, is therefore now anomalous. There is nobody for him to teach. All that he has to teach is precisely all which is most irrelevant to the pursuit of literature to-day—the veritable 'art' of poetry, the specific skill by which a poet is a poet and not something else. Whether that situation is in itself deplorable or not, the consequence of the situation, with which we are here concerned, is a simple one—namely, that Spenser is not appreciated

76

for the qualities that are peculiarly his own. He is judged, if judged at all, by standards which are not really germane to his intentions or his achievement; he is required to stand or fall by his intrinsic interestingness.

To require this of Spenser is unreasonable. But what seems unreasonable, to-day, is the assertion that the work of a great poet should be absolved from the application of a standard so obviously natural. If Spenser fails to interest, he fails in everything. But interestingness is relative. The criterion of interestingness which prevails under democratic conditions is that described by Dr. Johnson: 'Nothing can please many and please long but just representations of human nature.' It is, no doubt the most essential kind of interestingness. Chaucer and Shakespeare both possess it in abundance; Spenser scarcely at all. But Spenser, though he aimed at pleasing long, did not aim at pleasing many. He was not even very much concerned with his own subject matter, or at any rate he was concerned with it in a manner quite different from that in which he professed to be concerned with it. Its intrinsic interest for him, we may be sure, was very small. Provided that it was a subject-matter appropriate (by traditional canons) to a great poem in the English language; it could be about—anything that great poems were about.

Much is sometimes made of Spenser's moral intention in composing *The Faerie Queene*; and, indeed, Spenser rather paraded it himself. But in reality this moral intention amounts to little. We have only to read, with an advised ear, the passage of most sustained and various beauty in *The Faerie Queene* —the adventure of Sir Guyon in the Gardens of Acrasia— to be certain that Spenser's heart was not in his morality. When, as in this episode, it came to a struggle between his morality and his sense of beauty, the sense of beauty, very properly, triumphed. The sense of beauty did with Spenser precisely what it did with his pupil Keats, 'it obliterated all consideration'. Spenser as a philosopher was hopelessly inconsistent, as a moralist hopelessly divided. He was fairly caught between the old ascetic morality and the new enthusiasm for Beauty for its own sake. He did not know whether Beauty was from God or the Devil;

77

but it would not be true to say of him (as it would be true to
say it of Marlowe or Shakespeare) that he did not care: he was,
in this respect, a divided man.   There was that in him which
cared, and there was that in him—call it, with Coleridge, the
genius in the man of genius—which did not care.   This half-
conscious, instinctive or intuitive part of him was content to
suffer the sense of beauty to 'obliterate all consideration'.   This
was his destiny and he must follow it, even when it played havoc
with his allegory and his conscious morality.   Essentially, he
was in much the same case as Keats when he wrote *Endymion*,
inwardly impelled to trust to his sense of beauty, yet with his
consciousness mistrusting his own faith, ostensibly even dis-
owning it.   Keats did not do this; but Spenser was near to the
Middle Ages and Keats was far away.   Keats was committed to
find an individual solution for an individual problem, where
Spenser could still, in consciousness at least, support himself
with authority.   Besides, Keats had time to think, where Spencer
had not.   The business in hand was too tremendous, too urgent,
and too exciting to allow him to be   turmoiled with its implications.   The business in hand was making a great poem and
laying the foundations of English poetry.

That English poetry should be beautiful, subtle, and in-
exhaustibly capable: that the instrument should hence forward
have the capacity of ' divine respondence meet': that the
language and the forms of English verse should become sensitive
like that fair almond tree on Selinus, by whose vision Marlowe
was entranced—

> Like to an almond tree ymounted hye
> On top of greene Selinis all alone,
> With blossoms brave bedecked daintily ;
> Whose tender locks do tremble every one
> At everie little breath that under heaven is blowne—

this was the aim after which Spenser laboured as no English
poet has laboured, nor needed to labour, since.   The instrument
which he devised, and shaped, and inlaid and polished is still
the instrument of English poetry.   Strings were added, like the
blank verse of Shakespeare and Milton, or the rich stanza of
Keats's odes; or strings were taken away to make the heroic

couplet of Dryden or of Pope. But the *sermo communis* of English poetry was settled : the themes, the tunes, the immense liberty of absolute and intricate formality, were won. All the great poets of England have known by simple instinct to whom they must go to learn their craft.

And surely, for those who have ears to hear, the sheer patterning of Spenser's 'music' has never been surpassed. Take these few passages which follow hard upon one another :

> Her wanton palfrey all was overspred
> With tinsel trappings woven like a wave
> Whose bridle hung with golden bells and bosses brave . . .
> Ah, deare Sansjoy, next dearest to Sansfoy,
> Cause of my new griefe, cause of my new joy . . .

or this to link one stanza with another:

> Then turning to his Lady, dead with feare her found.
> Her seeming dead he found with feigned feare . . .

or this whole stanza :

> One day, nigh wearie of the yrksome way,
> From her unhastie beast she did alight ;
> And on the grasse her dainty limbs did lay
> In secrete shadow, far from all men's sight :
> From her fayre head her fillet she undight
> And layd her stole aside. Her angel's face,
> As the great eye of heaven, shyned bright,
> And made a sunshine in the shady place ;
> Did never mortall eye behold such heavenly grace.

But to attempt to exhibit the infinitely various modulations of Spenser's verse is a fantastic enterprise. Do we seek the characteristic music of Pope's heroic couplet? Here it is :

> Flesh without blood, a person without spright,
> Wounds without hurt, a body without might,
> That could doe harme, yet could not harmèd bee,
> That could not die, yet seemd a mortall wight,
> That was most strong in most infirmitee.

or take these two single lines from neighbouring stanzas and recollect what Keats made of them :

What hevens? what altars? what enraged heats? . .
And precious odours fetched from far away . . .

or the subsequent history of these :

Come then ; come soone ; come sweetest death to me
And take away this long lent loathed light :
Sharp be thy wounds, but sweet the medicines be
That long captived souls from weary thraldom free.

or this, for its own perfect felicity :

Withall she laughed, and she blushed withall,
That blushing to her laughter gave more grace,
And laughter to her blushing, as did fall.

or—to make an end of the endless—this single line:

Deep in the bottom of an huge great rock . . .

Lost in our admiration of this unbounded store of riches, we
can only say, in Spenser's own words of the painter of Leda
and the swan, ' O wondrous skill and sweet wit of the man! '

By common consent there is one perfect poem of Spenser's—
' one entire and perfect chrysolite '—the *Epithalamion*. The
reason of its universally recognised appeal is not far to seek : it
lies in that which is, for the reader of Spenser as a whole, the
subtle but immediately felt difference between this and all his
other work save the Sixth Book of *The Faerie Queene*—the
contained tremor of an intimately personal emotion. It is but
natural that those who have been rapt by the intoxication of
this silver music should feel a faint sense of disappointment
when they turn afterwards to his other work. But, rightly
regarded, the *Epithalamion* is not an introduction to, but a
culmination of, Spenser's poetry ; it is the accidental triumph
which he might easily never have had, but which none but
himself could have won. Twenty-five years of toil at the sheer
craft of poetry went to make that love-poem. And how many
times in the history of a nation's literature does it happen that
a mature and perfect poetic craftsman falls in love? Great
poets have fallen in love often enough, and often enough have
become great poets in part through that experience ; but
Spenser was complete when the experience came to him. If
he himself was disturbed, his poetry could not be ; it was

immune from perturbation, for it was an impersonal thing.

Impersonal, in the strictest sense, no form of art can be ; but the difference is immense between a form of art which is sustained by a pure aesthetic emotion and one which is primarily the expression of ordinary emotional and intellectual experience. The object in the one case is the making of a beautiful thing, in the other the communication of experience.   No doubt these two distinct aims have been variously mingled in various poets, and in the same poet at various times ; but in no English poet has the former aim been so completely dominant as in Spenser. He appears deliberately to have sacrificed to his ideal of formal poetic beauty a genuine personal emotion, even when the influence of that personal emotion was relevant and appropriate and even necessary.   We have no reason to doubt that his grief over Sidney's death was sincere ;   *Astrophel*, nevertheless, is completely frigid.   Matthew Roydon's companion elegy is simple and affecting beside it. And as this apparently deliberate sacrifice of personal emotion may be explained by the excessive strength of Spenser's passion for formal beauty, so the excessive strength of the passion itself may be explained by the evident difficulty which Spenser found in controlling his patterns.   The lack of balance and proportion in a poem relatively so personal as *Colin Clout's Come Home Again* is very notable ; so it is in *The Ruines of Time.*   One feels that Spenser had always to keep a tight rein on himself, and that the apparent ease of his formal patterning was achieved only by a rigorous concentration.

We might put it that he could afford to run no risks by entertaining other emotions than those aroused by the pure pursuit of form and formal beauty.   In such a statement there is inevitable exaggeration.   But it is remarkable that both the morality and the imagery of *The Faerie Queene* are largely formal.   In another, and perhaps a greater, kind of poet precisely these two elements are impassioned ;   his morality is what he intimately is, and his imagery is subdued to the urgency of his utterance.   But in Spenser the morality is a mere convenience, or a useful theme, and the imagery quite often mere decorative fantasy.   The meetings of a lion and a unicorn, or a gryphon

81

and a dragon, provide poor similes : they are there not from any inherent necessity, but because images are formally re· quired. It is only when he leaves for the time being the company of his patterns of virtue and comes nearer to the actual world of men that his imagery is more than abstract decoration. And in this regard one can mark a sort of progress towards reality. When Paridel has cast off Hellenore,

> Alone he rode without his Paragone ;
> For, having filcht her bells, her up he cast
> To the wide world, and left her fly alone :
> He nould be clogd. So had he served many one,—

when Trompart lays his snare for Malbecco,

> Yet stoupt he not, but lay still in the winde,
> Waiting advantage on his pray to sease . . .

the images do more than decorate, they define ; and by the time we have reached the pastoral loveliness of the Sixth Book we are scarcely surprised by the simple perfection of what is surely the most dramatically appropriate image in all Spenser, when Calidore makes the enchanting Tristram his squire :

> So he him dubbed, and his Squire did call.
> Full glad and joyous then young Tristram grew ;
> Like as a flowre, whose silken leaves small
> Long shut up in the bud from heavens vew,
> At length breakes forth, and brode displays his smyling hew.

The Sixth Book is perhaps no more truly characteristic of Spenser than the *Epithalamion*, with which it is probably contemporary ; into both alike enters a warm fragrance of reality. In Calidore morality steps down from the abstract empyrean and is incarnate and humane, wayward and lovely. In Calidore, as in young Tristram, it veritably flowers. And being humane, it does not even pretend to stifle in itself the lust of the eye and the pride of life. No whisper of conscience, nor monition of Palmer, warns Calidore that he is on the road to damnation when he peeps from the covert of the wood :

> There did he see that pleased much his sight
> That even he him selfe his eies envyde,
> An hundred naked maidens lily white

All raunged in a ring and dauncing in delight.

And since Colin Clout ('who knows not Colin Clout?') was in the midst of them, piping so merrily as never none, it is clear that Calidore was not in temptation, but in Elysium. It is woefully inconsistent with all that had gone before. Poor harried Acrasia and her lovely maidens, in sober justice, should have burst like a troop of Maenads into that naked conclave, for revenge. But the writ of sober justice does not run in the world of imagination. Colin Clout had no need to be abashed by the invasion ; he had only to trust his genius and let it speak for him. ' It was I,' his genius would have said to Acrasia and her maidens, ' who called you out of nothingness and made you lovely; it was not I who destroyed you. For I am Imagination, who, having once created beauty, can never destroy it again. Join in the dance.' And the enchantment of the Sixth Book is that we feel that Acrasia and her maidens have joined in the dance in virtue of that title which Keats proclaimed:' ' What the Imagination seizes as Beauty must be Truth.'

It is an old problem, this of Art and Morality, solved in fact easily enough by those who have the strength to make either a morality of their art or an art of their morality, but a cause of incessant perplexity to those without the courage to do either. Spenser, we know, did the former; and few who read him well will not be inwardly convinced that he did the latter also. The poet who conceived his ideal in the semblance of Sir Calidore, it is true, may not himself have been much like him; and perhaps that perfection of grace in conduct was no more the gift of the gods to Spenser than the perfection of grace in his poetry. After all, he half-confesses as much when he speaks of Sir Calidore's courtesy:

Thereto great help Dame Nature selfe doth lend;
For some so goodly gratious are by kind,
That every action doth them much commend
And in the eyes of men great liking find;
Which others that have greater skill in mind,
Though they enforce themselves, cannot attain;
For everie thing to which one is inclin'd

Doth best become and greatest grace doth gaine:
Yet praise likewise deserve good thewes enforst with paine.

Good thewes enforst with paine'—that is certainly the chief secret of Spenser's great and enduring achievement in poetry; quite possibly it was also the cause of his long wooing of his wife.

But the long wooing had a happy ending; and something of Spenser's moment of felicity is suffused through the Sixth Book, as it is through the *Epithalamion*. The five books which precede it are romance; the sixth is simply romantic, in the sense in which *As You Like It* and *A Winter's Tale* are romantic. The characters are real, their virtue and their love both credible and charming. We enter into a different world which, if it is not the world of every day, is at least a world into which if the fates were propitious and the stars dancing, the world of every day might be transmuted. And the tense atmosphere of derring-do is so mightily relaxed in this happy kingdom that nobody cares, though Sir Calidore forgets all about his blatant enemy for long months on end. The air is kindly here; the savage man discovers himself the pattern of courtesy, cruel ladies learn to be kind, and tyrannous husbands are taught to be gentle. *Redeunt Saturnia regna.*

[FEBRUARY, 1930]

METAPHOR

Discussions of metaphor—there are not many of them—often strike us at first as superficial. Not until we have ourselves made the attempt to get further do we begin to realize that the investigation of metaphor is curiously like the investigation of any of the primary data of consciousness: it cannot be pursued very far without our being led to the border-line of sanity. Metaphor is as ultimate as speech itself, and speech as ultimate as thought. If we try to penetrate them beyond a certain point, we find ourselves questioning the very faculty and instrument with which we are trying to penetrate them. The earth trembles and yawns beneath the explorer's feet. *Medio tutissimus ibis*; but the middle way is hard to find.

Suppose we take a familiar metaphor, as that the fiery spirit of Emily Brontë burned up her body. It cannot fairly be called *cliché*; it is rather a familiar and necessary idiom. Necessary, because we find that there is no way of saying what we want to say about Emily Brontë save by this metaphor or one of its variations. This obvious necessity of the metaphor, this absence of genuine alternatives, seems to make it clear that so soon as one person perceived in another and sought to describe such a quality as Emily Brontë's, a kindred metaphor was forced upon him. We may even say that the quality could not have been perceived without the metaphor. The imagination that the soul inhabits the body as fire inhabits the material which it burns must surely go back to the moment when the existence of the soul was first surmised; for only by such an image could the nature of the soul's existence be at all apprehended. And we may leave it undecided, or as impossible of decision, whether the creation of the metaphor was the result of a search for a description of the previously felt existence of the soul, or the existence of the soul was suggested by the manner of the flame's existence.

For, whichever it may have been, and perhaps the processes were equally prevalent, metaphor appears as the instinctive and necessary act of the mind exploring reality and ordering experience. It is the means by which the less familiar is assimi-

85

lated to the more familiar, the unknown to the known: it 'gives to airy nothing a local habitation and a name', so that it ceases to be airy nothing. To attempt a fundamental examination of metaphor would be nothing less than an investigation of the genesis of thought itself—a dangerous enterprise. Therefore we instinctively seek to circumscribe our own inquiries by leaving out of account as far as may be the countless host of dead or dormant metaphors of which the most part of language is composed, and concentrating on the living ones. We take for granted the past exploration of reality of which dead and dormant metaphors are the record, and try to focus our minds on the present, hazardous, incomplete, and thrilling exploration of reality which is represented by metaphors which still retain their vitality.

Such are the metaphors of what we call creative literature. These remain alive because they are the records of an exploration of reality by men who stood head and shoulders above their fellows, who discerned resemblances between the unknown and the known which the generality could not accept nor common speech assimilate. Their metaphors are felt still to be the vehicle of some immediate revelation to those who attend to them. As Aristotle said, 'But the greatest thing of all by far is to be a master of metaphor. It is the one thing that can not be learned from others ; and it is also a sign of original genius, since a good metaphor implies the intuitive perception of the similarity in dissimilars'. The statement, made so long ago, seems final still.

But before we hazard a small attempt to advance from it towards Coleridge's discussion of imagery, we need to inquire, for the sake of clarity, whether there is any but a formal difference between metaphor and simile and image. 'Far out, as though idly, listlessly, gulls were flying. Now they settled on the waves, now they beat up into the rainy air, *and shone against the pale sky like the lights within a pearl.*' The last words would be called indifferently an image. or a simile. Change them to 'shining lights in the pale pearl of sky', it becomes—not by any means to its advantage, for a reason we may discover— a metaphor. But the act of creative perception remains the same. And it seems impossible to regard metaphors and similes as different in any essential property: metaphor is compressed simile. The word 'image' however, which has come to usurp a prominent place in these discussions, is more recalcitrant. It not only narrows the content of the word 'simile', but tends to force unduly into the foreground the part played by the visual image. In the beautiful simile quoted above the visual image is preponderant; in Baudelaire's agonizing one:

> Ces affreuses nuits
> Qui compriment le cœur comme un papier qu'on froisse,

the visual image has no part at all. Again, it is obvious foolishness to persuade oneself that any visual image underlies the magnificent metaphors—

> Thou still unravish'd bride of quietness:
> Thou foster-child of Silence and slow Time.

Yet though the suggestion of the word 'image' is dangerous, the word is necessary. For metaphor and simile belong to formal classification. The word 'image', precisely because it is used to cover both metaphor and simile, can be used to point towards their fundamental identity; and if we resolutely exclude from our minds the suggestion that the image is solely or even predominently visual, and allow the word to share in the heightened and comprehensive significance with which its derivative 'imagination' has perforce been endowed—if we conceive the 'image' not as primary and independent, but as the most singular and potent instrument of the faculty of imagintion—it is a more valuable word than those which it subsumes: metaphor and simile. To them clings something worse than false suggestion: a logical taint, an aura of irrelevancy.

The image may be visual, may be auditory, may refer back to any primary physical experience—as those hoary metaphors which describe the process of thought itself as a grasping or apprehension—or it may be wholly psychological, the reference of one emotional or intellectual experience to another, as

> Then felt I like some watcher of the skies
> When a new planet swims into his ken . . .

The essential is simply that there should be that intuitive perception of of similarity between dissimilars of which Aristotle speaks. What we primarily demand is that the similarity should be a true similarity and that it should have lain hitherto unperceived, or but rarely perceived by us, so that it comes to us with an effect of revelation: something hitherto unknown is suddenly made known. To that extent the image is truly creative: it marks an advance, for the writer who perceives and the reader who receives it, in the conquest of some reality.

We also in our inquiry may take a step forward. That we demand more of imagery than this may be seen in our instinctive refusal of the image of a modern prose-writer, who speaks of the 'churches, like shapes of grey paper, breasting the stream of the Strand'. There are two images, and they war with each other. If the churches really breasted the stream of the Strand, they were not at that moment like shapes of grey paper. Possibly both perceptions are valid in isolation; in association they nullify one another. Yet how often does Shakespeare seem to commit the same offence.

> It is great
> To do that thing that ends all other deeds:
> Which shackles accident, and bolts up change;
> Which sleeps, and never palates more the dug,
> The beggar's nurse and Caesar's.

Yet the offence is only apparent. The images do not in fact disturb each other, whereas the modern writer's images do. This is partly because in the modern writer's imagery the stress lies wholly upon the visual: if we do not see what we are required to see, the sentence fails of its effect; and partly because of the characteristic swiftness of Shakespeare's language. We have not, and we are not intended to have, time to unfold his metaphors; and, moreover, the boldest and most abrupt transition among them is in its effect the smoothest. For the rhythm leaves no doubt that it is not 'the dug' but Death that is 'the beggar's nurse and Caesar's'. Death, which in the previous line was the child sleeping against the heart, becomes the bosom that receives mankind. We may say it is the mere verbal suggestion that links the metaphors. Yet, though it is true that verbal 'self-suggestion' is potent in high poetry ('Forlorn!

the very word is like a knell . . .'), it seems truer in this case to say that the one metaphor grows immediately out of the other. It is as though the vague 'thing', from which the images take their rise, swiftly groped after shapes before our mind's eye, and finally achieved a full realization—'the beggar's nurse and Caesar's'.

This is the work of the greatest of all masters of metaphor, and it would be preposterous to try others' achievement by its standard. The self-creative progress of Shakespeare's imagery is a thing apart. But by comparing small things with great we may see that the internal harmony which the modern writer fails to secure is a necessary quality of true imagery. Shakespeare's methods of securing it are indeed startling; he takes what seem to be impossible risks, and wins with ease. His success, when we examine it, is not really so surprising, for the extent to which images are discordant depends upon the extent we unfold them, and that is wholly within the great poet's control, for it in turn depends primarily upon the rhythm and tempo of his writing. And this, more than any other, is the reason why the successful use of metaphor is very much bolder in poetry than in prose. The poet's means of control—that is to say, the possibilities of tempo and rhythm in poetry—are much richer and more flexible than in prose. He has our sensibilities, our powers of realization and comparison, far more completely under his thumb than the prose-writer. So that we may hazard a generalization and say that the creative simile is by nature more appropriate to prose than the creative metaphor. Prose gives us time to bear upon the comparison, which if it be exact and revealing, will stand the strain of our attention, and is better frankly exposed to the inquiry it must receive. And, again, the function of imagery in poetry differs perceptibly from the function of imagery in prose. In poetry metaphor is chiefly a means to excite in us a vague and heightened awareness of qualities we can best call spiritual. Exactness and precision are seldom sought, and, if they are, are seldom valuable; and often where an apparent exactness exists, as in the Homeric simile, it is an incidental exactness and does not reinforce the point of specific analogy. Set two equally famous heroic portraits by great poets against each other.

His legs bestrid the ocean; his rear'd arm
Crested the world: his voice was propertied
As all the tunèd spheres, and that to friends;
But when he meant to quail, and shake the orb,
He was as rattling thunder. For his bounty,
There was no winter in 't; an autumn 'twas
That grew the more by reaping: his delights
Were dolphin-like; they show'd his back above
The element they liv'd in: in his livery
Walk'd crowns and crownets; realms and islands were
As plates dropp'd from his pocket . . .

                              He above the rest
In shape and gesture proudly eminent
Stood like a Tower, his form had not yet lost
All her original brightness, nor appear'd
Less than archangel ruin'd, and th' excess
Of glory obscur'd, as when the sun new risen
Looks through the horizontal misty air
Shorn of his beams; or from behind the moon
In dim eclipse disastrous twilight sheds
On half the nations; and with fear of change
Perplexes monarchs.

The Miltonic tempo, as ever, is far slower than Shakespeare's;
therefore we bear more heavily upon his comparisons, and in
sufficient measure they stand the strain; but the whole effect
is not precise, but rather vague, vast, and foreboding. So also,
in its totally different kind, the picture of Antony that is impressed upon our minds is of some thing (rather than some
one) immense, generous, genial, a careless and overflowing
force of nature—a dynamic phenomenon as peculiar to Shakespeare's view of the universe as the static figure of Satan to
Milton's. Exactness of this kind there is in both; but it comes
not from the exactness of the particular comparisons, it is a
total effect of many comparisons, as it were a painting of one
great and indefinable quality by many strokes of minor yet
allied analogies. To evoke such elemental spirits is seldom
the purpose of prose, nor of the imagery proper to it. It also
seizes, in so far as it is creative, indefinable qualities, but they

are more specific and more local.

> Soon after daybreak we were steaming down the arrowy Rhone, at the rate of twenty miles an hour, in a very dirty vessel full of merchandise. and with only three or four other passengers for our companions: among whom the most remarkable was a silly old, meek-faced, garlic-eating, immeasurably polite Chevalier, with a dirty scrap of red ribbon at his button-hole, *as if he had tied it there to remind him of something.*

It is perfect, it gives us the man—an individual and comic inhabitant of earth. Perhaps as an example it suggests that the prose use of simile must be more prosaic than we mean to imply. We have quoted solely to point an essential difference between the imagery of prose and poetry. The imagery of poetry is in the main complex and suggestive; the imagery of prose single and explicit.

But the three examples serve also to illustrate what is the highest function of imagery—namely, to define indefinable spiritual qualities. All metaphor and simile can be described as the analogy by which the human mind explores the universe of quality and charts the non-measurable world. Of these indefinite qualities some are capable of direct sensuous apprehension, while others can be grasped only by a faculty which, though obviously akin to sensuous apprehension, yet differs from it. Sensuous perception is of the qualities of the visible, audible, tangible world; of the spiritual qualities of the more recondite world of human personality and its creations there is intuition. Both faculties are necessary to the great poet, but there have been many who, though richly gifted with sensuous perception, have been deficient or altogether lacking in spiritual intuition. To the great poet his constant accumulation of vivid sense-perceptions supplies the most potent means by which he articulates his spiritual intuitions, for recognitions of spiritual quality can be most forcefully and swiftly conveyed through analogous recognitions of sensuous quality. One has only to imagine how much, and how much in vain, another writer might toil to render the quality of Antony that is given once for all in the words, grammatically confused though they are:—

>   . . . his delights
> Were dolphin-like; they show'd his back above
> The element they lived in . . .

or to consider the pregnant subtlety of these two kindred images:

>   This common body,
> Like to a vagabond flag upon the stream,
> Goes to and back, lackeying the varying tide,
> To rot itself with motion. . . .
> Her tongue will not obey her heart, nor can
> Her heart inform her tongue,—the swan's down-feather,
> That stands upon the swell at full of tide
> And neither way inclines . . .

to realize the enormous resources for describing the subtlest nuances of emotion and character which a vivid percipience the sensuous world can give.

But the greatest mastery of imagery does not lie in the use, however beautiful and revealing, of isolated images, but in the harmonious total impression produced by a succession of subtly related images. In such cases the images appear to grow out of one another and to be fulfilling an independent life of their own. Yet this apparent autonomy is as strictly subordinated to a final impression as the steps of a logical argument are to their conclusion. Such triumphs of imagery are to be conceived as a swift and continuous act of exploration of the world of imagination—though an obvious metaphor is in that phrase. A magnificent example of this peculiar movement of mind on a scale so large that it can be carefully exmained is Keat's *Ode to a Nightingale*. The strange combination of imaginative autonomy and profound total harmony in that poem is characteristic of the movement of creative imagery in its higest forms. We can perhaps get a clear glimpse of the nature of this contradictory process of creative imagery—the maximum of independence combined with the most complete and pervasive subordination—in one of the rare moments when we can honestly claim to be able to look over Shakespeare's shoulder. The famous picture of Cleopatra on Cydnus comes

substantially from North's Plutarch, of which the following
sentence is the original of Shakespeare's first seven lines:

She disdained to set forward otherwise, but to take her
barge in the river of Cydnus, the poope whereof was of gold,
the sails of purple, and the owers of silver, which kept stroke
in rowing after the sound of flutes, howboys, cytherns, violls,
and such other instruments as they played upon the barge . . .

It is often said that Shakespeare followed North as closely as
he could, with the minimum of original effort. It is not true.
North's sentence would fall quite easily into good blank verse,
but it would be nothing like—

> *The barge she sat in, like a burnish'd throne,*
> *Burn'd on the water*: the poop was beaten gold;
> Purple the sails, *and so perfuméd that*
> *The winds were love-sick with them;* the oars were silver,
> Which to the tune of flutes, kept stroke, *and made*
> *The water which they beat to follow faster,*
> *As amorous of their strokes* . . .

The phrases in italics are Shakespeare's additions: afterwards
he keeps more closely to North until he comes to the climax.
North has it:

Others also rann out of the city to see her coming in. So
that in the end, there rann such multitudes of people one after
another, that *Antonius* was left post alone in the market-place,
in his Imperiall seate to give audience.

Which is transformed into:

> The city cast
> Her people out upon her, and Antony,
> Enthron'd in the market-place, did sit alone,
> *Whistling to the air*: *which, but for vacancy,*
> *Had gone to gaze on Cleopatra too*
> *And made a gap in nature.*

The additions are worth attention. North's somewhat
amorphous prose is given a beginning and an end. The additions are all, in spite of formal differences, essentially similes
and metaphors; and, after the first, which gathers the vision into
one whole which it puts imperishably before the mind's eye,
the second and third develop the theme which is clinched in
climax by the fourth. In them the successive elements—the

winds, the water, the air—are represented all as succumbing to
the enchantment of love which breathes from the great Queen
and her burning barge; and by this varied return on a single
motive North's inconsequential panorama is given an organic
unity. It is quite impossible to conceive Shakespeare as dove-
tailing old and new together. Before his mind's eye as he read
North had risen a picture half visible, half spiritual, in short,
truly imaginative—the manifestation of Egypt, before whom the
elements made obeisance. All of North that was congruous
with his enchanted vision he incorporated with a flowing pen
into his new creation. And the added imagery, about which he
probably took no second thought, grew naturally into harmony
with itself and with the whole.

To this strange but strangely natural process Coleridge was
his often-quoted and sometimes violently interpreted words:

Images, however beautiful, though faithfully copied from
nature, and as accurately represented in words, do not of themselves characterize the poet. They become proofs of original
genius only in so far as they are modified by a predominant
passion, or by associated thoughts and images awakened by that
passion ; or when they have the effect of reducing multitude to
unity, or succession to an instant ; or lastly when a human and
intellectual life is transferred to them from the poet's own spirit.

Instances, and better instances than Coleridge himself gives,
of all the qualities which he demands of truly creative imagery
are to be found in the picture of Cleopatra. 'Multitude is
reduced to unity' by the first of the added images ; and in the
other three a human and intellectual life is transferred to the
images (Coleridge should perhaps have said, to the objects of
the images) from the poet's own spirit. This last desideratum
had been put forward long before by Aristotle in his discussion
of 'vividness' in the *Rhetoric*. Vividness, he there says, depends upon metaphor and on ' setting things before the eyes';
but ' setting things before the eyes ' turns out itself to be a
metaphor, and not, as one might imagine, a demand for the
visual image. ' This is my definition,' says Aristotle.

Those words set a thing before the eyes which describe it in
an active state . . , Or we may use the device often employed

by Homer of giving life to lifeless things by means of metaphor.
In all such cases he wins applause by describing an active state,
as in the line

Back to the plain rolled the shameless stone.

Whether the process is described thus dryly as by Aristotle,
or more transcendentally by Coleridge, as the working of the
poetic spirit ' which shoots its being through earth, sea, and
air,' the fact is indubitable. It seems to be an imperious need
of the creative spirit of the poet to impart life to the apparently
lifeless. This may appear a 'device' in the cold light of analysis;
but nothing is more certain than that when it is used as a
device it is intolerable. No conscious contrivance produced
' Thou still unravish'd bride of quietness,' or ' Joy, whose hand
is ever at his lips, Bidding adieu.' Such things as these—and
how many of the most magnificently natural achievements of
poetry belong to this kind—are, beyond all doubt, the effect of
some 'silent working of the spirit.' By the intensity of the poet's
contemplation the lifeless thing lives indeed.

Probably the world of true imagination of which these miracles
are the common subtance is for ever inviolable by intellectual
analysis. Even to apprehend its subject-matter the intellect
must suffer a sea-change, so that it is no longer itself and cannot
perform its proper function. Restore its power to the intellect
again, and that which it seeks to understand has ceased to exist
as what it really is. This world of imagination is a universe
wherein quality leaps to cohere with quality across the abysms
of classification that divide and categorize the universe of intellectual apprehension. Its true citizens are few and far between ; they are the masters of metaphor, and the authentic
messages they bring from that near yet distant country perplex
our brains and comfort our souls with the half-assurance that
the things that are may be otherwise than as we know them.

Towards this exalted region, as to the sole reality, Coleridge
was ever groping ; and what he meant by the ' predominant
passion ' which modifies the images of original genius is the
power by which genius comprehends its chosen region of this
world of qualitative interpenetration. The passion is a passionate contemplation of the unity which pervades the chosen

region : a creative passion to correspond with an organic unity. Whether the unity proceeds from the passion, or the passion from the unity, it would be profitless to inquire. They are knit together, as knower and known, in one act of creative comprehension. But if we are shy of the notion of Coleridge which seems to give the poetic spirit an actually plastic power over the material world, we have only to reflect that the predominant passion of the poet's mind is but the counterpart of a predominant quality of the region of the universe which he contemplates. His passion roused by the quality is reflected back upon the quality, and gives it redoubled power; so that it begins to dominate all other qualities and properties, to suffuse them with itself till it becomes as it were the living and governing soul of that which the poet contemplates. By means of his passion the actual realizes its own idea.

However much we struggle, we cannot avoid transcendentalism, for we are seeking to approximate to a universe of quality with analogy for its most essential language through a universe of quantity with a language of identities. Sooner or later, a transcendentalism (which is only the name for a prodigious metaphor) is inevitable. But the process may be brought a little closer to the light of common day if we take once more that region of the qualitative universe which Shakespeare embodied in Cleopatra. She was, we may say, the incarnation of love : the mighty, elemental power which, in Shakespeare's experience, was love, was made corporeal in her. She is possessed by it ; from her it radiates and compels obeisance from the elements. But she is not merely a contemplated but a self-uttering thing ; and this power that informs her body informs her soul also. All her thoughts are shaped by it. Without her love she will die, she must die ; but when she imagines death, she imagines it as a consummation of love, as the thing

Which sleeps, and never palates more the dug,
The beggar's nurse and Caesar's . . .

She dies, and her dying she imagines as a reliving of her triumph on Cydnus. 'I am again for Cydnus, to meet Mark Antony." And it is a more wonderful triumph. ' Yare, yare, good Iras.' The flower-soft hands that yarely framed the office frame one

last office more ; and at the aspic's touch the Queen is wholly
dedicate to the love she is and serves. The winds, the water,
the air obeyed on Cydnus ; now the most fickle element of all
obeys—her own secret self, from which well up the images of
love in death, and death in love :

> The stroke of death is as a lover's pinch
> That hurts and is desired . . .
>
>   Peace, peace!
> Dost thou not see my baby at my breast
> That sucks the nurse asleep?

In the intensity of Shakespeare's imagination the great property
takes utter and complete possession of that it dwells in. By the
alchemy of Cleopatra's images death is transmuted into a sleep
of love. But her thoughts are Shakespeare's thoughts, her predominant passion his. Therefore it is not strange that Caesar,
who in the waking world knows nothing of her dying words,
should echo them, and prolong her triumph beyond her death.

>   She looks like sleep,
> As she would catch another Antony
> In her strong toil of grace.

But Caesar did not know what Shakespeare knew, that it was
the self-same Antony whom she had taken.

[1927]

THE POETRY OF WALTER DE LA MARE

Since Plato turned his eyes, weary with the flux of things. to a celestial city whose aëry burgomasters kept guard over the perfect and unblemished exemplars of the objects of this bungled world, and not long after, Jesus told his fishermen that they could find their peace only in the Kingdom of Heaven, where the mansions were innumerable, the subtle and the simple mind alike have been haunted by echoes of an unceasing music and dreams of imperishable beauty. Men's hearts have been swayed between a belief that the echoes and the dreams reached them from a distant eternal world more real than ours, and a premonition that the voice they heard was that of their own soul mysteriously calling them to self-perfection. And even those who have spoken with most conviction and persuasiveness, as though seeing face to face, of the perfect world immune from the rust of time have been the foremost to let fall the warning that their words were a parable. The rare spirits which steer the soul of humanity unite within themselves the contrary impulses of men. They live so intimately with their ideals that they are half persuaded of their reality ; they think so highly of the soul that a truth for it alone becomes a truth. Therefore they can say in the same breath that the Father's house has many mansions and that the Kingdom of Heaven is within us, and no man can tell for certain whether *The Republic* is an allegory.

This dream or desire is one of the eternal themes of poetry, not because it is superficially more 'poetic' than any other, but because it contains one of the persistent realities of the soul. For if the soul lives in its own right, having a core of active being, it lives by an ideal. There is no escaping the fact of the Kingdom of Heaven which is within you, because it is the condition of the soul's vitality. Once begin to make choice between a worse and a better, and you are inevitably bound to recognise its validity ; and to live without making the choice, whatever the intellect may tell us, is not life at all. Life, as we know it, cannot bar the gate against the ideal. If it is a dream it is a dream we live by, and a dream we live by is more real than a reality we ignore.

But if this opposition of the ideal and the real is one of the great essential themes of poetry, it is also one which yields most to the impress of the poet's personality. Between the one pole of a complete belief in the existence of a kingdom of eternal beauty and imperishable perfection, and the other of an unfaltering recognition that these beatitudes exist in and for the soul alone, are infinite possibilities of faith and doubt, inexhaustible opportunities for the creative activity of art. For, apart from the precise mixture of certainty and hesitation in the poet's mind, one of the sovereign gestures of art is to make the ideal real, and to project a dim personal awareness on to a structure of definite inventions. The sense that we are exiled from our own country, that our rightful heritage has been usurped from us, we know not how, may impel one poet to create his kingdom in words and name it with names, people it with fit inhabitants, and another to record the bare fact of his consciousness as a homeless wanderer.

Mr. de la Mare is a poet of the great theme who is distinguished chiefly by his faculty of pressing invention and fancy to the service of his need. He has named his other kingdom with many names; it is Arabia,

> Where the Princes ride at noon
> 'Mid the verdurous vales and thickets
> Under the ghost of the moon.

It is Tartary; it is Alulvan. Queen Djenira reigns there, and when she sleeps she walks through

> The courts of the lord Pthamasar,
> Where the sweet birds of Psuthys are.

Or again it is Thule of the old legend, upon which the poet beautifully calls:

> If thou art sweet as they are sad
>> Who on the shore of Time's salt sea
> Watch on the dim horizon fade
>> Ships bearing love and night to thee . . .

Within its shifting frontiers are comprised all the dim, debatable lands that lie between the Never-Never country of nursery rhyme and the more solid fields to which the city mind turns for its paradise, the terrestrial happiness which only a shake of the gods' dice-box has denied :

> Had the gods loved me I had lain
>   Where darnel is and thorn,
> And the wild night-bird's nightlong strain
>   Trembles in boughs forlorn.
>
> Nay, but they loved me not ; and I
>   Must needs a stranger be
> Whose every exiled day gone by
>   Aches with their memory.

That, surely, is a kingdom of solid earth. And yet we wonder. Is it not also rather a symbol and projection of the poet's desiderium, his longingness (to use his own word), than an earthly kingdom from which fate has exiled him? We do not wonder long. The peace that comes from the satisfaction of this haunting desire is not to be found in any actual countryside. Nature has no medicinable balm for this unease. The poet himself tells us that he

> Oft marvelled who it was that sang
> Down the green valley languidly,
>   Where the grey elder thickets hang.
>
> Sometimes I thought it was a bird
>   My soul had charged with sorcery;
> Sometimes it seemed my own heart heard
>   Inland the sorrow of the sea.
>
> But even where the primrose sets
>   The seal of her pale loveliness,
> I found amid the violets
>   Tears of an antique bitterness.

Wherever the flux of things endures, this antique bitterness endures also. The loveliness of earth comes to the poet with the perpetual shadow of regret ; and even the memory of it dissolves into nothingness :

> . . . Beauty vanishes ; beauty passes ;
> However rare—rare it be ;
> And when I crumble, who will remember
> This lady of the West Country?

Life haunted by death, beauty by decay. What remedy will avail against this malady of mankind? Nothing but the courage of a dream. It is fitting, therefore, that the first, and presumably the earliest, of Mr. de la Mare's collected poems is an attempt to turn, as all the great idealists have tried to turn, the ephemerality of earthly beauty into a proof of the existence of a beauty which endures for ever :

> The loveliest thing earth hath, a shadow hath,
> A dark and livelong hint of death,
> Haunting it ever till its last faint breath.
>   Who then may tell
> The beauty of heaven's shadowless asphodel?

But how to keep the courage of that dream—there is the question. The poet belongs to the world of existence ; it is not possible for him to elude it. The shadowless asphodel is haunted by the shadows of the earthly flowers that have died. When the delight of fancy and invention has begun to fade where shall the poet place his other kingdom? What if Arabia and Tartary and Thule and Alulvan cease to delight, and Queen Djenira dream no more? Not all the princes of Arabia, with their splendours and their music, can lull the poet's mind into forgetfulness that he seeks not only a symbol, but a satisfaction for his longing. There comes a time when he knows that the delight of discovering a new name is not the delight of discovered peace. -The urgent, incessant question begins to dominate, the pattern in the carpet to appear.

The other kingdom is the kingdom of peace, the country where the soul can rest. And now the poet no more makes a triumphant deduction of immortality from mortality, of the eternal from the temporal. He declares his need, but the haven where it will be satisfied is one which no earthly ship will find :

> Where blooms the flower when her petals fade.
> Where sleepeth echo by earth's music made,

101

> Where all things transient to changeless win,
> There waits the peace thy spirit dwelleth in.

And so, by nuances almost imperceptible of emotion and expression, we pass from this undiscoverable country to the clear, comfortless conclusion of what we must consider on this and on other grounds to be Mr. de la Mare's finest poem so far. In a sense *The Tryst* marks the end of his poetical journey. The curve is complete. The dream is only a dream.

> Think! in Time's smallest clock's minutest beat
> Might there not rest be found for wandering feet?
> Or 'twixt the sleep and wake of Helen's dream,
> Silence wherein to sing love's requiem?
>
> No, no. Nor earth, nor air, nor fire, nor deep
> Could lull poor mortal longingness asleep.
> Somewhere there Nothing is ;   and there lost man
> Shall win what changeless vague of peace he can.

On the path of that curve all Mr. de la Mare's memorable poetic achievements—and they are many—will be found. On it too will be found the greater part of those rhymes for children which, to the casual glance, seem to be eccentric to it. For, as we have said, Arabia is on the same continent as the Never-Never land of the nursery rhyme ; they march with one another. They were created to satisfy the same impulse. In the magic kingdom of childhood ' the shadowless asphodel ' seemed really to exist, in a realm where all perfections and splendours and beauties persisted without change ;   and one might truly regard Mr. de la Mare's 'grown-up' poetry as an effort to recapture the simple certainty of that childhood belief, or to express the regret at the shadows that have encroached upon it. Therefore, his rhymes for children take a definite place in his poetry as a whole, and are also essentially different from other rhymes of the kind ; they are the natural, inevitable expression of the poet's deepest feeling. How natural and in-evitable can be seen, if not from the tenor of this exposition, from the final verse of the exquisite poem, *Dreams* :

> What can a tired heart say,
> Which the wise of the world have made dumb?

Save to the lonely dreams of a child,
' Return again, come! '

To recognise that the dream is a dream, yet to refuse to put it away, this is the crucial act of comprehension which animates the enduring part of the poetry of the present age. It is a reflection of our devastating experience and our shadowy faith; for even while we know that the dream is a dream, having no counterpart in the reality without us, it cannot be wholly surrendered because we live by its enchantment. For to live is to make ourselves of a certain quality, to fashion ourselves to a certain temper; and if the dream is impotent to reshape the stubborn world beyond us, its power to work upon our own souls is undiminished.

When we say, therefore, that Mr. de la Mare's poetry is characteristic of the age, it is not in the sense that there is much poetry of the same quality to be found in our magazines and bookshops to-day—there is, alas, very little—but that it makes an appeal to, and in a way satisfies minds which have been tempered by the common experience. The strings have been so tightened that they respond to this touch. At a price we have purchased wisdom ; clamour rings empty in our ears, we turn a mistrustful eye upon ambitious structures ; superficialities —and these are commonest in the poetry of to-day—inspire in us an extreme repulsion. We respond only to the expression of the truth of our experience, and turn away from the pompous platitude and the laborious paradox which are generally offered to us as poetry.

In the vast wreckage of faiths with which the modern consciousness is strewn, there remains one thing in which we may believe without fear of disillusion ; we may believe in beauty. We may even in the exaltation of despair, say with conviction that the wreckage of our hopes and the ruin of the world is beautiful. But the effort of contemplation so austere and self-regardless is too great to be maintained ; we have not the strength to be Spinozas for more than a moment. And, even if we cannot make our beauty so all-inclusive we can still believe in the more partial and more human beauty we discern. But the condition of our belief is that we shall not deceive

103

ourselves. Beauty is transient, we cannot by doting make it changeless. Where changeless beauty exists, there, indeed, our home may be ; but we have only a dim memory of it to set against the certainty that the road leading back has been lost for ever.

Nevertheless, and in spite of the regret with which beauty must ever be attended, the faith in it endures ; for the discernment of beauty is a mode of perception that is adequate to all the fates can bring. Disillusion has no power against it ; it can not merely conquer, but make part of itself its regret for its own impotence. If it inspires men to build dream cities whose walls are proof against ephemeral corruption, it also inspires them to discover beauty in the recognition that their city is unsubstantial.

> And some win peace who spend
> The skill of words to sweeten despair
> Of finding consolation where
> Life has but one dark end ;
> Who, in rapt solitude, tell o'er
> A tale as lovely as forlore,
> Into the midnight air.

The winning of peace that haunts the mind of the poet is nothing other than communion with beauty. And if this beauty, which in spite of all can still be discerned and won, yields but a precarious peace, where the brave dream of youth promised one that would be secure, it could not well be otherwise, and the lovers of beauty are perhaps more fortunate than the lovers of justice, or of love.

In Mr. de la Mare's poetry we discover a trembling poise between the longing for an eternality of beauty and an acquiescence, an almost ecstatic acquiescence, in its transitoriness. Between those two conditions lies the gamut of emotional suggestion on which he plays with a consummate skill. They correspond to the deep, antithetical realities of the soul that have vexed men and poets and philosophers through the ages. The old debate between the One and Many is indeed changed, as it must be in the glancing mirror of an artist's mind. It is no longer a question which is true, but which the poet desires to be true. And can he tell? How shall he really choose between the static, eternal beauty whose ghost haunts the beauty that vanishes and passes, and the beauty which has sorrow 'more beautiful than beauty's self' to attend its passing?

The one whispers to the heart of the man; the other is a magnet to the soul of the artist. The beauty the poet perceives, the transitory gleam at which he snatches, cheats him with a mirage of unchanging perfection, of an imperishable beauty beyond the beautiful thing; yet the peculiar preciousness of the gleam he captures comes not least from its mortality. It is, indeed, more beautiful because it is evanescent. No lasting comradeship with happiness could bring half the enchantment of the vision of

> Joy, whose hand is ever at his lips
> Bidding adieu.

And if poets have indulged the child and the man within them with memories of the clouds of glory which they trailed, and the thought that here they have no abiding city, they have done it in part in order that they may more exactly respond to the strange quality of their true condition. If we can once persuade ourselves that we are princes of the blood-royal who wander unknown in rags, how much keener grows our sense of the infinite variety of life's vicissitude. It is, in short, neither the ideal nor the real which fascinates the true poet, but their incessant and conflicting interplay. Each is a light which illuminates the other with 'an unearthly gleam'; without the real to give it substance, the dream is clear, calm, and colourless; without the dream to give it shadow, the real is a vague and confused chaos.

Beauty, which we may truly worship, is a jewel of many facets. It gathers the radiance of the Many; it diffuses the ray of the One. The poet seeks to borrow both its powers, according to his mood; and we may contrast and compare his moods, but to find them contradictory is to make ourselves guilty of the old crime of seeking logic where logic has no place. Mr. de la Mare writes symbolically of the soul:

> Why did you flutter in vain hope, poor bird,

105

Hard-pressed in your small cage of clay?
'Twas but a sweet, false echo that you heard,
　Caught only a feint of day.

Still is the night all dark, a homeless dark.
　Burn yet the unanswering stars.　And silence brings
The same sea's desolate surge—sans bound nor mark—
　Of all your wanderings.

Fret now no more; be still.　Those steadfast eyes,
　Those folded hands, they cannot set you free;
Only with beauty wake wild memories—
　Sorrow for where you are, for where you would be.

There beauty diffuses the radiance of the One, vexes the soul with the memories of a lost perfection.　Man, like the Adam of another poem, 'still must roam a world where sin and beauty whisper of home'.　But in *Fare Well*, which is the envoy to the collection called *Motley*, beauty appears as the power which gathers the radiance of the Many and brings to the soul the comfort of a fleeting, but earthly, paradise:

Look thy last on all things lovely
Every hour.　Let no night
　Seal thy sense in deathly slumber
　　Till to delight
Thou hast paid thy utmost blessing;
Since that all things thou wouldst praise
Beauty took from those who loved them
　　In other days.

Yes, Mr. de la Mare belongs to the company which has sought 'the principle of beauty in all things'.　It is a quest which, followed in singleness of heart, takes the great poet into strange countries by strange roads.　And if Mr. de la Mare has not been led into the wilderness, never stumbled across the temple floor to face the awful question of Moneta, he has none the less given a perfect expression to some of the deepest and most characteristic moods of this generation.

[SEPTEMBER, 1920]

ANTON TCHEKHOV

For some reason or other it seems a very bold thing to write a book about Tchekhov. One would need in one's words the voice which Gorki said Tolstoy was wont to use when speaking of the beloved writer, a voice with some delicate, intimate modulation, with the quality of a caress. To be less than exquisitely true in one's appreciation of what he wrote and was holds the menace of complete disaster.

What is the cause of this strange and particular inhibition? Why this particular fear? The would-be critic thinks ahead and imagines his essay or his book before him. There in the midst of his own words is a paragraph of quotation, a sentence that might be taken from almost anywhere in Tchekhov's works; and suddenly in the light of its rainbow radiance all that he himself has said appears fumbling and clumsy and vulgar. It is the menace of one's own self-revelation that is frightening.

To write about Tchekhov is nothing less than an ordeal. One cannot hope to emerge from it unscathed. Mr. Gerhardi has not managed that, in his book on Tchekhov.* But it is no small thing for any one who has felt within himself the subtle and secret spell of Tchekhov to have the courage of the ordeal. It may be in Mr. Gerhardi's case partly the courage of youth; in another ten years, perhaps, when Tchekhov might appear to him still wiser, still truer, and still nearer, his confidence might have failed him. He might then have been gently excruciated, as we are, by his juxtaposition of sentence after sentence from Mr. Wells's *The Undying Fire*, with sentence after sentence in which Tchekhov has allowed his characters to declare his faith. Mr. Wells is a man of genius, but his genius is of another order than Tchekhov's. Where Mr. Wells fumbles, Tchekhov is certain; where Mr. Wells is crude, Tchekhov is exquisite. To set them side by side is to deal unfairly by the one and to show a lack of understanding of the other, and all to no real purpose : for their faiths like their sensibilities are of a different kind.

Let us admit then that in such an attempt it was impossible

Anton Tchekhov, by William Gerhardi: The first book on Tchekhov by an English writer.

for Mr. Gerhardi to avoid making us wince by touching upon a nerve occasionally; and let us remember that it is probably true that such a thing had to be done young or not at all. Then we can freely rejoice that the thing has been done; for it is certainly better that it should be done than left undone. Still, we have not yet touched even the fringe of the obdurate main question: Why do we feel this intimate and personal loyalty to Tchekhov? Why is he set so close to our hearts that even the critic's minor misphrasings, even the choice of a mistaken word, should be felt as a physical pain? We try to think calmly. We are being ridiculous (we say to ourselves), foolishly hypersensitive. If any one were to make these small mistakes about Shakespeare, or Tolstoy, or Dickens, why, we should not care at all. But alas, the reply to this attempt at sober reasoning with ourselves is simply that the argument is only too true. If it were Shakespeare, if it were Tolstoy, we certainly should not care; but it is Tchekhov, and we do.

So in the last resort it seems that we are sensitive about Tchekhov because he is a writer about whom, if we feel deeply at all, we feel in this intensely personal way. His case is unique. Our reaction, our queer desire to protect him from our own roughness, to save him from the coarseness of all critical approximation, at first appears to be quite independent of his greatness. He is not a Shakespeare; he is not a Tolstoy— never, in our wildest enthusiasm, have we made a mistake in proportion about him: somehow he does not invite such mistakes. And, after all, this period of 'wild enthusiasm' is a phrase, not a reality. There never was such a period. Our enthusiasm for Tchekhov never grows, never diminishes: we take him into ourselves, and he is part of our lives for ever.

He is not great, we say, and then we wonder : whether it is not precisely because we feel him so near to us that we refuse him the name. We cannot tolerate that he should be removed from us to a mountain-top, and enveloped in a cloud. Perhaps it is not that he is not great, but that we cannot afford to let him be; and it may be that his greatness consists not least in this, that no writer of whom we know more obstinately avoided the attribute. Or we may put what is ultimately the same paradox in this way: Here is a writer who is more intimately dear to us than any other, whose truth is exactly our own truth, whom we do not have to interpret, for whom we never at any moment have to make allowances; and yet his writing seems to us new, not new in parts and old in others, not new in method and old in substance, but simply and wholly new.

It is passing strange, this mystery of no mystery; and exceedingly hard to hold firm before the eye of the mind. There is no point on which to fix, no visible mark of joining between his world, his consciousness and ours. Tchekhov calls for no efforts, demands no abjurations,—nothing of 'that willing suspension of disbelief which constitutes poetic faith,' which was the inseparable condition of all literature before him. We have, it seems, only to open our eyes, and his world will be in front of us: we open them, and it is not there. If we are writers, we think for a vain moment of assimilating Tchekhov's method —Mr. Gerhardi thinks of it—and the method slips through our fingers like quicksilver: we try to fix it, and we are left with a handful of airy negations—no plot, no ornament, no construction, no lies—and the smiling despair of this conclusion, that Tchekhov wrote like Tchekhov because he was Tchekhov, and that if we want to write like him—and who would not?— we must *be* like him. To see his world is not, after all, merely a question of opening our eyes, but of opening other eyes than ours.

In Harnack's *History of the Western Church* is told the story —from which of the Fathers it comes we have forgotten—of a Christian who was haled before a Roman magistrate. The magistrate asked him how it was possible for him to believe in such a simple religion—it was in the *very* early days of the Church—a creed so naked that it gave the mind nothing to take hold of, whereas the superb complications of Roman mythology offered an hand-hold to the least prehensile of minds. And the Christian answered that the secret of his faith was the mystery of simplicity—*mysterium simplicitatis*. This haunting Latin phrase, cavernous with spiritual profundity, yet in its whole effect so lucid and child-like, is the one we should choose if we were summoned to describe Tchekhov's work in a word.

He is still accused, as he was accused by Merezhkovsky thirty
years ago, of writing about ' failures,' of being grey and depressing and painful ; and it would be vain even to attempt to
reply to a charge so manifestly based on insensitiveness to
what he was, were it not that his own comment on the criticism
has the luminous directness of the mysterious simplicity that
was his. ' One would need to be God,' he said, ' to decide which
are the failures and which are the successes in life.'   And
when we read that, we suddenly remember that the great Tacitus
had no doubt to which class belonged the fellow of the name
of Christ.

Most of all, it is this quality of mysterious simplicity in
Tchekhov's presentation of life which first prevents us from regarding the depths of understanding below.   It is as though
he understood not only that life was so, but also that it must
be so ; as though he knew a secret.   And the secret, as all true
secrets must be, is very, very simple, so simple that we cannot
recognise it ; we can recognise only a strange enchantment in
what he shows us, a strange and haunting quality in his words.
We look and listen, and we feel that we are trembling on the
brink of knowledge so incredible that it cannot be. We do not
know what to say ; we cannot understand what is happening
in ourselves ; we are overwhelmed by a single feeling, which
when we try to hold it before our eyes, splinters like light
through a crystal into contradictory emotions : laughter, tears,
pity, love, and one knows not what infinite and unfamiliar tenderness from our depths. Yet these are blended and made one by
a kind of sacramental solemnity : we have been made partakers
of a mystery.   And Tchekhov works this magic on our souls
again and again and again.   We could choose the endings of
twenty of his stories, quote sentences by the hundred from them,
in which, with no essential diminution through the veil of a
foreign language, the miracle is accomplished.   For a single
instance, take the ending of *The Lady with the Dog* :

> Then they spent a long while taking counsel together,
> talked of how to avoid the necessity of secrecy, of deception,
> of living in different towns and not seeing each other for long
> at a time. How could they be free from this intolerable

110

bondage?

'How? How?' he asked, clutching his head. 'How?'

And it seemed as though in a little while the solution would be found, and then a new and splendid life would begin; and it was clear to them both that they still had a long, long way to go, and that the most complicated and difficult part of it was only just beginning.

The response which that awakens within us is an inaudible *Nunc dimittis* set to some new and unknown melody. We are grave, we are quiet, we are gathered to ourselves; for our eyes have seen, and our hearts have understood, a mystery.

That which Tchekhov makes us feel, he felt: we cannot maintain the vision, but he could: what is a miracle to us was to him a faculty of nature. He saw what seem to our bewildered eyes immeasurably complicated and subtle things *sub specie simplicitatis*. From where he stood life was—exactly what life is, yet it was one. He did not need to exclude anything; not a single one of the thousand seemingly insoluble discords which in our lives we know had to be set aside and ignored by him. On the contrary, where the discord is at extremity and the tangle most obviously beyond all solution this side the grave, to that point before all others he turns: and lo! the harmony is there. In our everyday language, in the framework of our everyday belief, the situation in *The Lady with the Dog* would be to some impossible, to others immoral, to both, manifestly intolerable and beyond all human remedy. 'Look again,' Tchekhov seems to whisper; we look, and everything in transfigured. There is only one gesture for us, if we have eyes to see—to bow our heads, in the knowledge that it must be so and not otherwise.

There are dangers in this word simplicity. It seems that few people understand (or if many understand, few remember) that there are two kinds of spiritual simplicity. There is the simplicity of the child, and the simplicity of the man: the one comes before the great struggle of self-discovery begins, the other when it is ended. There is the simplicity of *Love's Labour's Lost*, and the simplicity of *The Tempest*; of birth, and of rebirth. And our language is still so far from a final perfection that we are compelled to use one name for both, or to describe the second condition by metaphors taken from the first. The simplicity of Tchekhov is very wise and very old; it is an achievement wrung out of much knowledge and surpassing inward honesty. Tchekhov began to learn very early in his life: at a time when most Englishmen are still schoolboys he had learned not only to bear but to accept an overwhelming burden of responsibility. Read the letter to his brother which he wrote when he was only twenty-six: it is an incredible document, for it contains the humanity and the wisdom and the humour which even men of genius are not wont to acquire till they are old. And this personal heritage of experience, important though it was, is less important than his impersonal inheritance of the great explorations of Tolstoy and Dostoevsky, who had brought the European consciousness to a verge. There was nothing for it, if Tchekhov was to *be* at all, but to be a new man.

And that is what we feel he was. Those amazing letters of his which come so near to us, are simple and strange in a new way ; they seem to us perfectly natural, more natural than any letters we have ever read, yet they are quite unlike any other letters we have read ; they belong to a different kind, they are informed by a new consciousness. They are simple, the attitude of which they are the natural product is simple, but we sense in that simplicity a complete knowledge of all the complexities with which the modern consciousness is laden. Tchekhov had somehow passed beyond all this. Mr. Gerhardi's instinct is surely right when he protests against the attitude of those who regard a Marcel Proust or a James Joyce as the advanced out- posts of the literary consciousness to-day. Tchekhov is far in advance of them; by his side they are almost antiquarian survivals of a superseded past. Tchekhov's work is indeed a resolution of their illimitable intellectualisms. His simplicty completely undercuts their complexities.

For Tchekhov knew where the intellectual consciousness was impotent ; and he knew it was impotent precisely for the apprehension of the eternal livingness of life. Entangled in the maze of complicated accidents, it misses the essence. In *The Duel*, von Koren gropes in vain after some understanding

112

of the impossible Laevsky, until at the last the rigidity of his honest mind is melted by a simple intuition into the nature of Laevsky's being ; and the reconciliation which ensues is as profound as any of the more striking reconciliations in which the great drama of old used to culminate. For Tchekhov, who preached nothing deliberately, in reality preached no less than this : a reconciliation here and now, achieved by an understanding not from the mind, but from the soul, or more truly from a reborn soul. And, as though expressly for our illumination, Tchekhov in his Notebooks isolated the quintessence of the reconciliation which is his.

Essentially all this is crude and meaningless, and romantic love appears as meaningless as an avalanche which involuntarily rolls down a mountain and overwhelms people. But when one listens to music, all this is—that some people lie in their graves and sleep, and that one woman is alive and, grey-headed, is now sitting in a box in the theatre, seems quiet and majestic, and the avalanche is no longer meaningless, since in nature everything has a meaning. And everything is forgiven, and it would be strange not to forgive.

This condition which Tchekhov experienced when he listened to music, we experience when we listen to Tchekhov. It would be not impossible, not inhuman, not stupid, but simply strange not to forgive.   This forgiveness is not the result of an effort ; indeed it is not what we understand by forgiveness at all ; the name has been carried from the past to define a new condition of the consciousness.   If one were truly conscious of some fundamental harmony, if one steadily knew that everything had a meaning, then forgiveness and unforgivingness would have none : for they have meaning only in a world which is ignorant of its own.

And here, perhaps, we come nearest to the newness of Tchekhov.   What in other men would be some kind of intermittent and bewildering mystical perception, in him was a steady mode of apprehension; and because it was that, it seems extraordinarily simple and intangible. He makes no claim for himself : he is perfectly ready to admit that he is lemonade ' compared to the strong drink of the great men before him, or that they had purposes—'axes to grind'—and he has none. Yet imperceptibly we realise (more with our hearts than our heads) that he is single as those great men never were single ; he was harmonious, where they were still divided ; he did not have to struggle his life long to forgive, he forgave. Yet so soon as we begin to use these ambitious phrases, we are afraid. He, who knew so much, whose writing was so incomparably subtle, who when we try to analyse him becomes so complex, in reality astonishes us by the impression of his simplicity. And it may be that, after all, the truest description of him is the most elementary : that he was a different *kind* of man. It happens with us in regard to Tchekhov, as it happened with the man in his story, *The Wife*, in regard to the doctor.

I listened to the doctor, and, according to my habit, applied my usual measures to him — materialist, idealist, money-grubber, herd-instincts, and so forth, but not a single one of my measures would fit even approximately ; and, curiously, while I only listened to him and looked at him, he was, as a man, perfectly clear to me, but the moment I began applying my measures to him he became, despite all his sincerity and simplicity, an extraordinarily complex, confused, and inexplicable nature.

And nothing could, in fact, be simpler in itself and in its manifestations than this new consciousness of Tchekhov's. There are in his letters, for instance, hardly any 'profound thoughts,' and yet the most trivial incident recorded in them seems to have a profound importance ; if he makes a joke, we feel that nobody ever made a joke like that before. It is not in the least, as he sometimes pretends, that he is too trivial to pay attention to the deep speculations and debates of the *intelligentsia*, or that he is one of those would-be hierophants who reduce life to terms of some undifferentiated origin out of which life has differentiated itself. He accepts all the complexities, he sacrifices nothing ; he simply makes us feel that everything has a meaning, and he knows it. Of course, he cannot tell us the meaning : no man will ever be able to do that, for knowledge of meaning can only come with a change in the nature of consciousness.

The more we try to make clear to ourselves the unique and

114

essential reality of Tchekhov, the more inevitable appears the conclusion that some such prophetic change had actually occurred in him, so that he saw things with some simple and direct apprehension of their nature, of which we can recognise the truth though the process eludes us. The transparent simplicity of his descriptions of things which to other minds are intricate and complicated is disconcerting. He wants to show that a man is in love with his wife : this is how he does it :

> That which in her words was just, seemed to him uncommon, extraordinary ; and that which differed from his own convictions was, in his view, naive and touching.

Astonishing effects achieved by simple means have always been the prerogative of the finest art; but these effects of Tchekhov's are different from those attained before him. They do not make the impression of flashes of incredible intuition, and far less of some superhuman gift of creation, but of some quite human faculty of knowledge which unfortunately we do not possess. The illumination is so steady and unemphatic that at first it often escapes us altogether; then comes a period when we do notice it and put it down to some sort of deliberate method employed by Tchekhov—Mr. Gerhardi shows some of the signs of this period—but finally we are forced to the conclusion that it was a natural function of Tchekhov's consciousness, and his consciousness a natural function of his being. Tchekhov does not insist, but his lack of insistence comes not from a deliberate artistic purpose, but by nature. He is not resisting a temptation—as we feel Flaubert is resisting a temptation in, for instance, *Un Cœur Simple*—he is merely expressing a vision and stating a knowledge which are natural to him. In his world it would be as strange to insist as it would be strange not to forgive.

It seems that at this point we begin to touch the secret of the intense and sensitive personal loyalty which Tchekhov's admirers feel towards him. Much more immediately than in the case of any other writer all that he wrote appears to us as a function of all that he was. It is not easy to explain why the closeness of the relation between his seeing and his being should be so striking, or so unmistakably acknowledged by us. We have and know the Letters and the Notebooks, it is true, and these are, more than such things are wont to be, of one piece with his stories and plays; but that is not the cause. We knew the connection long before the Letters and the Notebooks were revealed to us. The cause is rather that, if we leave aside a few comic stories of his nonage, there is an all-pervading unity in his work. There is a point in his too brief life (and it occurs very early) after which there is no perceptible evolution in his work, and above all no perceptible struggle. Suddenly he is mature, and he remains mature; and it becomes almost impossible to say that one piece of work is better than another. At most, we can have personal and irrational preferences. Every story, every play, every letter, after this moment, is new; but all alike belong to the same order. There was a moment when Tchekhov possessed his knowledge and possessed himself in a new way.

But why, it may be asked, because he possessed his knowledge did he necessarily possess himself? There are two answers · one, that knowledge of this kind cannot be achieved without possession of oneself: that sounds almost mystical. Therefore it is better to insist on the second, which is, that if the knowledge of the writer—and by knowledge we mean his comprehension of life—outstrips his own inward development, no power on earth can conceal the traces of the conflict and contradiction in his work. In Tchekhov's work these traces are invisible; instead his powers are steady and equable; there is neither sign of disturbance nor evidence of hesitation. As is the work, so is the man: the work is new and true, the man also.

If we could know the process of this inward development in Tchekhov, we should know something of infinite value to humanity. But like all things of the highest spiritual value, it cannot be *known*; if it were put into words we should not understand them, any more than we understand the words into which still greater souls than Tchekhov have put their secret. Moreover, Tchekhov was reticent about it. Practically all we have is a letter he wrote to Suvorin when he was twenty-eight (in 1888) soon after his play *Ivanov* had drawn upon him the attention of Russia. He is speaking of the play :

> As far as my design does, I was on the right track, but the execution is good for nothing. I ought to have waited! I am glad I did not listen to Grigorovich two or three years ago, and write a novel! I can just imagine what a lot of good material I should have spoiled. He says : ' Talent and freshness overcome everything.' It is truer to say that talent and freshness can spoil a great deal. In addition to plenty of material and talent, one wants something else which is no less important. One wants to be mature—that is one thing ; and for another *the feeling of personal freedom* is essential, and that feeling has only recently begun to develop in me. I used not to have it before ; its place was successfully filled by my frivolity, carelessness, and lack of respect for my work. What writers belonging to the upper class have received by nature for nothing, plebeians acquire at the cost of their youth.

It was Tchekhov himself who underlined the words: 'the feeling of personal freedom.' Of course, it is a mere momentary fancy of his that personal freedom of the kind he means is the gift of nature to the aristocrat. It is something which no man has by nature, and very few, be they aristocrats or plebeians, achieve at all: it is a sense of one's own personal existence and validity independent of all circumstance : it is the profoundest of all kinds of self-knowledge, and no one can receive it without paying the full price. Tchekhov leaves us in no doubt what he meant if we read his letters carefully. ' I believe,' he wrote elsewhere, ' in individual people, I see salvation in individual personalities scattered here and there all over Russia— whether they belong to the intelligentsia or to the peasants— they are strong though they are few.' For this feeling of personal freedom of which he knew the importance and the cost is the mark of the true and completed individuality, the sign of independent self-existence. Such individuals are the pioneers of humanity, and on them the future of true civilisation does indeed depend. At another time, also in a letter to Suvorin, Tchekhov described the process as 'squeezing the slave out of oneself.'

117

Write a story (he says) of how a young man, the son of a serf who has served in a shop, sung in a choir, been at a high school and a university, who has been brought up to respect every one of higher rank and position, to kiss priests' hands, to reverence other people's ideas, to be thankful for every morsel of bread, who has been many times whipped, who has trudged from one pupil to another without goloshes, who has been used to fighting, and tormenting animals, who has liked dining with his rich relations, and been hypocritical before God and men from the mere consciousness of his own insignificance—write how this young man squeezes the slave out of himself, drop by drop, and how waking one beautiful morning feels that he has no longer a slave's blood in his veins, but a real man's.

Tchekhov states it so unobtrusively that we may easily pass it by, and even, if we notice it, may forget how vital this inward achievement was to his real maturity as a writer.

So vital indeed that the truest of all his brief definitions of his writing would be that it is the writing of a perfectly free man : a man who has freed himself from all fears and has found that within himself which enables him to stand completely alone. When a man has attained this freedom and unity in himself, he does not need to send his intellect any more on fruitless expeditions after meanings : somehow he knows the meaning. And such a man can afford to love humanity as Tchekhov loved it, for he is in no danger of entanglement ; he does not love for the sake of being loved. And the knowledge of a free man is steady and unfaltering—a possession for ever—because there is, in that which knows, no variableness, neither any shadow of turning.

We catch a glimpse of Tchekhov's secret; we cannot know it wholly : if we did, we should be like him, and to be like him would be to be far in advance of what we are. But in so far as we do understand what he wrote and was, and have a sense of the simple unity of his seeing and his being, we are not surprised that Tchekhov's method has found so few followers. nor do we wonder why the one conspicuous attempt to imitate him (in Mr. Shaw's *Heartbreak House*) is merely a revelation of a strange insensibility in Mr. Shaw, or why the juxtaposition of Mr. Wells's declarations of faith with Tchekhov's is impossible. nor are we any longer perplexed for the reason why we feel an intense and unique loyalty to a writer whom most of us know only in translation: for we know that Tchekhov made himself a new man by a great spiritual victory, that a kindred victory in ourselves is the condition of using his method, and that the victory, like all victories of this high kind, was won on our behalf.

[NOVEMBER, 1923]

GOGOL

'We all,' wrote Dostoevsky, 'come out from under Gogol's "Overcoat".' This derivation of one of the great literatures of the world from a young man's single story—*The Overcoat* was written in Gogol's early twenties—is easier to appreciate than to define. Over and over again in reading *The Overcoat* we come upon sentences and paragraphs in which we feel as if were a new life stirring, the birth of a new sensitiveness to human experience. The range of man's responsiveness is being definitely extended.

This sense of new possibilities that he gives us is Gogol's great fascination. Old limitations are breaking down; the face-to-face vision of eighteenth-century 'common sense' is giving way not so much to a new method as to the potentiality of many new methods. Gogol now looks more intently at what is before him, now he glances altogether sideways. His scrutiny is, sometimes more microscopic, sometimes more fantastic than that of his predecessors in his own country and abroad. He looks harder, and he looks from a different direction. But indeed he glances rather than looks. He opens the new window just long enough for the vision to excite us; then he turns abruptly aside and opens another. We have not time to see the whole world as we do through the eyes of the greatest, but we may have many glimpses. They are unsettling, for Gogol's eyes are restless. We feel that he is being driven on by a greater power: he has no time to pause. On this side and that he leads us to a brink and turns abruptly away. He sets our imaginations racing and pulls them up short at the crucial leap. What he does to us must in some sort have happened to himself, so that we might describe him also as the man of a racing imagination. And the moment we have written those words we remember the strange description of the racing troika with which *Dead Souls* rushes to its illimitable end.

Gogol's work is essentially incomplete; because of that it is the more exciting, so exciting in its peculiar way that we can not only see the Russian literature we know springing out of its beginnings, but we have glimpses also of a literature which not even the Russians have achieved. There is what we can only call a 'mad' streak in Gogol; and madness, applied to the human imagination, is an unsatisfactory term, the more unsatisfactory since we are using it to define a queer imaginative tempo in Gogol by which the first things at moments are brought perilously near to the last. It might be argued that Dostoevsky himself followed this particular road of Gogol's opening to the bitter end. But there is, or there seems to be, a real difference between them. The 'mad' element in Gogol's vision is not an inevitable extension of the intellectual and the speculative, as it is in Dostoevsky. Gogol's is not a mind considering the problem of evil and pain with an implacable imaginative logic. The tremendous discipline of Dostoevsky is not his at all. Gogol's phantasmagoric vision is more immediate and more primitive. When things and creatures begin to loom before his mind they are not embodied principles; they are more elemental. They are grotesque and gigantic and comic; they are terrifying also.

The more we feel that Dostoevsky's sentence concerning the derivation of Russian literature from *The Overcoat* is true, the more definitely we feel that all the seeds contained in certain pages of *Dead Souls* and in such an extraordinary story as *The Nose*, did not come to fruition. These possibilities were never fulfilled. Perhaps they never could have been; perhaps, in fact, they are not there. But so much undoubtedly was there that it is wiser to allow the benefit of the doubt. *The Nose*, for instance, persists in appearing as something more than a rather crude comic fantasia. Major Kovalyov's nose suddenly turns up in the middle of a loaf of bread. Major Kovalyov as suddenly finds that his nose has disappeared leaving a space 'as smooth as a pancake.' The barber into whose breakfast loaf it has smuggled wraps it up in a parcel which he finds it very hard to dispose of. Even when Major Kovalyov goes to the newspaper office to advertise for his missing nose, and is taken aback at being told that such an advertisement cannot possibly be accepted, the story remains within the limits of an excellent fantastic invention. But when the Major, with his face muffled, stops 'as though rooted to the spot before the door of a house,' the 'mad' streak is suddenly visible.

> Something inexplicable took place before his eyes: a carriage was stopping at the entrance; the carriage door flew open; a gentleman in uniform, bending down, sprang out and ran up the steps. What was the horror and at the same time the amazement of Kovalyov when he recognised that this was his own nose!

The effect which this makes in its place and context, upon one mind at least, is queer indeed. It is, perhaps, only an Aristophanic invention, but it is so curiously sinister. The last thing we feel inclined to do is to laugh; it should, it *ought* to, be uproariously funny; but it is not funny in the least. It is impressive, indeed, but in quite another way. And this, after all, is only a single instance, and in some respects rather a crude one, of a kind of vision which is continually manifesting itself in Gogol, and is invariably disconcerting when it does.

Again, consider the tailor's toe-nail in *The Overcoat*. It sticks in the mind first because there is another famous toe-nail in Russian literature. It belonged to Dmitri Karamazov, who gazed at it with a disgusted fascination when he was arrested at Mokroe. One wonders whether Dostoevsky had a subconscious memory of Gogol. But they are very different toenails. That of Gogol's tailor was almost a thing-in-itself. It had no relation to Akaky Akakievitch's consciousness, as Dmitri's had to his.

> The feet, as is usual with tailors when they sit at work, were bare; and the first object that caught Akaky Akakievitch's eye was the big toe, with which he was already familiar, with a misshapen nail as thick and as strong as the shell of a tortoise.

That is all; but it is surprising and more than a little frightening to discover how monstrous that toe-nail is, and how monstrously it abides in the memory. It dwarfs the tailor and his room.

But this was not the Gogol from whom Russian literature descended. This is the Gogol of the most disturbing parts of *Dead Souls*, and not of *The Overcoat*, even though the toe-nail comes in that story, simply because Gogol found it impossible to be only one thing at a time. After all, he was Gogol, and not, save for the purposes of literary history (which are always laudable but never essential), the original germ of Russian literature. *The Overcoat* itself, which is in this historical context a 'realistic' story, telling of the disaster of 'a creature whose cause no one had championed, who was dear to no one, of interest to no one, who never even attracted the attention of the student of natural history,' is in right of its own reality something different. That is quite clear from the fact that there is plenty of room in it for the ghost of the dead Akaky Akakievitch, who, with scant courtesy and a total forgetfulness of what was due to a general, roughly pulled off the overcoat of a civil councillor who had refused to help him in his search for the overcoat he had lost. That unseemly ghost is not at all discordant in Gogol's own story; but he had no place in the literature which derived from it. Ivan Karamazov's Devil, Kolya's Black Monk, are quite another kettle of fish. Gogol's ghost was a real ghost: Dostoevsky's and Tchekhov's were projections of a consciousness.

Russian literature took what it wanted from Gogol, and it did not want the whole of him. It is hard to say quite how central to Gogol was the part it took. Probably the pound of flesh was pretty near the heart; but it was on one side of it, and there were other sides. Nevertheless, in the description of Akaky Akakievitch at his work as copying-clerk, we can hear not merely faint intimations of the note which was to be sounded, but the very voice itself. This speech is unmistakable.

The young clerks jeered and made jokes at him to the best of their clerkly wit, and told before his face all sorts of stories of their own invention about him; they would say of his landlady, an old woman of seventy, that she beat him, would inquire when the wedding was to take place, and would scatter bits of paper on his head, calling them snow. . . . Only when the jokes were too unbearable, when they jolted his arm and prevented him from going on with his work, he would bring out: 'Leave me alone! Why do you insult me?' And there was something strange in the words and in the

123

voice in which they were uttered. There was a note in it of something that aroused compassion, so that one young man, new to the office, who, following the example of the rest, had allowed himself to mock at him, suddenly stopped as though cut to the heart, and from that time forth everything was, as it were, changed, and appeared in a different light to him. Some unnatural force seemed to thrust him away from the companions with whom he had become acquainted, accepting them as well-bred, polished people. And long afterwards, at moments of the greatest gaiety, the figure of the humble little clerk with the bald patch on his head rose before him with his heart-rending words: 'Leave me alone! Why do you insult me?' And in those heart-rending words he heard others: 'I am your brother.'

Perhaps not the whole of Russian literature can be derived from that, but the whole of Dostoevsky can. And probably that is what Dostoevsky really meant.

[SEPTEMBER, 1923]

STENDHAL

No one has better described the impression made by Stendhal than Goethe, who wrote in 1818: 'Er zieht an, er stosst ab, interessiert und ärgert, und so kann man ihn nicht loswerden.' ('He attracts, repels, interests, irritates, and one can't get away from him.') That was written after reading *Rome, Naples, and Florence*, which M. Edouard Champion has republished in his superb edition of the complete works, and the description fits the particular book perhaps a little more exactly than any of the others. It so obviously ought to be a dull work, and it so obviously is not. It has neither system nor shape; it is concerned with a society that has passed out of mind; it is studded with the irrelevant, tangential speculations of a perpetually curious mind, with odd facts of history, with long and enthusiastic appreciations of forgotten Italian operas and unremembered singers. Yet we are held. Stendhal's facts are not like anybody else's facts. They are like objects looked at from a peculiar and unexpected angle. We only half recognize them. The proportions are queer. At first they are almost silly, then they become bizarre, then fascinating, and then—at least for a period in most literary lives—all-absorbing.

Stendhal was a man of many surfaces. There are bold men who call themselves *stendhaliens* and profess to be adept in in *le beylisme*; but they are not to be trusted. It is true that Stendhal had an attitude to life, a philosophy of conduct, which might be imitated. But the man who actively followed Beyle's precepts would, by the mere fact, be very different from Beyle. For this seeming *rusé* realist was the embodiment of timidity; this amateur of the *amour-passion* was one of the most backward love-makers who ever existed. In M. Arbelet's admirable biography, *La Jeunesse de Stendhal*, which is published as part (and a worthy part) of the collected edition, you may read of the comedy or the tragedy of young Beyle's initiation into love at Milan. It is an unfamiliar but characteristic episode in the man's life, which was as it were stained through and through with a dye of some paradoxical uniqueness. One feels that he was born in a momentary interregnum of the *Zeitgeist*, just as in the actual world he happened to be educated in one of those strange schools which were the immediate product of the Revolution, where masters and pupils alike were fired by a passion for *la Raison*—schools which lasted barely three years, just long enough to give a unique impress to the one boy with a touch of genius who might, on merely statistical grounds, be expected to be born in the period.

If one were writing the book upon Beyle which has still to be written—it will be the work of the English critic, for no Frenchman could have sufficient detachment, or even sufficient understanding—one would begin by showing how a cornucopia of uniqueness was made ready to be emptied upon the head of the infant Henri Beyle. M. Arbelet has gathered most of the material for a study of his astonishing parents and relations, those bourgeois aristocrats (like the Rênals of *Le Rouge et le Noir*) who were so much more exclusive even than the *grands bourgeois* of modern France. When one comes to know them a little more closely, to see them a little more clearly, than is possible through the melodramatic kaleidoscope of *La Vie de Henri Brulard* one comes to look upon Beyle as a kind of infant Samuel dedicated to one knows what deity of contrariety and paradox. One feels, rather than understands, the reason of the inevitability which imposes itself upon any one who attempts even in the scope of a brief essay to define the substance of Beyle, the man and the writer. Every comparison turns into paradox. The outward garment of his style suggests the influence of Voltaire; in fact, Beyle hated Voltaire, and the real influence was much rather Jean-Jacques. His whole manner is that of an aristocrat of aristocrats; he was, in fact, and most profoundly, a republican, a libertarian, and a radical. Most sincerely in the literary controversy of his age Beyle insisted that he was a romantic; in fact, he detested Chateaubriand, and he was pretty exactly what we call a realist. His lucid and exact psychological analysis recalls no dramatist in the French tradition so directly as Racine: in fact, Beyle could not abide Racine, and most honestly and for the most substantial reasons idolized Shakespeare. 'Adorava Shakespeare' was the alternative epitaph to the one which he finally chose: 'Arrigo Beyle

Milanese: vissè, scrissè, amò.' The art of Shakespeare and the life of Italy —between Rivoli and the Risorgimento, be it understood—may fairly be said to have been the two passions whose rule over him endured throughout his life.

Beyle is, perhaps, the smallest of great men; but he is also one of the most compact, and his title to be called great is proved not least by the wholly peculiar persistence with which he seems to avoid all classification. He makes a queer final impression—how delighted he would have been to read it!—as of a miniature, desiccated Shakespeare, and, indeed, one can easily conceive a definition of him in terms which in a richer, riper world of perceptions would apply to Shakespeare. His universe of men was also blank between the aristocrat and the peasant, and it may be for the same reason. He confesses that because he was a bourgeois, the bourgeois had become as intolerable to him as the taste of oysters to a man who had a surfeit of them; he had supped too full of the horrors of the bourgeoisie in childhood ever to contemplate them again. The middle class were ciphers in his system of values, and even an ideal member of it remained a cipher, just as zero, raised to the nth power, remains zero. 'Ce qui est exactement raisonnable ne donne pas prise aux beaux-arts; j'estime un sage républicain des Etats-Unis, mais je l'oublie à tout jamais en quelques jours· ce n'est pas un homme pour moi, c'est une chose.' Therefore, although he was by impulse a realist, he was nevertheless a romantic because he had a theory of what was real. Not all that existed in the shape of human beings was real to him. This anti-bourgeois speck in his telescope, he wrote in *Henri Brulard*, had been very useful to him with the characters of his novels. It was true; but the word 'bourgeois' had by that time come to denote for him not so much a social class as a type of being. The reality of a man for Stendhal lay in his faculty of allowing all that is prudential and calculating in him to be swept aside by what is instinctive and passionate.

That is a fairly complete and coherent attitude towards life: it certainly has its counterpart in Shakespeare, it is, moreover, what we might call a very good working basis for a literary artist. But it does not in the least resemble that enlightened hedonism which the 'Beylistes' profess to find in their idol. Beyle, indeed, makes a poor showing as a hedonist. The overwhelming impulses of soul which he set highest, and counted most real among human capacities, the precious *élans d'âme*, were likely to prove annihilating to their vehicles. Indeed, they not only annihilated his heroes and heroines, Fabrice, Julien Sorel, Mademoiselle de la Môle, Clélia, and the rest, but they came near to being his own undoing at one or two points of his own career. To be interesting to Beyle people must be ready to surrender their lives at the summons of a *grande passion*; to be interesting to himself he had to believe that the same readiness lay in him. It is therefore inexact to call him a romantic, even though he called himself one. Your true romantic is ready to surrender himself only to his dreams; his *élan d'âme* has little or no repercussion in the visible world. The real world is altogether too sordid, and perhaps too difficult a place for him to be concerned with it. His passions are veritably passive. It, was, however, the essence of Stendal's conception of passion that it should issue, and issue immediately in act. Whether the act seems grandiose or ridiculous, momentous or merely bizarre, was of small account ; it was precisely indifferent. He prefaces almost every one of his stories of *la vie passionelle* in *Rome, Naples et Florence* with the warning that it will seem ridiculous, but the implication behind the warning is that if you find it ridiculous, you are a poor creature. The faculty which he admired in men had two complementary aspects. Looked at from the inside it was passion, the *élan d'âme*, from the outside was *la force.* This is the meaning of his paradox: 'J'aime la force, et de la force que j'aime, une fourmi peut en montrer autant qu'un éléphant.'

Stendhal's attitude to life was not romantic, therefore ; it was tragic. It falls in between the classical and the romantic attitudes. His ideal is neither the harmonious man of the Greeks nor the gesticulating, dreaming hero of romanticism ; it is, really, the hero of a Shakespearean tragedy, a hero who plays his part in the active life of a real world. In order to give literary expression to this tragic hero-worship, Stendhal had to become what is generally called a realist. But just as

128

the term ' romantic ' has to be given an unfamiliar and improper meaning to fit him, ' realist ' has also to be given a precise and particular sense. Realist in the proper critical meaning he was not. A good deal more than half human life was supremely uninteresting to him. But the part he was interested in had a sort of super-reality to compensate. The problem was how to convey and communicate this, how (in the expressive phrase of the working artist) ' to get it across.' An unobtrusive sentence in *Rome, Naples et Florence*—we are endeavouring to explain Stendhal on the evidence of this single book—gives us his solution. ' On n'a jamais du feu,' he writes, ' qu'en écrivant la langue qu'on parle à sa maîtresse et à ses rivaux.'

Now there is much more in Stendhal's style than is indicated here ; but that dictum contains the solid basis of some of his most remarkable achievements—passionate episodes expressed in the natural language of passion. On the creative side one can think immediately of a dozen passages in the two great novels where the theory is superbly exemplified—for instance, the ' Qu'avez-vous dans la poche de côté de votre habit? ' of Mathilde de la Môle—on the critical, it is a main count in his one-sided, but convincing case against Scott. ' Ses personnages passionnés semblent avoir honte d'eux-mêmes'; therefore they are unreal. This principle is the chief of the two tendencies that unite to form Stendhal's ' realism.' From his childhood upwards he was, in regard to literature, a dissatisfied rather than a disillusioned romantic. M. Arbelet has unearthed a singularly interesting passage from one of his unpublished notes which bears upon this. It was written before he was twenty :

Dans les romans on ne nous offre qu'une nature choisie: nous nous formons nos types de bonheur d'après les romans. Parvenus à l'âge où nous devons être heureux . . . nous nous étonnons de deux choses: la première, de ne pas éprouver du tout les sentiments auxquels nous nous attendions; la deuxième, si nous les éprouvons, de ne pas les sentir comme ils sont peints dans les romans.

Two year later he re-read his note, and added : ' Voilà l'histoire de ma vie; mon roman était les ouvrages de Rousseau.'

Stendhal himself was destined to offer to future generations a *nature choisie,* more sedulously selected, perhaps, than that of any other considerable novelist. It was not the ignoring of half reality that shocked him, but the being unreal in the expression of the reality you choose. Because he was consistently and profoundly a ' romantic,' he hated with a threefold hatred romantic falseness and pomposity ; because he really had a tragic attitude to life, the high falutin' of French classical tragedy goaded him to a frenzy. It was making his heartfelt realities ridiculous. From this he directly derived his detestation of the phrase and the circumlocution, which remained with him all his life, and his at first sight strange desire, which lasted to middle age, to write a good comedy. An instinct told him that the drama was the most perfect vehicle for his tragic view of life ; another instinct told him that a genre in which you had to write *coursier* for *cheval* and the precious word *pistolet* was taboo, was intolerable. To get natural speech on to the stage he must write comedy. It may seem a fantastic conclusion ; fantastic it must seem if you have read the outline of any of his projected ' comedies '—irrefutable evidence that he had not a shred of a sense of humour—but yet it was inevitable.

The other component of his style, a bare and vigorous clarity of analytical exposition, came from two sources. He was, as we have said, a devout believer in the tragic attitude. Tragic heroes were real people ; he had met plenty of them in the Italian society he loved. He wanted to prove that they existed, to take them to pieces, as it were, in the intervals when they were not expressing *élans d'âme* in the natural language of passion. Here the ideologists who had been triumphant in the French educational system for the three brief and impressionable years he spent at the Ecole Centrale at Grenoble lent him powerful aid. Those forgotten psychologists, Destutt de Tracy and Condillac, whose names recur so often in his pages, were indeed his masters of method here. Hence came the passion for *la lo-gique* which in his curious drawl he so often impressed upon Mérimée, and his recourse to the Code Napoléon as a model of descriptive style. His education and the demands of his theory of life and art worked together for good. His heroes, being heroes of action, were saved from perishing in a maze of super-subtle psychology ; since their supreme moments had to be expressed in the natural language of passion, they were also saved from becoming ' desiccated.'

Stendhal, in brief, was a tragic realist. Tragic realism is, on the whole, an unusual kind ; but some of the greatest works of literary art belong to it, the *Medea* and *Antony and Cleopatra, Anna Karenina*, and *The Possessed*. Stendhal differs from the writers called up by these names in that he held his faith a perceptible shade more naïvely than they. It was for him not merely the attitude of an artist towards life, not merely a philosophy which enabled the artist to express his vision of the truth and quality of life, it was also, and perhaps chiefly, a philosophy of conduct. Tragic heroes did not merely exist because their destiny was forced upon them ; it was man's duty to be one. The first thing was to be *une âme supérieure* (his beloved phrase), the second to assert it in act, the third— and a bad third—was to write about it. And here is the reason why, although there is no real incongruity in naming Stendhal with Euripides and Shakespeare and Tolstoy and Dostoevsky, a vital difference remains. To a casual glance it presents itself as a constant amateurishness in Stendhal the artist. We must look deeper than that, however ; and, looking deeper, we shall discover it to be a profound naïvety. What satisfies only a part of the great writer's mind satisfied the whole of his : in other words, Stendhal was even less a creator of heroes than a hero-worshipper.

[SEPTEMBER, 1920]

GUSTAVE FLAUBERT

There were two Flauberts. One was born on the 12th of December, 1821, in the surgeon's house at Rouen hospital; the other in enthusiastic minds in the last quarter of the nineteenth century. One was a broad, big-boned, lovable, rather simpleminded man, with the look and the laugh of a farmer, who spent his life in agonies over the intensive culture of half a dozen curiously assorted volumes; the other was an incorporeal giant, a symbol, a war-cry, a banner under which a youthful army marched and marches still to the rout of the bourgeois and the revolution of literature.

To distinguish these beings from each other is not so difficult as to understand how they came to be so completely interfused that the separation of the legend and the reality may appear an act of wanton inconoclasm. So much has been derived from the legendary Flaubert, so many advancing waves have borne his name on the crest of their attack, that he has acquired the dignity of an institution. We have a critic of the stature of Remy de Gourmont declaring that Flaubert is the very archetype of the creative writer, for two reasons; because he devoted his life and his personality to his work, suffering nothing to be wasted in the exigencies and delights of mere living, and because he was pre-eminently gifted with visual imagination.

It is not easy to see why the value of a writer's work should depend upon the completeness of his incineration on the altar of Art. A good writer has to make sacrifices, of course, but he need not (indeed, he had better not) burn himself to ashes Greater writers than Flaubert have not felt the necessity. To one who is not a born Flaubertian the astonishing tortures he inflicted upon himself would naturally suggest, not that his genius was pre-eminent, but that his creative impulse was not of the strongest. While the truth about his visual imagination is that it was not of the finest quality. Flaubert adored images; he believed, truly enough, that the highest poetic faculty is mastery of metaphor; he fancied that when he was wholly free to write what pleased him—though when was he not?—he would triumphantly indulge his passion. Yet, in fact, Flaubert's use of

132

imagery is almost invariably strained or commonplace, and often both. Take the similes with which *L'Education Sentimentale* begins and ends: neither is successful. Here is the first:

> Enfin le navire partit; et les deux berges, peuplées de magasins, de chantiers et d'usines, filèrent comme deux larges rubans qu'on déroule.

The image is forced, and it gives the wrong tempo to the opening movement. A torpedo-boat destroyer could not steam fast enough to justify it wholly, and this was a river-steamer on the Seine. The second simile is used by Madame Arnoux when she revisits Frédéric Moreau:

> Elle s'étonnait de sa mémoire. Cependant, elle lai dit:
> —Quelquefois, vos paroles me reviennent comme un écho lointain. comme le son d'une cloche apporté par le vent; et il me semble que vous êtes là, quand je lis les passages d'amour dans les livres.

This is, indeed, not a visual image ; but its discrepancy is not less remarkable for that. Had the words been given to the second-rate romanticism of Emma Bovary they might have been in place. But Madame Arnoux was designed to be Emma's opposite. For the sake of a worn-out poetical metaphor, Flaubert was willing to make his heroine speak out of character. It would be hard to find an absolutely convincing metaphor in the whole of his work. Some of them are really comic, as this of Rosanette. 'Toutes ces images qu'elle se créait lui faisait comme autant de fils qu'elle aurait perdus, *l'excès de la douleur multipliant sa maternité* . . . .

The fact is that Flaubert did not possess the very finest kind of literary discrimination. He had an unusual visual faculty which he turned to good account, but the use he made of it was primitive. Most of his descriptions are visual pageantry, sometimes impressive, sometimes beautiful, sometimes as tedious as the tail-end of a Lord Mayor's show when we are waiting to cross the Strand. Of the faculty which employs visual imagery to differentiate the subtler emotions of the soul, Flaubert had little or nothing at all. The true faculty of metaphor was denied him.

133

Lacking this a writer cannot be reckoned among the greatest masters of style. But Flaubert lacked something more fundamental still. If we consider his works in the order in which they were writen we are chiefly struck by the strange absence of inward growth which they reveal. The surface texture of *L'Education Sentimentale* is more closely woven than that of *Madame Bovary*, but the scope of the story itself is, if anything, less significant. Flaubert's vision of life had not deepened in the long interval which separates the two works. He saw a larger extent of life, perhaps, but he saw no farther into it ; he had acquired more material, but no greater power of handling it ; he manipulated more characters, but he could not make them more alive. Though the epicure of technical effects may find more to interest him in the later book, it is impossible not to endorse the general verdict that *Madame Bovary* is Flaubert's masterpiece. Undoubtedly the choice lies between those books, for *La Tentation de Saint Antoine* and *Salammbô* are set-pieces which will not kindle, and *Bouvard et Pécuchet* which Remy de Gourmont declared the equal of *Don Quixote* cannot be redeemed from dullness by the mildly amusing bubbles which float to the surface of its viscous narrative.

We may suspect that a writer who does not really develop, the vitality and significance of whose latest work is less than that of his first, has not the root of the matter in him. And Flaubert had not. It may not be given to mortal men to understand life more deeply at the end than at the beginning of their share of it ; but they can more keenly feel its complexity and its wonder ; they can attain to an eminence from which they contemplate it calmly and undismayed. The great writers do this, and convey the issue of their contemplation to us through the created world which they devise. But of this unmortified detachment Flaubert was incapable. He lived and died indignant at the stupidity of the human race. As he was at thirty, so he was at sixty ; in stature of soul he was a young man.

' Récriminer,' asks Baudelaire in *L'Art Romantique*, ' faire de l'opposition, et même réclamer la justice, n'est-ce pas s'emphilistiner quelque peu? ' In those three occupations

Flaubert spent all his time when he emerged from his *gueuloir*, and it is not too much to say that he was a good deal of a Philistine. He had a bourgeois horror of the bourgeois, and it was this repulsion rather than a natural attraction which kept him chained to his desk at Croisset. Literature was to him an ascetic revenge on life, not a culmination of it, he tore himself up by the roots and planted himself in the most highly artificial atmosphere which a considerable writer has ever breathed. Under this unhealthy stimulation he evolved for himself the doctrine of the sovereign autonomy of art.

He could do no less. Having chosen the ivory tower, he had to justify its existence. Hating life, he had to be convinced that literature was also indifferent to it. Accordingly he tried to persuade himself that the subject-matter of a work of literature was of no account. A structure of beauty could be raised upon no matter what foundation, and beauty was absolute and incommensurable.

Two things are remarkable about this aesthetic theory of Flaubert's ; the theory itself, and his manner of holding it. Though it seemed to resemble the doctrine held by other French romantics of his generation, it was profoundly different. Baudelaire, for instance, who claimed for the poet the right to deal with subjects generally held to be immoral, made this claim on behalf of what he considered to be the higher morality of art. He believed that the importance of a subject was independent of the moral estimation in which it was held, but he insisted that the subject should be important. Flaubert, on the other hand, tried to believe that the significance of a subject was an unessential quality. The writer actually endowed it with importance by the beauty of the language in which he treated it. Pressed to its logical conclusion, the theory is almost meaningless, for the writer must choose a subject and must have motives for his choice. So that it is not surprising that Flaubert never wholly satisfied himself He wavered. At one moment he asserted that 'tout découle de la conception,' at another that style was 'the soul beneath the words,' at yet another that everything in literature depended on character. These beliefs do not necessarily conflict with one another, but not one of them can really be reconciled with the notion that the subject-matter is indifferent. For some reason Flaubert was incapable of thinking the question out to a conclusion. His formulated theory of writing went no farther than the injunction—valuable enough—to think clearly, express precisely, and read aloud to test the rhythm.

All this he did, and did so well, that our feeling when we contemplate the years he spent upon works so inwardly hollow as *Salammbô, La Tentation*, and *Bouvard et Pécuchet*, is one of utter dismay. It seems that it was only by accident that he stumbled on a subject of any significance at all ; and indeed it was. It was not the fault of his theory ; that had little influence on his practice, and was rather (as most literary theories are) a justification of an accomplished fact. His choice of subjects was governed by his temperament and his temperament was governed by his two predominant emotions : indignation and aversion. Indignation drove him to Yonville and Nogent and Paris ; aversion gave him wings to fly to Carthage and the Thebaid. His realism was of disgust, his romanticism of predilection ; the realism was in part triumphantly successful, the failure of the romanticism complete. Never was a literary achievement more deeply paradoxical. Flaubert's natural expression was satire, but as we know from *Bouvard et Pécuchet*, and as he himself also recognised, his hand was as heavy in satire as his thought was cumbersome.

Indignation and aversion, unless they find their proper satisfaction in satire, are treacherous emotions for a writer to build on ; too frequently they turn to petulance and superficiality. Flaubert was saved from this by the qualities of his character. He had an immense capacity for work, a passionate love of truth, and most important of all, he worshipped the great writers before him ; as he said, ' he had the bump of veneration strongly developed.' Though he recognised, with a clearness that should be disconcerting to his own idolaters, that he was of another and lower order than his demigods, he saw that they had one quality which he too might aim to possess. They were objective ; they did not intrude their personalities into their work ; they were content to represent

136

and to record. Long before he began *Madame Bovary* his determination to emulate them in this was fixed ; when he was only twenty-three he declared that ' dans la première période de la vie d'artiste il est mieux de jeter du dehors tout ce qu'on a de vraiment intime, d'original, d'individuel.' It sounds rather forbiddingly professional for twenty-three, and in fact Flaubert had a fling on St. Antony before sitting down to *Madame Bovary*, his first real exercise in his self-imposed discipline. It was much more than an exercise, of course, for Flaubert had a passion of indignation that needed vent ; but without his resolve to be impersonal it would have wasted itself in vain.

In sacrificing his personality Flaubert thought he sacrificed much. He believed that he was ' born lyrical.' Born romantic would have been nearer the truth, for we have to qualify lyrical by his repeated and truthful confession that his talent was not ' primesautier.' His natural bent was towards romantic dream and romantic tirade, and his gift of lyrical expression very small. But the strength of a desire cannot be measured by the capacity of satisfying it, and there is no cause to doubt Flaubert's sincerity when he rebelled, as he rebelled continually, against the ' ugliness ' of his work on *Madame Bovary*. Ah, what he would do when he had a subject of his own! He was tired, tired to death of the bourgeois. It was time to drop them for ever. But the subject of his own never came. At first he imagined that *La Tentation* and *Salammbô* were completely congenial, but the illusion was brief ; and though he never went so far as to declare that these subjects were ugly, his complaints and his torments were the same. It was not surprising that in his last two books he should return to the detested bourgeois. In one sense at least all subjects were the same to him ; he suffered equally from them all.

Two demons stood always between Flaubert and his dreams — the demon of style and the demon of truthfulness. Of the two it was the demon of truthfulness that tormented him the more. It drove him to fantastic efforts of documentation ; his researches for *Salammbô* were prodigious and at the very commencement of *Bouvard et Pécuchet* he

137

confessed that he had read 1,500 volumes for it. Yet he seemed never to have asked himself jesting Pilate's question. What was this truth for which he laboured? Had he asked, he would have been forced to reply ; the truth of history, not of art. But he was never able to disentangle them. His letters sometimes make nightmare reading. He must find an actual piece of France for Bouvard and Pécuchet to farm in. It was not enough to invent the episode of their geological expedition to the coast ; young de Maupassant must provide him with a stretch of real cliff where the complicated event was possible: and he wrote again and again till he got it. A passion for truth of this kind is a purely morbid condition in a writer ; he must indeed be 'drunk with ink' to feel it. Such truth has no value in itself, and the search for it is bound to prejudice the truth which is proper to literature. The verisimilitude of art does not depend on documents—neither indeed does the verisimilitude of history—but upon the creative imagination and the sensibility from which the imagination is replenished. In both these Flaubert was deficient ; the range of his sensibility was not large, nor his creative imagination robust. He tried to eke them out with a reference library, with the result that in all his books, save *Madame Bovary* and *Un Cœur Simple*, his tenuous characters dissolve away into their own background.

With the demon of style, as he understood style, his struggle was more successful. But in order to appraise his victory we must remember how he understood it. So many passages in his letters reveal his conception that the choice is embarrassing ; one may suffice :

> Ce qui distingue les grands génies c'est la généralisation et la création: ils résument en un type des personnalités éparses et apportent à la conscience du genre humain des personnages nouveaux; est-ce qu'on ne croit pas à l'existence de Don Quichotte comme à celle de César? Shakespeare est quelque chose de formidable sous ce rapport: ce n'était pas un homme, mais un continent; il y avait de grands hommes en lui, des foules entières, des paysages; ils n'ont pas besoin de faire du style, ceux-là, ils sont forts en dépit de toutes les

138

fautes et à cause d'elles; mais nous, les petits, nous ne valons que par l'exécution achevée. Hugo en ce siècle enfoncera tout le monde quoiqu'il soit plein de mauvaises choses, mais quel souffle! Je hasarde ici une proposition que je n'oserais dire nulle part: c'est que les très grands hommes écrivent souvent fort mal, et tant mieux pour eux.

A style of which the greatest writers have no need, to the want of which they owe their greatness, is a dubious light to follow. It was less dangerous for Flaubert, who saw his own limitations clearly, than for those who have blindly followed him. But probably Flaubert also paid a price for his obsession ; probably it distracted his attention from the content of his work and induced him to spend energies that might have gone to the expansion of his sensibility upon the painful polishing of a hollow surface ; the substance which could have made it solid his starved sensibility could not provide. One dare not dogmatise. Who knows for certain that a writer by taking thought can add a cubit to the stature of his soul? Possibly Flaubert, being the man he was, made a right choice ; possibly he persevered where he could make some progress and abandoned the road along which advance was barred. But the probability and the evidence point the other way. The book whose style he laboured least—a Flaubertian minimum is not as other men's—is the one by which he is chiefly remembered. The youthful *Madame Bovary* has a validity which he was to achieve only once again, in *Un Cœur Simple*. *Madame Bovary* alone answers to his own definition of a great work of literature ; it gathers scattered personalities into a type and brings new personalities to the consciousness of the human race. Emma Bovary and Monsieur Homais are figures of this kind ; they are (except perhaps Félicie) the only ones in Flaubert's work.

Flaubert began his career with what is, take it all in all, a masterpiece; he was to write no other. *L'Education Sentimentale* is not one. It may be life, but it is not living; it is a work of history rather than literature. Flaubert had no certain hold of his characters, and his handling of his theme at the crucial moment falls to the level of melodrama. The most famous passage in the book is the death of Dussardier:

Mais, sur les marches de Tortoni, un homme—Dussardier—
remarquable de loin à sa haute taille, restait sans plus bouger
qu'une cariatide.

Un des agents qui marchait en tête, la tricorne sur les yeux,
le menaça de son épée.

L'autre alors, s'avançant d'un pas, se mit à crier,—

—"Vive la République!"

Il tomba sur le dos, les bras en croix.

Un hurlement d'horreur s'éleva de la foule. L'agent fit un
cercle autour de lui avec son regard; et Frédéric, béant, reconnut
Sénécal.

Il voyagea.

Il connut la mélancolie des paquebots, les froids réveils sous
la tente, l'étourdissement des paysages et des ruines, l'amertume
des sympathies interrompues.

Il revint.

'Et Frédéric, béant, reconnut Sénécal,' has been for years the
object of an esoteric admiration as a masterpiece of style. In
a different book it might, indeed, have been overwhelming; in
the gray monotone of *L'Education Sentimentale* it is a splash of
discordant red. The dramatic artifice tears through the even
texture of the narrative: it belongs to another world of seeing and
feeling, and the measure of its discordance is our astonishment
at Sénécal's surprising change. If a respectable solicitor were
to slip behind a screen and reappear in a cardboard nose and
a pair of huge moustaches, it could not be more disturbing than
this *coup de théâtre* in the most laboriously realistic story ever
written.

Only if style could be separated from content, the surface
from the perceptions which make it solid, could Flaubert's
style be praised without reserve. The distinction, as he knew,
cannot be be made. And Flaubert's style is sometimes perfect,
sometimes bad, more often indifferent than either. It is at its
highest level in *Un Cœur Simple.* There it follows the contour
of his thought with a perfect economy.

Elle se levait dès l'aube, pour ne pas manquer la messe, et
travaillait jusqu'au soir sans interruption; puis, le dîner étant

fini, la vaisselle en ordre et la porte bien close, elle enfouissait la bûche sous les cendres et s'endormait devant l'âtre, son rosaire à la main. Personne, dans les marchandages, ne montrait plus d'entêtement. Quant à la propreté, le poli des ses casseroles faisait le désespoir des autres servantes. Econome, elle mangeait avec lenteur, et recueillait du doigt sur la table les miettes de son pain—un pain de douze livres, cuit expès pour elle, et qui durait vingt jours.

En toute saison elle portait un mouchoir d'indienne fixé dans le dos par une épingle, un bonnet lui cachant ses cheveux, des bas gris, un jupon rouge, et par-dessus sa camisole un tablier à bavette, commes les infirmières d' hôpital.

Son visage était maigre et sa voix aiguë. A vingt-cinq ans, on lui endonnait quarante. Dès la cinquantaine, elle ne marqua plus aucun âge;—et, toujours silencieuse, la taille droite, et les gestes mesurés, semblait une femme de bois, fonctionnant d'une manière automatique.

Elle avait eu, comme une autre, son historie d'amour.

How exquisite—to descend to particulars—is the order of the words in 'recueillait du doigt sur la table les miettes de son pain'; it gives the gesture its significance and yields to the rhythm of the paragraph. And the final sentence, which opens the second chapter, is characteristic of Flaubert at his best. He was a master of the short sentences even more than the period. The effects he wrung from it are sometimes astonishing. Here the contrast between the movement which ends 'une femme de bois fonctionnant d'une manière automatique' and the short sentence which follows is carefully modulated by the insertion of 'comme une autre' where we should not expect it. It not only gives us the very substance of Félicie, but saturates the narrative with a sense of time.

The power of awakening in us a sense of the process of time was Flaubert's most individual achievement as a writer. We might almost say that wherever we are struck with the apparently inexplicable beauty of a page or a passage in his work we shall find the secret of the enchantment in this presentation of time. *Un Cœur Simple* unrolls a life from beginning to end in ninety short pages, and we feel every year of it drop slowly into the past. In the passage we have quoted from *L'Education Sentmentale* the significance of 'Il voyagea' is unmistakable, and there again Flaubert uses the division of a chapter to achieve his effect. His devices are innumerable. In the last sentence of *Hérodias* it is the choice and placing of an adverb. 'Comme elle (the head of Jokanaan) était très lourde, ils la portaient alternativement.' There it is too deliberate. But the first twenty pages of *Madame Bovary* are a splendid example of Flaubert's resource. The story is swift and unhesitating up to the eighteenth page. Charles Bovary's schooldays and the events of his first marriage flow by in a steady stream; it is one life among many. Suddenly the tempo is changed in a paragraph. Emma Rouault has appeared.

Elle le reconduisait toujours jusqu'à la première marche du perron. Lorsqu' on n'avait pas encore amené son cheval elle restait là. On s'était dit adieu, on ne se parlait plus: le grand àir l'entourait, levant pêle-mêle les petits cheveux follets de sa nuque, ou secouant sur sa hanche les cordons de son tablier qui se tortillaient comme des banderolles. Une fois, par un temps de dégel, l'écorce des arbres suintait dans la neige sur es couvertures des bâtiments se fondait. Elle était sur le seuil: elle alla chercher son ombrelle, elle l'ouvrit. L'ombrelle, de soie gorge-de-pigeon, que traversait le soleil, éclairait de reflets mobiles la peau blanche de sa figure. Elle souriait là-dessous à la chaleur tiède; et on entendait les gouttes d'eau. une à une, tomber sur la moire tendue.

It is like a sudden oasis of calm in which everything can be seen, everything heard. The languorous beauty of the last sentence echoes on like the sounds of the drops it registers. We feel that that day was the first in his life for Charles Bovary.

If one were to press home the analysis of those characteristic effects of Flaubert, they would be found to depend generally on two elements, an unusual use of the verb tenses which an English reader can more easily feel than describe, and the manipulation of the rhythm. A period like this from *Madame Bovary* has the complicated rhythm of a fine piece of blank verse. Flaubert learnt something of this from Chateaubriand, and another part from Voltaire and Montesquieu, from whom he quoted with delight: 'Les vices d'Alexandre étaient extrêmes comme ses vertus; il était terrible dans sa colère; elle le rendait cruel.' A thousand sentences after that pattern can be found in his work. The quality that fascinated him in it was not so much the rhythm as the close texture on which the larger effects of rhythm depend. Each one of those pronouns helps to bind the parts of the sentence into one inseparable whole. Flaubert, as always, turned his admirations to account. He worked upon the hints they gave him indefatigably, and he fashioned for himself an instrument upon which no tones were impossible.

Because of this Flaubert is indeed a great master; but not of the greatest. In the years he spent on perfecting the instrument he forgot, if he ever knew, what tunes are most worth playing; and too often in his work we hear him sounding idly for their own intrinsic beauty notes which have no part in any larger plan. He was never passionately possessed by a comprehens-ive theme, and he never clearly saw that the rendering of such a theme was the final purpose of all the explorations of language on which he lavished himself. His sacrifice was as pathetic as it was noble. When we read such a passage as this in his letters—and there are many of them—we feel as sad as he.

Néanmoins, il y a une chose triste, c'est de voir combien de grands hommes arrivent aisément à l'effet en dehors de l'art même: quoi de plus mal bâti que bien des choses de Rabelais, Cervantes, Molière, et Hugo? Mais quels coups de poing subits? Quelle puissance dans un seul mot! Nous il faut entasser l'un sur l'autre un tas de petits cailloux pour faire nos pyramides qui ne vont pas à la centième partie des leurs lesquelles sont d'un seul bloc.

What is this 'Art' which the masters triumph by ignoring If they have no 'Art' what is the value of 'Art' at all? And why call it 'Art'? Flaubert never answered the question: the greatest writers remained prodigies for him; there was no room for them in his philosophy.

But for Flaubert, though they existed on heights unapproach-able, they did exist, and he never forgot them. What are we to say of a generation that has seen in Flaubert's 'Art' the highest achievement of literature, and in Flaubert himself the perfect type of the great writer? Were it not the fact, the collective hallucination would appear like a chapter in a fairy tale. We can see the cause of the aberration. Flaubert's 'Art' is an art which minor writers can understand; in pretending to surrender themselves to it—for the patient labour of a real surrender is much too painful—they have the satisfaction of manipulating a mystery. But the mystification has lasted too long. The invention of 'Art' has done no good to art, and it has interposed a veil between Flaubert's work and the general judgment. To be critical of Flaubert is to prejudice a vested interest, so large an edifice has been built up upon the insecure foundation.

Flaubert came as near to the highest literary genius a man can come by the taking of pains. Just as his example will be a perpetual encouragement to all honest craftsmen of literature, it will be a will o' the wisp to those who presume to measure the giants by it. Flaubert's work can never cease to smell of the lamp, but by the writing of one fine book and one perfect story, and his devoted researches into the capacity of language, he is one of the greatest heroes in the second rank of letters. More than this, his correspondence shows him to us as one of the most lovable of all writers, for though we smile at him tearing his hair in the silence of his study, our smile is the smile of sympathy and admiration. But those who claim more for him than this would lose all, if it were possible, for they can exalt him only by deposing greater men than he. Flaubert stands in no need of such extravagant admiration, and we know him well enough to be certain that he would have resented bitterly a worship paid to himself at the cost of divinities he adored.

[OCTOBER, 1921]

AMIEL

'If we look,' says Benedetto Croce at the end of the most suggestive chapter of his book on the writing of history, ' merely at the enormous amount of psychological observations and moral doubts accumulated in the course of the nineteenth century by poetry, fiction, and the drama, those voices of our society, and consider that in great part it remains without critical treatment, some idea can be formed of the immense amount of work that it falls to philosophy to accomplish.' Whether the traditionalist would call the work that Croce indicates philosophy or history or criticism is of no particular account; what is important is that it remains to be done. Until it is done the twentieth century will always be liable to be puffed up with a conceit of its superiority to a century which it has not yet troubled to understand.

It is true there are signs in England of a fashionable reversion to the Victorian era ; it is being exhibited as a curiosity with patient skill. But the Victorianism which may have a present vogue is a very local and limited variety of the consciousness of the nineteenth century ; it does not contain England's contribution to that consciousness. The work of isolating and estimating that contribution is eminently a work of seriousness, and seriousness—the ' spoudaiotês' for which Matthew Arnold so strongly pleaded—is not the quality most frequently demanded or supplied today. The very word jars on a modern ear. To be serious is to be solemn, to be solemn portentous. Yet it is silly to approach the England of the Oxford Movement, of Carlyle and Faraday, of Clerk-Maxwell, and Huxley, and Arnold, of Thomas Hardy in a superficial mood. The depths of these men were troubled. If we can see their agonies only as grimaces, we had better leave them alone.

But the time will come, and the work will be done. Not until the twentieth century is fully aware of the nineteeᶜth and has exerted itself to put a valuation upon its achievement, will it have the strength for an achievement of its own. When the work is being done and nineteenth century England is being seen in its true relation to the European consciousness of the period, Henri-Frédéric Amiel will be one of the landmarks in the survey. He may even be a basis for the triangulation, as a piece of flat, unbroken, compact ground serves best for the certain measurement of the great peaks on the horizon.

The nineteenth century was complex and titanic, a *saeculum mirabile* if ever there was one, a century difficult to comprehend by reason of the magnitude of the peaks that rose from it. In it Amiel appears like one of those little convex mirrors which reflect, in bright and distinct minuscule, the splendid landscape on to which the window opens. All the potentialities are there, none of the realizations. He is a microcosm of the moral effort and moral perturbation of a century in which moral effort and perturbation reached a climax. Now that we are in the trough of the wave, weary and impatient beforehand of the attempt to penetrate into the significance of a Tolstoy, a Nietzsche, or a Dostoevsky, it is well that we should have a miniature in Amiel to remind us that this was a pigmy in the days when there were giants.

From the days of Rousseau until the end of the nineteenth century the European mind was concentrated upon a moral problem. It is sometimes said that the nineteenth century was the century of science ; but it was the moral, the religious, in a word the humane interest of science which riveted men's minds. They waited on tiptoe to see what light science would cast on the problem of man's place in the universe. It was a century which accepted the fact that the universe could no longer be regarded as anthropocentric. It opened with Rousseau's intoxicated chant of freedom, proclaiming that 'man was born good'. The paraphernalia of divinely sanctioned institutions could be swept away without fear, for the kingdom of Heaven was within men. Within a few years his uncomprehending disciples were teaching the world that the kingdom of Hell was there also.

The problem of the nineteenth century was the problem of morality without institutions. The institution of the state was reduced to a matter of majorities and progressively worse educated majorities, the institution of the church to a department of the state or an antiquarian relic. Religion and morality

146

might possibly be psychological needs, but they might prove to be psychological illusions or, at least, no more than psychological habits evolved for the better protection of the triumphant herd; certainly the structure of the universe and the processes of animal life provided no endorsement for them. The earth and all that is therein was a trivial incident in the incomprehensible cosmic adventure.   How were men to live? Where was a sanctioned principle of conduct to be found? In pursuit of the answer arose that amazing company of 'God-seekers', to use the simple and impressive Russian name: Tolstoy, Dostoevsky, Nietzsche, Hardy or their fellows, like Baudelaire and Stendhal, who affected the Stoic part and turned an impassive face on the chaotic and incomprehensible world. Whatever their differences, these great figures of the nineteenth century were occupied with a single problem: to discover a morality.

To this company Amiel belonged.   Probably he was the smallest and least vigorous among them, but to them he indisputably belonged.   With his intellect 'he accepted ¦the universe of science, with his heart he admitted the necessity of religion and morality.   He spent his life trying to find a place for the one in the other.   In his intense and unremitting effort to reconcile them he reached strange ecstasies and strange despairs.   He sounded in his soul the whole octave of the nineteenth century conciousness and left a record of his experiences in`a book which has become, as it deserved to become, a minor classic of the century he lived in.

Amiel lived his life as a professor of aesthetics and philosophy in the Academy of Geneva. He wrote some poetry and translated more; he also wrote a little criticism. But the finest passages of his *Il Penseroso* are so reticent that they need the *Journal* to give them substance, and the best of his deliberate criticism is below the level of the incidental estimates in the *Journal*.   All Amiel is there.   Only there did his rare and delicate gift of expression find the protective atmosphere in which it could expand; it was not strong enough to endure any but the tempered and incense-laden air of posthumous publication.   The true creator does not fear to give hostages to fortune, and to deliver to the mercies of the world books in which is only half his thought and that imperfectly expressed; he risks misunderstanding in the confidence that what is to come will correct the insufficiency of what is past. 'Continuez vos ouvrages,' said Galiani to Madame d'Epinay, 'c'est une preuve d'attachment à la vie que de composer des livres.' But Amiel was not attached to life; to him the thought of incompleteness and misinterpretation was a perpetual terror; and he chose, in the little work he did publish, rather to conceal than to reveal his thought, and preferred in poetry minutiae of form to adequacy of content.

This horror of exposure which stultified the literary production of his lifetime was only a particular manifestation of the fear of life which marked him from the beginning for its own. In his inward experience it emerged as a terror of moral responsibility. Like all the elements of his composition, in the process of his painfully scrupulous investigation of himself, it assumed the most unlikely disguises. And perhaps the most striking quality of Amiel's introspection—a perfect type of intellectual introspection—is the self-deception it contained. Sometimes, indeed, he had a blindingly clear sight of his own nature, but quite as often the illusion was complete. Time after time he diagnosed his disease as *la maladie de l'idéal*. He was so enamoured of perfection, he believed, that he could not to accept the imperfect, so desirous of the whole that he could not be satisfied with the part, whether of knowledge or even of life itself. He could not love for fear his love might be less than the perfect consummation he dreamed of; he could not give himself to work, because to know one thing perfectly meant to know all things. In other words, he refused to be anything less than God. That is, of course, an uncharitable description of a nature so fine as Amiel's; but in a nature so subtle it is peculiarly necessary to separate, even with a blunt and brutal instrument, the part of self-deception from the core of truth. That Amiel was in love with the ideal no one can doubt. Perfect truth, perfect love, perfect beauty, perfect harmony were dreams that truly haunted him. But it was not the contrast between the poverty of the real and the richness of the ideal that froze the veins of action in him, it was 'thinking too precisely on the event'; it was fear.

The *malade de l'idéal* is a *malade imaginaire*. The ideal, if it is present to a mind at all, as it was to Amiel's, is a spur, not an obstacle, to action. When it is put forward as the cause of inaction, we may be sure that the diagnosis is romantic and untrue. It recurs continually in the earlier portion of Amiel's *Journal*, but it disappears in the later years. Then Amiel recognized that his disease was fear. He was afraid of the menacing universe which his mind held before him: he was devoured by the misgiving that every act was a mere venturing of the hand into the spinning cogwheels of the huge, implacable machine—'l'engrenage terrible de la souffrance humaine et la responsabilité humaine'—just as in the microcosm of literature he felt that to express his thoughts was only to draw the clumsy misinterpretations of a hostile criticism upon his head. It was a consciousness of the sheer danger of living that drove him back upon himself; he peeped out of his tiny window on to the grim waste of life, unlit by any purpose, and he drew back in dismay.

Amiel could not take the plunge into life, not because it was imperfect, but because it was cruel. This was the fundamental verity in the man. What is of absorbing and permanent interest are the strange metamorphoses which this fear underwent in the crucible of his intellect. Melancholy and diffidence were familiar to the human spirit long before the Copernican revolution; probably *taedium vitae* is as old as humanity. The conviction that the universe is mechanical and therefore indifferent only opened a new chapter in the history of the 'ennui commun à toute personne bien née'. The distinction between the instinct and the intellect of Amiel is therefore logical rather than psychological. His intellectual apprehension of the indifference of the universe was the nurse, though not the parent, of his fear.

It was natural that the effort to overcome this fear in the realm of the intellect should hold the chief place in Amiel's record of his inward struggles. The process of the intellect is clear; a man's deeper evolution is not. Besides, he had

149

somehow to *prove* that the universe was not indifferent. That was impossible as it has always been. An inward *change* is necessary, as Dostoevsky knew when he created Alyosha. But that inward change, in spite of all his passing self-deceptions, was impossible for Amiel to achieve, and it may even be that in this one respect his analysis was keener than that of the great Russian. Amiel tried to accept the process of becoming, of birth and death and pain in the universe, as a mighty and indivisible whole. It was one; therefore, surely, it was a harmony. Man could fall down and worship it, he could acknowledge in his soul that, like a great work of art, it could not be otherwise. To take away the suffering and the evil would be to separate the warp from the woof of the sublime pattern. Man could bow himself, not ignobly, not without joy, to this vision of necessity. Who can tell whether it was not this doubtful beatitude which entered Alyosha's soul when he fell upon the earth and wept at the vision of harmony? We do not know what lay in store for Dostoevsky's latest hero.

But Amiel, who knew this condition of frozen ecstasy, also knew that it was not real acceptance.

Il n'y a pas de paix que dans la réconciliation avec la destinée quand la destinée paraît religieusement bonne, c'est-a-dire quand l'homme se sent directement en présence de Dieu. Alors seulement la volonté acquiesce. Elle n'acquiesce même tout à fait que lorsqu'elle adore. L'âme ne se soumet aux duretés du sort qu'en découvrant une compensation magnifique, la tendresse du Tout-Puissant.—(*August* 16, 1875.)

Perhaps he never formulated quite clearly to himself the difference between a true religious acceptance and the ecstasy of self-immolation on the altar of the cosmic process; they are extremely subtle states of mind. The basis of the former is moral, the basis of the other aesthetic. It may be that language is impotent to distinguish these impulses in their supreme manifestations; but they are not the same. Amiel may not have defined the difference, but he knew it, as doubtless many saints within and seers without the Christian Church have known it.

One thing is necessary, Amiel repeats again and again,

L'abandon à Dieu. But where and what could God be for him? Try as he may—and the agony of his effort is apparent to the least sympathetic reader of his *Journal*—to give his Deity substance, he finds him always dissolving away into the same indifferent and undifferentiated cosmic process. In his earlier days he managed to persuade himself that he could enter by force of imagination into all beings and forms of life, and that this illusory expansion of the self was communion with God. When the illusion began to fail he comforted himself, like the men of Athens, by erecting an altar to the Unknown God. 'Sois dans l'ordre toi-même et laisse à Dieu le soin de débrouiller l'écheveau du monde et des destinées. Qu'importe le néant ou l'immortalité? Ce qui doit être, sera ; ce qui sera, sera bien.'— (*April* 24, 1869). There he is on the road to a pure agnosticism Three years later his disintoxication is complete.

La sagesse consiste à juger le bon sens et la folie, et à se prêter à l'illusion universelle sans en être dupe. Entrer dans le jeu de Maïa, faire de bonne grâce sa partie dans la tragi-comédie fantasque qu'on appelle l'Univers, c'est le plus convenable pour un homme de goût qui sait folâtrer avec les folâtres, et être sérieux avec les sérieux.

To play a game of which you can never know the rules, to act a part of which you can never know the lines, is a difficult morality. It is true Amiel goes on to explain that this is the end of a pure intellectualism, and that the heart of man can never accept it ; but he has nothing more to offer, and the passage closes on a note of complete despair.

L'esprit en tant que pensée arrive à l'intuition que toute réalité n'est que le rêve d'un nêve. Ce qui nous fait sortir du palais des songes, c'est la douleur, la douleur personnelle; c'est aussi le sentiment de l'obligation, ou ce qui réunit les deux, la douleur du péché; c'est encore l'amour; en un mot c'est l'ordre moral. Ce qui nous arrache aux enchantements de Maïa, c'est la conscience. La conscience dissipe les vapeurs du kief, les hallucinations de l'opium et la placidité de indifférence contemplative. Elle nous pousse dans l'engrenage terrible de la souffrance humaine et de la responsabilité

151

humaine. C'est le réveille-matin, c'est le cri du coq qui met en fuite les fantômes, c'est l'archange armé du glaive qui chasse l'homme du paradis artificiel. L'intellectualisme ressemblait à une ivresse qui se déguste; le moralisme est à jeun, c'est une famine et une soif qui refusent de dormir. Hélas! Hélas!

The moral fact, as Amiel elsewhere says, is also a fact. The consciousness of sin and the longing for duty are indeed facts. But they are very variable facts which could offer hardly more resistance to his analysis than the fact of a divinely ordained universe. Was the notion of duty to which he clung so desperately more substantial than the straw clutched at by a drowning man? What was he in fact to do? To play his part in the game of Maïa? Whatever he did he would be doing that, no less than the murderer and the liar. To do good to his neighbour? But what was good? Was it good, for instance, to tell his students at Geneva the truth about the Universe as he perceived it? His conscience gave him no answer to that. To do his part in diminishing the suffering of the world? To that and nothing more the duty of the sceptic slowly dwindles down. It is, indeed, not a little ; but, alas, it also may be dissolved away. Amiel did not choose the method of Dostoevsky's terrifying heroes who deliberately violated this last dictate of conscience to see what might happen, and discover whether the whisper of conscience was only the last illusion of all. Amiel was not the man to put his radical scepticism into action ; but scepticism itself was potent enough to dissolve away the duty of diminishing suffering. The part of suffering in the history of humanity was undeniable. If it was unnecessary, then the Universe was either a chaos or the work of a satanic power ; if it was necessary, it was lost labour to try to diminish it. So the tender-hearted Amiel, to whom in his youth war had seemed the last futility of a blind ignorance, was driven at the last into the hateful position of justifying war.

Les maudisseurs de la guerre ressemblent à ceux qui maudissent la foudre, les orages ou les volcans; ils ne savent ce qu'ils font. La civilisation tend à pourrir les hommes, comme

les grandes villes à vicier l'air. *Nos patimur longae pacis mala.*
—*(March* 20, 1880).

These are the very accents of the philosophers of militarism.
On the lips of Amiel, a year before his death, they sound
strangely indeed.

Thus the last duty of man turned to ashes. Amiel spent his
life in obeying a conscience he could not believe in, and fulfilling a duty that was meaningless to him.   Everything he
touched with those timid, delicate, reverential fingers crumbled
into dust.   The words remained, but the substance was lost.

L'être moral peut moraliser ses souffrances en utilisant le
fait naturel pour son éducation intérieure. Ce qu'il ne peut
changer, il l'appelle la volonté de Dieu, et vouloir ce que Dieu
veut lui rend la paix.—*(September* 1, 1874).

Again it is the unsubstantial God of a pure agnosticism.
Though he may have deceived himself for the moment he knew
there was no peace to be found in that submission.   Not a
year had passed before he declared that ' il n'y a pas de paix
que lorsque la destinée paraît religieusement bonne.' A destiny
which consists only in the things which we long to change but
cannot, and a God whose single attribute it is that he wills
those things, were not to be worshipped by Amiel ; he could
not so far abrogate his humanity.

Nothing but Stoic renunciation was left.   The word ' God '
emptily reverberates through the last pages of his *Journal.* By
some curious process of self-hallucination he declared to the last
that he believed in God ; but it was an assertion of the desire
to believe, not of belief.   He was utterly cast out from life ; his
rebellion had ended in nihilism, his promise in disaster.   He
thought back on what he had done.   Nothing.   *Omnis moriar,*
he wrote bitterly.   Let us hope that even then he knew that
the record of his seeking was imperishable.   Centuries hence,
when the struggles and disenchantments and despairs of the
nineteenth century may be no more real than the vague memory
of an uneasy dream. Amiel will be known and loved and pitied.

Perhaps the healthy and tough-minded pity him now, if they
read him.   But their pity is more likely to be the pity of

ignorance than understanding. Amiel's travail of mind cannot be thrust aside. It does not belong to the past, but to the present, and still more to the future. Men have discovered God in our own day. But it is doubtful whether the Invisible King is more substantial than Amiel's Maïa. God, to be God, must be seen and known and loved, or he is no more than eternal illusion, a romantic expansion of the self into a universe which is not self at all. On the one side there is religion, which can abate nothing of its claim to a truly personal God ; on the other side there is an indifferent universe. Amiel's *Journal* is a demonstration that will hold good for all time that the attempt to find a third way between these opposites is a barren self-deception.

The search for a morality remains, unsatisfied ; it even seems that it is neglected now as an unfashionable relic of a bygone era. The misty religion of the new evangelists will not provide one ; and the new psychology is so interpreted that it is become a mere corrosive of responsibility. Nevertheless, an intellectual age which neglects morality will itself be neglected, for the desire to be good is one of the deepest longings of the human heart. Without the discipline of morality life wastes itself in the desert sands. A culture which is blind to this necessity is inevitably futile ; it has lost the power of seeing life steadily and whole, it has lost the driving force of the creative passion which springs only from a deep acknowledgement that morality is essential to the conduct of human life. The strength of a truly great writer endures either because he builds upon the foundations of a morality which he accepts, or because he is animated by the intense desire to discover one. The greatest writers, as Tchehov said, have always had axes to grind.

Amiel's title to remembrance rests in the last resort upon his profound conviction of the necessity of morality. However dark the nihilism into which his analysis led him, he proclaimed the truth that ' le fait moral est aussi un fait.' The moral fact, it is true, was the desire for morality and not morality, as his declaration of belief in God was a declaration of his desire to believe, not of belief. But he saw also that ' la civilisation est surtout une chose morale.' That is to say, he never lost touch with the prime reality of life. It is this moral preoccupation which gives dignity and significance to his *Journal*. Matthew Arnold's failure to respond to this dominant quality in Amiel makes his essay irrelevant and superficial. That Amiel had a singularly acute critical intuition is true, though Arnold managed to miss the finest manifestation of it. Amiel's analysis of Chateaubriand's relation to Rousseau belongs to an order of criticism altogether higher than the remarks on Sainte-Beuve which Arnold quoted admiringly. By discovering no more in Amiel than a literary critic who had missed his vocation he came near to showing that he had missed his own.

In the last balance the positive morality of Amiel is purely Stoic, but he was a Stoic who had a clear intuition of the insufficiency of Stoicism. Morality, he knew, was a discipline , he knew also that it was not enough to suffer the discipline: he must surrender himself to it. This act of surrender was impossible to him, but he thought he saw how it might be achieved without disloyalty to the truth his intellect declared to him.

L'amour sublime, unique, invincible, mène tout droit au bord du grand abîme, car il parle immédiatement d'infini et d'éternité. Il est éminemment religieux. Il peut même devenir religion. Quand tout autour de l'homme chancelle, vacille, tremble et s'obscurcit dans les lointaines obscurités de l'inconnu, quand le monde n'est plus que fiction et féerie et l'univers que chimère, quand tout l'édifice des idées s'évanouit en fumée et que toutes les réalités se convertissent en doute, quel point fixe peut encore rester à l'homme? C'est le cœur fidèle d'une femme. C'est là qu'on peut appuyer sa tête, pour reprendre du courage à la vie, de la foi en Providence, et, s'il le faut, pour mourir en paix avec la bénédiction sur les lèvres. Qui sait si harmonie universelle des choses, n'est pas la meilleure démonstration d'un Dieu souverainement intelligent et paternel, comme elle est le plus court chemin pour aller à lui? L'amour est une foi et une foi appelle l'autre. Cette foi est une félicité, une lumière, et une force. On n'entre que par là dans la chaîne des vivants, des reveillés, des heureux, des rachetés, des vrais hommes qui savent ce que

155

vaut l'existence et qui travaillent à la gloire de Dieu et de la vérité. Jusque-là on ne fait que babiller, bredouiller, perdre ses jours, ses facultés et ses dons, sans but, sans joie réelle, comme un être infirme, invalide, inutile et qui ne compte pas.

'It can even become religion.' When we have sifted away all the contradictions in Amiel, this positive indication alone is left in our hands ; when we have followed him along all the paths by which he sought peace in vain, this road alone remains open through ' the high, uno'erleaped mountains of necessity.' It was Amiel's bitter fate that he could not enter upon it.

[August, 1921]

AMIEL'S LOVE STORY

It was common knowledge that previous to the 1920s only a fraction of the whole of Amiel's *Journal* had been published. The entire manuscript contains 16,900 pages. In 1929, under the title *Philine*, were published those portions of the unpublished *Journal* which deal with Amiel's relations to women, and chiefly to one particular woman, whom Amiel discreetly named Philine, or X, or Hg. Amiel met her, after some correspondence, in 1859, and for the ensuing twelve years their relations were extremely intimate, though not in the cant sense of the phrase. Philine became Amiel's lover on one sole occasion, in October 1860, the only occasion when Amiel had experience of physical love. But for many years he was on the brink, or what he supposed to be the brink, of marrying her. He drew back his timid foot, and died as he had lived, celibate. Philine's letters to Amiel are unmistakable evidence of a passionate devotion to him. She was a young widow who had endured a painful past ; moreover, according to the rigid classifications of the Genevan *bourgeoisie*, she was not quite Amiel's social equal. This was one of the excuses he seized upon to justify to himself his refusal to marry her, though naturally, since he was Amiel, it took the form of a refusal to expose her to the gossip of Genevan society and the hostility of his own family. In this he was no doubt sincere. Difference in social rank had, in such a situation, little real influence with him ; he was genuinely afraid of the inevitable complications. But the root of the matter lay deeper, in his radical fear of life, not in his fear of this particular manifestation of life.

Hence the absorbing interest of this volume of his *Journal*. It reveals Amiel's weakness, or Amiel's self, as it were at the centre; for love and marriage, as he well knew, are the forms under which life chiefly makes its demand upon the individual that he should be prepared to sacrifice his individuality. At this point a man must risk himself in that mysterious process of which Amiel had an almost superstitious dread: 'l'engrenage terrible de la souffrance humaine et de la responsabilité humaine.' About this fearful machinery Amiel fluttered like a fascinated bird. Isolated, sensitive, delicately understanding, he longed to be delicately understood; he was for ever seeking for love, and, as was inevitable with such a nature, he aroused not a little of it. But what he roused would not remain delicate, silken, and Platonic; he discovered, to his incessant dismay, that love is passionate and primeval, however, frail may be the vehicle in which it is embodied. 'Une femme comprise,' he wailed, 'se croit une femme aimée.' He managed, quite often, to convince himself that this was altogether unreasonable, and that the ideal woman would lend herself freely to his penchant for soul-investigation without being in the least disturbed by his inquiries. He reached the comfortable conclusion that a man, if he does not love more, 'loves better' than a woman. But 'loving better', if we look closer, simply meant, in Amiel's thinking, loving with detachment. He begged the question.

Amiel knew it. There was, indeed, very little about him-self that Amiel did not know. Those who are well acquainted with his *Journal* are familiar with the rhythmical regularity with which first he persuasively justifies himself for a certain attitude, and then, a little more persuasively, at a few days' interval— time enough to have forgotten his previous self-defence—tears his own justification to shreds. In the record of his relations with Philine the phenomenon is remarkable. Whenever he has complained of her lack of 'limpidity', her failure to meet his frankness with an equal frankness, or his consistency with an equal consistency, the moment inevitably follows when he accuses himself bitterly for his cowardice in refusing the life which she had to give, and longed to give. Though there are moments when one feels a robust impatience with him, it is impossible to blame him. The same fundamental terror of life which made him draw back frightened from the flame that he had kindled had driven him to seek consolation and com-panionship in women's love. He could not bear his own loneliness; neither could he bear the breaking-down of that loneliness in the only way that was possible for him. 'Ma nature est ainsi faite', he wrote at the beginning of his relation with Philine, 'elle s'ingénie à faire le désert autour d'elle, et ne peut souffrir le désert.'

158

So he poured himself into enchanted feminine ears, in the belief that he could thus escape his own isolation yet still remain isolated. He would, so to speak, face life on the narrowest possible front; and then he was astonished and pained to discover that the whole force of life was concentrated behind a single woman. What she required of him was precisely what life as a whole had been requiring of him; but whereas in the general conduct of his affairs he could find plausible excuses for himself, in the particular instance it was more difficult. He felt that he was not playing fair; he was not giving as good as he got; and, since his conscience, like his consciousness, was acute, he was miserable about it. His general failure he could explain away conveniently enough in metaphysical terms: it was his belief in Maïa that prevented him from action, and by refraining from action he did no harm. But now his weakness appeared to him without metaphysical disguise, in personal terms. He, the kind and sensitive Amiel, was inflicting suffering upon another human being—suffering for which he was wholly responible. He had indulged himself and brought Philine to a condition of soul of which love and marriage were the rightful consummation. Then he shrank away. His conscience never ceased to accuse him.

As ever with Amiel, he had perfectly clear glimpses of the true situation almost from the beginning. The entries in the Journal in October, 1860, are extraordinarily illuminating. On the 6th he had been, for the first and only time in his life, Philine's lover. Immediately afterwards he wrote:

> Mais comment dois-je appeler l'expérience de ce soir? Est-ce une déception, est-ce un enivrement? Ni l'un ni l'autre. J'ai eu pour la première fois une bonne fortune, et franchement, à côté de ce que l'imagination se figure ou se promet, c'est peu de chose. C'est quasi un seau d'eau fraîche. J'en suis bien aise. Cela m'a refroidi en m'éclairant. La volupté elle-même est aux trois quarts ou plus encore dans le désir, c'est-à-dire dans l'imagination. La poésie vaut infiniment mieux que la réalité. Mais l'intérêt vif de l'expérience est essentiellement intellectuel; je puis enfin raisonner sur la femme sciemment, sans cette demi-niaiserie de l'ignorance, ou cette idéalisation

159

fautive de la pensée, qui m'ont gêné jusqu'ici. Je vous le sexe entier avec le calme d'un mari, et je sais maintenant que, pour moi du moins, la femme physique n'est presque rien. La moralité de l'histoire, c'est que l'affection, la sympathie, l'attachment d'une femme est bien son tout, et que sa faveur dernière ne grossit pas notablement (et à peine sensiblement) son compte. Quant à la femme même, cela ne m'a autant apprisque je l'espérais. En dernière analyse, je suis stupéfait de l'insignifiance relative de ce plaisir dont on fait tant de bruit . . .

It is an astonishing piece of self-revelation. In spite of Amiel's disclaimer it is an almost perfect example of *deminiaiserie;* but still more wonderful is the underlying and uncriticised assumption that he now knew all that was to be known about physical love. The notion that, if it was indeed so insignificant a thing as he had found it, the general attitude of humanity towards it was inexplicable seems not to have entered his head. His naïve presumption brings to mind the youthful scorn of Hippolytus and the fearful vengeance exacted by the dread Queen.

But Amiel was psychologically incapable of physical love. That something deeper was at work to disturb his facile intellectual conclusions the note of four days later is witness:

Comme l'estomac et les poumons réclament impérieusement la nourriture de l'air, un autre de nos systèmes organiques réclame insolemment sa pâture et se moque de nos réticences comme de nos objections. L'instinct du sexe travaille en nous sans nous; la nature nous somme de satisfaire ses droits, ses vœux, ses ordres. Son but ici, c'est la cessation de la vie individuelle, et l'entrée dans la vie générique, l'identification avec un autre. Cette combustion de l'égoïsme, cet abandon de l'individualité, cet oubli total du moi, je ne l'ai éprouvé dans sa douceur que par l'admiration poétique et par l'emotion intellectuelle ou morale; mais jamais, je crois, jusqu'au fond de l'etre, jusqu' aux moelles. Ni l'extase, ni la pâmoison, ni l'ivresse, ni l'étourdissement ne m'ont encore arracheé à la conscience de moi-même, ne m'ont vaincu,

anéanti, absorbé; j'ignore la transhumanisation, et je ne
connais que l'impersonnalisation.

Here Amiel came close, perhaps as close as he ever came, to
acknowledging that the fault lay in himself. The reality of what
is *en nous sans nous* he could not truly admit. He could admit it
as a fact intellectually apprehended; he could even admit that
in the scheme of things it had a right to be and fulfilled a
function and a purpose; but to submit himself to it was impossible. The ecstasy of self-annihilation, he said, had not
visited him; he chose not to remember that the ecstasy visits
no one who is not prepared to receive it. One cannot stipulate
the terms upon which one will receive life. Sooner or later the
demand comes, in one or other of a thousand forms, that we
must lose our life to save it.

Amiel could not suffer it to be so. In his infinite sophistication
he told himself that he could obey nothing but an irresistible
impulse; but to a completely conscious man, as Amiel was, no
impulse is irresistible, not even the impulse to maintain complete self-consciousness. There is a very deep self-deception
in his final conclusion after the years-long debate whether he
should or should not marry Philine. He was writing in 1878,
nearly twenty years after their first meeting.

> J'en conclus qu'un mariage n'est à conseiller que s'il est
> irrésistible. Il ne faut prendre pour époux que l'être néces-
> aire. Dans ce cas, quelle que soit l'issue, on peut se dire c'était
> écrit, c'était mon destin! Dieu l'a voulu, résignons nous.
> Comme un œuvre d'art ne vaut rien sans inspiration, une
> décision irréparable ne vaut rien sans un entraînement sur-
> naturel. Il nous faut l'illusion que Dieu y a mis la main.

It is the voice of an inheritor of centuries of Calvinism.
Election is necessary, even in marriage, and Amiel is not of the
elect. Indeed, we are inclined to believe that the only complete
explanation of Amiel is to be found in his theological inheritance. For we have to explain not only his shrinking from action,
but his immense and unique perseverance in composing his
Journal. To act, to venture himself in the 'engrenage terrible',
he needed the grace of God: more of the grace than another

161

because he was aware of more of the dangers. The grace was never vouchsafed to him. But to do nothing, in the moral sense, was impossible. Somehow, somewhere, he had to surrender himself to destiny, and to perform a heroic task. His *Journal* was the opportunity. Only a man of extreme conscience and unconquerable will could have accomplished it. We cannot measure Amiel by common standards, for what we must deny him as a man we must give him again as a writer; and even that separation is finally untenable. It needed nothing less than a hero to make so ruthless a record of his own timidities.

[1929]

BAUDELAIRE

Perhaps no word has been more prolific of literary mis-understandings in the last half-century than the word decadence. Critics with the best will in the world, which is the will for exact description, have called writers decadent. The unfortunate writer has been damned by a definition that no one had troubled to understand. In the general mind to be decadent is to be impure, immoral, or, in the now more frequent and really more damaging phrase, to be 'unhealthy.' Many poets were branded as decadents in the nineteenth century. All of them suffered by the name ; some deserved to suffer, and some did not. Charles Baudelaire, who was the first and greatest of the line, suffered most and deserved it least. He suffers still, because every critic who is convinced of his high excellence as a poet and is anxious to elucidate it is driven to dwell on the element of decadence in the man and his work. The word is as necessary to the understanding of Baudelaire as a particular instrument to a surgeon for a particular operation.

Decadence is essentially a word of the historian who applies it to those periods in the history of a society when its old institutions are breaking down and being obscurely replaced by new ; to ages when the transition is being made from one social ideal, one social fabric, to another. The word can be applied to literature, or art in general, in one of two ways. It can be used historically to distinguish the literature that is created during an age of decadence, or it can be used meta-phorically to describe the literature of a period of transition between two literary ideals. These meanings are utterly different yet the word is generally made to carry them both at the same time, as though a literary decadence were the necessary con-comitant of a social decadence. Worse still, to the vagueness created by the fusion of these two meanings has been added a misty recollection of orgies under the Roman Empire. A tincture of fiddling Nero, Caligula, and Elagabalus gives a piquant flavour to the bolus of haziness. Writers and artists are called 'decadent' by people who mean that they are merely bad artists, or artists who deal with 'unhealthy' subjects. Thus a valuable word is ruined because it is used to save people the trouble of thinking.

It may be true, though it remains to be proved, that the literatures of all periods of decadence have certain elements in common; it is certainly untrue that the literature of such a period is necessarily inferior as literature (indeed Nietzsche argued, very plausibly, that the veritable heights of literature can be attained only in an age of decadence). In the case of Baudelaire it is extremely necessary that we should be clear in what sense the epithet decadent is used when it is applied to him. Baudelaire is the poet of an historical decadence; he is not in any useful sense of the word a decadent poet. On the contrary, he was one of the greatest and most assured poets that France has produced. As a poet, he was strong, masculine, deliberate, classical; not a puny successor of great men, but the heroic founder of a line; and the peculiar quality of his work derives from the interaction of these two very different factors, the decadence of the age in which he lived and his own poetic strength and determination. Not that his choice of subject may not sometimes be called perverse; but the perversity of his work is the least important, the least relevant, and, to the unbiased reader, the least noticeable of its qualities. It is easy for any poetaster to be perverse; it is extremely difficult for a poet to be perverse in Baudelaire's way. For Baudelaire was not a furtive dabbler in unclean things; he was the deliberate and determined poet of an attitude to life to which we cannot refuse the epithet heroic. The driving impulse of his work was not a predilection, but a conviction.

Baudelaire was convinced that the age in which he lived was a decadence, and we who know it not only by his own passionate protest against it, but by Balzac's romantic anatomy of its corruption, must acquiesce in his conviction. The old aristocratic order had fallen; there was no new democratic order to supply its place: in the interval arose, like a growth of weeds on the site of a demolished building, as the sole principle of spiritual and social order, that reverence for wealth for its own sake which distinguished nineteenth-century France. Guizot's *Enrichissez-vous* marked a social nadir. It was the age of rampant industrialism and violent and abortive revolution ; of the hideous and uncontrolled eruption of the great cities ; of all the squalor of a victorious and hypocritical materialism. Against this tyranny Baudelaire conceived it his duty to protest, not merely by the poetic utterance of cries of revolt but by the actual conduct of his life. The French romantic movement as a whole was animated to some extent by a spirit of protest against the sordidness of the age ; but Baudelaire belonged to a curious section of the movement which had very little in common with romanticism as we generally conceive it now. His affinities were with the disciplined and contemptuous romanticism of Stendhal and Mérimée. This romanticism was rather a kind of sublimated realism, based upon an almost morbid *horreur d'être dupe*—romantic in its aspiration away from the *bourgeois* society which it loathed, realistic in its determination to accept the facts as they were. It was romantic also in its conception and elaboration of the attitude which it considered inevitable for the chosen spirits who would not bow the knee to Baal.

It is important to grasp these two intimately woven strands of realism and romanticism in Baudelaire and his two predecessors. This strange but natural combination plays a great part not in the literature of France only, but in that of Europe as a whole during the last century. A single thread runs through the work of Stendhal, Mérimée, Baudelaire, Nietzsche, and Dostoevsky ; in spite of their outward dissimilarity, and the great differences between their powers, these men are united by a common philosophical element which takes bodily shape in their conceptions of the hero. They are all intellectual romantics, in rebellion against life, and they imagine for themselves a hero in whom their defiance should be manifested. The three Frenchmen had in common, and put into actual practice, the ideal of 'le Dandy.' ' Le Dandy' is an imperturbable being above the law, inscrutable, contemptuous of the world, silent under the torments which it inflicts upon his sensitive soul, continually experimenting at his own risk with morality,

165

exercising a drastic discipline upon himself, and adopting, as a symbol of his inward discipline, that elegance of outward appearance which we generally associate with the word 'dandy.' On the one side the conception of the Dandy touches the romantic literary ideal of the poet in his *tour d'ivoire*, on the other it reaches out in anticipation towards the superman of Nietzsche and the still subtler and more impressive antinomian hero of Dostoevsky's novels. In both these forms it influenced Baudelaire's life as a man and activity as a poet.

From this angle it is perhaps easier to understand and analyse the almost massive impression of unity we receive from so small a work as Baudelaire's. A volume of poetry, a volume of prose (of which fully one third is a paraphrase of De Quincey's *Opium Eater*), two volumes of scattered criticism, chiefly of painting, three volumes of translations from Poe—these are the complete works of Baudelaire. What is really original in them could easily be contained in three pocket volumes. Yet the abiding impression made by them is one of solidity. This is in the main because the inspiration is single and the foundations firm and invariable. As an artist Baudelaire works from a single centre ; his attitude to life and his attitude to art lend each other aid and confirmation. Even his vices as a poet have the merit of being deliberate, and of contributing to the total effect at which he aimed. They are the vices proper, one might almost say essential, to his achievement. When Baudelaire is rhetorical, his rhetoric is never entirely empty ; it has a dramatic propriety and significance in the mouth of the *âme damnée*, the rebellious angel hurling defiance at the powers of heaven. When he indulges his desire to astonish, he is asserting his immunity from conventional fears. Both these vices, it is true, betray in Baudelaire's mind some confusion between the laws of heroism in life and in art. They are not the less vices because they are intelligible. Nevertheless, it does make a difference that they are not irrelevant. A writer's weaknesses are to some extent condoned when they are seen to be the condition of his strength.

It is Baudelaire's chief distinction that, in spite of these one or two failures, he made a successful and undeviating effort to

166

translate his ethical attitude towards life into a purely poetical gesture. He might so easily have been a poet of the confessional, pouring out his wounded soul in lyrical *cris de cœur* ; but his ' Dandyism' helped him to a more truly poetic conception of his task. The fox might be tearing at his vitals, but there must be, if not a smile, an inscrutable expression of Spartan impassivity on his face. The self-sacrifice demanded of him by his moral creed coincided with the self-sacrifice demanded of him as a poet. That the original impulse was partly moral discounted nothing of his achievement, for he was in the fortunate position of one whose effort in life seconded his endeavours in art ; and if he more often formulated his purpose in ethical terms, it was more because he was enough of a romantic to prefer the hero of life to the hero of art than because he was unable to evisage it as a poetic problem alone.

> Bien d'autres que moi' (he writes in *L'Art Romantique*), ont pris soin d'appesantir sur les conséquences fatales d'un génie essentiellement personnel; et il serait bien possible aussi, après tout, que les plus belles expressions du génie, ailleurs que dans le ciel pur . . . ne pussent être obtenues qu'au prix d'un inévitable sacrifice.

Still, in spite of this unequivocal declaration of faith, it would be a mistake to suppose that Baudelaire admitted any clear distinction between his 'Dandyism' and his poetry. Though he saluted the artistic heroism of Flaubert when *Madame Bovary* appeared, he did not particularly admire it; much less would he have admired the attitude of Cézanne towards his painting or Mr. Hardy towards his poetry. He would have found them lacking in gesture.

Here again Baudelaire was fortunate. The desire for a gesture is not so dangerous in French poetry as it is in English. Traditional French prosody, and above all the prosody of the Alexandrine, is a perpetual invitation to rhetoric, just as the blank verse prosody of Milton sooner or later compels the English poet who adopts it to become more tremendous than he wants to be; but whereas the Miltonic prosody is an aberration from the true English tradition, the prosody of the French Alexandrine is the tradition itself. Wordsworth said of the English sonnet that in Milton's hands 'the thing became a trumpet'; the French poet's difficulty with the Alexandrine has always been to prevent the thing from becoming a trumpet. Luckily Baudelaire wanted a trumpet—one might almost say he wanted a cavalry bugle. The Alexandrine was made for a man possessed by the burning desire to send his challenges ringing up to heaven. Had it not been that his Satanic defiance was moderated by a Satanic sense of *comme il faut*, Baudelaire might have gone the way of Victor Hugo and largely wasted his lesser genius in a mere fury of blowing.

Baudelaire's power of concentration saved him from rhetorical disaster. In the matter of prosody he willingly accepted the severest limitations. He made no technical innovations himself, and he rejected some of those which Victor Hugo had made before him. He saw that for him it was much more important to blow a few blasts that were piercing than many that were merely loud; and he early set himself to the task of finding an equivalent in pure poetry to his destestation of the world and his defiance of the powers that ordained it. He sought the equivalent by making his poetry as metallic in sound and suggestion as he could; he would change the psychological oppression of life into a plastic oppression. To make concrete the immaterial is, of course, a familiar process of the poet's activity, and the effort lies at the source of all metaphor. But Baudelaire went far beyond this phase; he made it his deliberate aim to expel all elasticity from his verse, all bright and ethereal perspectives from his vision. He built himself a house of metal and went from room to room, shutting, bolting, and barring all the magic casements. The surface of his vision and the texture of his verse should alike be hard and impenetrable; thus he would render in poetry his sense of the stifling oppressiveness of life. He would meet steel with steel.

His methods of achieving his end were manifold. The most obvious and the most successful is his endeavour to reduce all living things to a condition of immobile solidity. There is a curious example of this in the *Réve Parisien*, where the poet dreams of a symbolic landscape:

Je savourais dans mon tableau
L'enivrante monotonie
Du métal, du marbre et de l'eau.

Even at the outset only one-third of his universe—the water—has any chance of moving; within a half a dozen lines he has (literally) petrified even that third.

Et des cataractes pesantes
Comme des rideaux de cristal
Se suspendaient obéissantes
A des murailles de métal.

Here Baudelaire has indulged his obsession at the cost of an artistic blemish; his stately pleasure-house needed the movement of water to make the contrast of his motionless marble more intense and oppressive. In a poet so scrupulous of his plastic effects the blunder and the underlying motive are the more striking. But in Baudelaire the strangest things are turned to stone and brass; he speaks of a woman's 'granite skin' in one poem, and in the next, 'j'aiguisais lentement sur mon cœur le poignard'. The beautiful Dorothea, his mulatto Venus, is 'belle et froide comme le bronze.' His dreamland of happiness is 'un vrai pays de Cocagne, où tout est riche, propre et luisant, comme une belle conscience, une magnifique batterie de cuisine, comme une splendide orfévrerie, comme une bijouterie bariolée'. It is not necessary to accumulate examples; one has but to open *Les Fleurs du Mal* at random to find them. Baudelaire makes solid everything he can. His very ideal of Beauty is an absolute immobility; Beauty itself declares:

Je haïs le mouvement qui déplace les lignes
Et jamais je ne pleure et jamais je ne ris.

We are not surprised that Beauty should define itself in terms exactly descriptive of the inscrutable Dandy; nor even that an immobile Beauty should be a symbol of the poet's oppression by an adamantine and inexorable world. In Baudelaire's vision of the cosmos, as we have said, steel is opposed to steel. The oppressor and the oppressed are equally ruthless, equally immobile, equally conscious, and equally beautiful. Only the poet-hero knows the Adversary, but to know him is to salute the splendour of his majesty.

> Etre maudit à qui, de l'abîme profond
> Jusqu'au plus haut du ciel, rien hors moi ne répond!
> —O toi, qui comme une ombre à la trace éphémère.
> Foules d'un pied léger et d'un regard serein
> Les stupides mortels qui t'ont jugé amère,
> Statue aux yeux de jais, grand ange au front d'airain!

To this Moloch of existence the poet sacrifices himself in an ecstasy which is concealed beneath a mask of bronze. In harmony with the clangour of this meeting of metallic opposites, Baudelaire conceived himself as working like a smith at an anvil on the very words of his poems, hammering and shaping them till they rang with a steely resonance. It is something more than a metaphorical flight when he speaks of

> mes vers polis, treillis d'un pur métal,
> Savamment constellé de rimes de cristal.

That is not fancy, but a precise description of them; they are tempered: and even if the poet had not himself given the hint, one might without any violent exercise of the imagination have compared them to sword-blades, cunningly damascened.

Within this metallic resonance which is the large and general characteristic of Baudelaire's poetry we may distinguish many variations and undertones; or rather we may say that in one continuous and predominant physical sensation—for Baudelaire's verse is physically oppressive—we can detect various separate pulses. Of these the most remarkable might be called an exacerbation of the image. It appears in many forms: in some it is used to give to a vague emotion the acuteness of a physical sensation, as in 'Ces affreuses nuits Qui compriment le cœur comme un papier qu'on froisse'. Sometimes it is a peculiar variation of the dominant endeavour after solidity which has already been discussed. Thus he writes of the beautiful Dorothea:

> Ta gorge qui s'avance et qui pousse la moire,
> Ta gorge triomphante est une belle armoire

> Dont les panneaux bombés et clairs
> Comme les boucliers accrochent des éclairs.

The varieties are, indeed, too many to be separately defined; but a small collection of examples will show some of the curious tones that Baudelaire extracted from this singular instrument:

> Le ciel! couvercle noir de la vaste marmite
> Où bout l'imperceptible et vaste humanité . . .

> Cœur acorni, fumé comme un jambon . . .

> La nuit s'épaississait ainsi qu'un cloison . . .

> Sous le fardeau de ta paresse
> Ta tête d'enfant
> Se balance avec la mollesse
> D'un jeune éléphant . . .

> Le plaisir vaporeux, fuira vers l'horizon
> Ainsi qu'une sylphide au fond de la coulisse . . .

> Quand, ainsi qu'un poète, il [le Soleil] descend dans les villes
> Il ennoblit le sort des choses les plus viles . . .

> On voit un chiffonnier qui vient, hochant la tête,
> Buttant et se cognant aux murs comme un poète,
> Et, sans prendre souci des mouchards, ses sujets,
> Epanche tout son cœur en glorieux projets.

Some of these attempted effects may be traced to the desire to astonish which is permitted to the Dandy on the condition that he himself betrays no astonishment. But the explanation would certainly not cover them all, even if the desire to astonish were not closely related to the desire to compel a response, which is not lawful only but essential to the poet. Some of them are curiously beautiful; they have a novel and bizarre beauty that lingers in the mind. The Dandy is not only looking steadily at facts; he is extracting from them some quaint and vivid essence that escapes the duller or more cowardly eye. His world may be hard, repellent even, but it is full of a number of interesting things.

Nevertheless, the importance of these quaint vistas opening on to things grotesque or beautiful must not be exaggerated.

Baudelaire's exacerbation of the image was destined to play a considerable part in the subsequent evolution of French poetry, and, at second hand, of our own; but he himself used it sparingly, as one aware that the method was scarcely on a scale with the large effect of solidity at which he aimed. His main road of escape from his iron-walled world lay elsewhere, and was as ample as the prison-house was huge. His symbol of deliverance was the sea. The sea appears as often in his poetry as the metals themselves. It was for him a terrestial infinite that led 'anywhere out of the world'; and even in that famous and beautiful poem *Le Voyage*, the last of *Les Fleurs du Mal*, when the voyagers have returned with their mournful message that in every corner of the world 'the eternal bulletin' is the same, the poet calls to Death as the great ship's captain. After the failure of all voyages, a voyage remains:

> O Mort, vieux capitaine, il est temps! levons l'ancre!
> Ce pays nous ennuie, ô Mort! Appareillons!
> Si le ciel et la mer sont noirs comme de l'encre,
> Nos cœurs que tu connais sont remplis de rayons.

Doubtless, in the constant recurrence of the vision and imagery of the sea throughout Baudelaire's poetry, we may detect the profound impression made upon him as a young man by the voyage on which his perturbed parents sent him to cure his passion for poetry. But the sea is, after all, only a symbol; if he had not found the sea to express his intentions he would have found something else; hardly anything, however, that would have served him so well, or have made so universal an appeal. Even those who know nothing of Baudelaire's disdains and detestations, and would dismiss his attitude of rebellion as a mere theatricality, cannot fail to respond to the suggestion of his recurrent imagery of the sea. We may call it a simple or a naïve emotion that finds in a 'splendid ship with white sails crowding' the perfect symbol of the freedom and happiness that are hidden beyond our mortal horizon; it is a profound emotion, and, what is more, an emotion peculiarly of our time. An age of industrialism drives men to treasure the symbol of the sea and its ships. Baudelaire made a magnificent

172

use of this great modern commonplace. 'Grand style: rien de plus beau que les lieux communs', he notes in his Journal, where we also find this delicate statement of the fundamental theme:

> Ces beaux et grands navires, imperceptiblement balancés (dandinés) sur les eaux tranquilles, ces robustes navires, à l'air désœuvré et nostalgique, ne nous disent-ils par une langue muette: Quand partons-nous pour le bonheur?

The image appears in an innumerable variety of forms and contexts. Music is a sea opening on to he knows not what freedom:

> Je mets à la voile
> La poitrine en avant et les poumons gonflés
> Comme de la toile.

The lovely Dorothea sails along his memory like a ship. Again, 'notre âme est un trois-mâts cherchant son Icarie'. Every desire for the illimitable, every hope that some final freedom lay behind the brazen wall of circumstance, took concrete form in this image. If in a rare moment his fascinated loathing of the octopus city gives place to a delightful contemplation, it is because the beloved vision has interposed between him and the reality. 'Les tuyaux, les clochers', have become 'ces mâts de la cité'. Here finally are two passages from the *Poèmes en Prose*; placed side by side they render exactly the quality of significance which the sea and the ships possessed for the poet's mind:

> Moi seul, j'étais triste, inconcevablement triste. Semblable à un prêtre à qui on arracherait sa divinité, je ne pouvais, sans une navrante amertume, me détacher de cette mer si monstrueusement séduisante, de cette mer si infiniment variée dans son effrayante simplicité, et qui semble contenir en elle et représenter par ses jeux, ses allures, ses colères et ses sourires, les humeurs, les agonies et les extases de toutes les âmes qui ont vécu, qui vivent et qui vivront (*Déjà*).
>
> Un port est un séjour charmant pour une âme fatiguée des luttes de la vie. L'ampleur du ciel, l'architecture mobile des nuages, les colorations changeantes de la mer, le scintillement

des phares, sont un prisme merveilleusement propre à amuser les yeux sans jamais les lasser. Les formes élancées des navires, au gréement compliqué, auxquels la houle imprime des oscillations harmonieuses, servent à entretenir dans l'âme le goût du rythme et de la beauté, et puis, surtout, il y une sorte de plaisir mystérieux et aristocratique pour celui qui n'a plus ni curiosité ni ambition, à contempler, couché dans le belvédère ou accoudé sur le môle, tous ces mouvements de ceux qui partent et de ceux qui reviennent, de ceux qui ont encore la force de vouloir, le désir de voyager ou de s'enrichir (*Le Port*).

The sea is life, and the ship that rides over it is that triumphant, impossible beauty which haunts the mind with the promise that by its power the terrors of life may be overcome. It is only a dream, as Baudelaire well knew, but he dreamed it continually.

For Baudelaire was truly an *âme damnée*, because he was in love with the ideal. The fox of illusion and disgust really tore at his vitals. Like Ivan Karamazov, he persisted in his determination to give God back the ticket; because his sensitiveness was such that the degradation and misery of life left him no peace. Ennui and spleen had 'magnified themselves into divinities'; they were not petulant and momentary outbreaks of emotionalism, but constant factors of his being. To maintain himself he adopted an attitude, he became Satanic after the pattern of the Miltonic Satan, whom he considered the perfect type of manly beauty; and in the parallel world of art he sought to transform the reactions of his sensibility into the elements of a cosmos of his own making, a little universe that should produce in us the emotions that had tormented him in the world of everyday. Sometimes the original emotions show through the mask he wore; not through any artistic failure on his part, for no man was ever more resolute in his determination to sacrifice himself to his achievement, but because in the later work in prose he was intentionally loosening the rigour of his artistic creed. He was looking for a more precise equivalence to his feeling. In the texture of the *Poèmes en Prose* we can distinguish the separate threads of emotion which are lost in the stiff brocade of *Les Fleurs du Mal*. The prose is more

lightly and in a sense more delicately woven; the unity of effect
which the little pieces give derives more from complicated
harmony than from the resonant unison which marks the poetry.
In his prose Baudelaire is content to be ironical, compassionate,
lyrical, and symbolic by turns; each piece has the contour of
a single mood, together they have the complex solidity of an
attitude. There, if we look, we may find as much of Baudelaire
the man, as much of his human sensibility, as we shall ever
find; there his pity, his irony, his dreams have their original
quality, their individuality is not submerged. And there we
discover an exquisite compassion and sympathy with the
oppressed, of which we may be sure none of those who
denounced his immorality was ever remotely capable; and
even now few people know that it was Baudelaire who wrote
in *Le Veuves* one of the most compassionate phrases in all
literature:

> Avez-vous quelquefois aperçu des veuves sur ces bancs
> solitaires, des veuves pauvres? Qu'elles soient en deuil ou
> non, il est facile de les reconnaître. D'ailleurs il y a toujours
> dans le deuil du pauvre quelque chose qui manque, une
> absence d'harmonie qui le rend plus navrant. *Il est contraint
> de lésiner sur sa douleur.* Le riche porte la sienne au grand
> complet.

'They are compelled to save on their grief.' No wonder the
inventor of this phrase gave toys to the waifs of Paris and
watched them 'steal away like cats who take the bit you give
them far away to eat, having learned to mistrust men', and
recorded with a delicate precision the plans four little children
were making for their lives; or that the most cynical of all his
cynicisms about love is the little story, *Les Yeux des Pauvres.*
The poet and his mistress are sitting outside a new and splendid
café. Suddenly he is aware of a poor man holding two tiny
children by the hand; all three are staring, 'extraordinarily
serious', with large and fascinated eyes into the café:

> Non seulement j'étais attendri par cette famille d'yeux mais
> je me sentais un peu honteux de nos verres et de nos carafes,
> plus grands que notre soif. Je tournais mes regards vers les

vôtres, cher amour, pour y lire *ma* pensée; je plongeais dans vos yeux si beaux et si bizarrement doux, dans vos yeux verts, habités par le Caprice et inspirés par la Lune, quand vous me dites: "Ces gens-là sont insupportables, avec leurs yeux ouverts comme des portes-cochéres! Ne pourriez-vous pas prier le maître du café de les éloigner d'ici?"

Tant il est difficile de s'entendre, mon cher ange, et tant la pensée est incommunicable, même entre gens qui s'aiment!

This suppressed yet passionate sympathy with the sufferings of the poor is one of the deepest strains in Baudelaire's nature; it helps to give to his ennui and his spleen the decisive, creative force which a passing mood of disenchantment could never have. Unlike Verlaine, Baudelaire is a constructive poet; he works from a constant centre and builds on a firm foundation. It was easy for Verlaine to react against his first admiration for Baudelaire and say, 'Prends l'éloquence et tords-lui son cou'. He had very little to be eloquent about; but Baudelaire's moods have all the force of convictions, they have the backing of an accumulation of unforgotten injuries. Even when he is deliberately striving to express a mood, the effect is massive and overwhelming. To compare with Verlaine's plaintive songs his *Chant d'Automne*:

> Bientôt nous plongerons dans les froides ténèbres;
> Adieu, vive clarté de nos étés trop courts!
> J'entends déjà tomber avec des chocs funèbres
> Les bois retentissant sur le pavé des cours.

is to apprehend 'the difference between poetry of an eternal intensity and poetry that is merely beautiful'. The grave austerity of *Recueillement* belongs to the same rare order of achievement, the highest of which French poetry is capable:

> Sois sage, ô ma Douleur, et tiens-toi plus tranquille.
> Tu réclamais le soir; il descend; le voici.

There were one or two enthusiastic critics who welcomed the appearance of *Les Fleurs du Mal* with references to the great name of Dante. They were generous; but their instinct was sound. Baudelaire stands to Dante in a relation not unlike

176

that of Keats to Shakespeare.

We need not describe in detail the misery of the poet's life. Behind his mask he waged an incessant but a losing battle against a strange paralysis of the will. Only in the last two years, during which his letters to his mother and the fragments of his intimate journal have been published, has it been possible to appreciate his sufferings. Even now much of his life remains mysterious; but enough is revealed to show how striking are the points of resemblance between him and Dostoevsky. The two men were born in the same year. Certainly Baudelaire's powers were less than those of the Russian, but had Dostoevsky died when Baudelaire did, in 1867, he would have left only *Crime and Punishment* of his greater novels. Baudelaire did not live to push his exploration into the possibilities of rebellion so far. But Dostoevsky would have found in him all the material for one of his inscrutable heroes. This heroic side of Baudelaire, his prolonged and passionate attempt to live up to his own conception of heroism, is the part of his private life which most excites our curiosity, for it has a direct bearing upon his work as a poet. We may take his actual existence in the underworld for granted, as we take Dostoevsky's; it is his endeavour to establish himself in a place midway between the *âme supérieure* of his compatriot Stendhal and the Stavrogin of Dostoevsky that needs illumination. In his journals we catch only fitful glimpses of his immense exercise of will. We grasp at odd, fragmentary phrases like 'Self-purification and Anti-Humanity' (written in English and in big letters), or 'Etre un grand homme et un saint pour lui-même, voilà l'unique chose importante', or this—with its curious anticipation of an uncanny scene in *The Possessed*—'Le Dandy doit aspirer à être sublime sans interruption: il doit vivre et dormir devant un miroir.' And how unexpected to those who persist, like Mr. Arthur Symons in his recent study, in seeing in Baudelaire only a Swinburnian singer of 'strange sins,' will this be! 'Il ne peut y avoir du progrès (vrai, c'est-à-dire moral) que dans l'individu lui-même.' Yet all these professions of faith are perfectly consistent. Baudelaire's pursuit of the ideal of the rebellious angel called for a rigorous self-discipline and aimed at an

177

ethical victory ; but it also demanded enormous courage and physical endurance. The isolation of the man who adopts an individualist morality is complete ; he cannot expect sympathy or even understanding. Even a friend and admirer like Théophile Gautier confessed that he knew nothing about Baudelaire the man. We see the evidence of the tortures which he suffered from his spiritual loneliness in the almost hysterical way in which he clung to the affection of his mother and of Jeanne Duval, to both of whom he was, and knew he was, quite incomprehensible.

'One cannot live in rebellion,' said Ivan Karamazov. Just as Baudelaire used the symbol of the sea in his poetry for a way of escape from the adamantine world he had made, so in his life he was haunted by the thought that a simple domesticity might liberate him from the oppression and fascination of Paris. He will live in suburban rusticity with Jeanne at Neuilly in a quiet little 'home'—it is the English word he uses ; and nothing is more pathetic than his hysterical attempts to escape to his mother's villa in Honfleur. Again and again the plans are made, the day fixed. In vain. A month or more of silence precedes the inevitable letter, with its pages of feverish explanation why it was impossible. When he did break away from Paris, it was only to be drawn into the vortex of another great city ; and when at last he made the journey from Brussels to Honfleur his mother herself brought him, for he was paralysed and speechless.

So, too, in his inward consciousness he dreamed of a way of escape by a belief in God. In his moments of doubt of his own endurance came the thought that there still might be an explanation of all that was intolerable to him in life : the veil of the mystery might be lifted. We have for evidence the pitiful prayers which are scattered through his Journal, and the appeal with which he ends *Mademoiselle Bistouri* :

> La ville fourmille de monstres innocents.—Seigneur, mon Dieu! vous le Créateur, vous, le Maître; vous qui avez fait la Loi et la Liberté; vous, le Souverain qui laissez faire, vous le Juge qui pardonnez; vous qui êtes plein de motifs et de causes, et qui avez peut-être mis dans mon esprit le gôut de

l'horreur pour convertir mon cœur, comme le guérison au bout d'une lame; Seigneur, ayez pitié, ayez pitié des fous et des folles! O Créateur! peut-il exister des monstres aux yeux de Celui-là seul qui sait pourquoi ils existent, comment ils *se sont faits* et comment ils auraient pu ne pas se faire?

' Healing at the point of the knife.' Baudelaire was never to believe it wholly, but it was a possibility which haunted him. Perhaps it weakened his resolution ; certainly it was a cause of that paralysis of the will—the faculty by which he chiefly lived—which most afflicted him in his later days. The poignant notes in his Journal, 'Travail immédiat, même mauvais, vaut mieux que la rêverie,' his repeated references to ' le sentiment du gouffre,' give us an inkling of what he endured.

Baudelaire was a great poet of a decadence. In other words, he was a great modern poet ; for the decadence which shaped him by compelling him to revolt against it was the ' civilization of industrial progress ' which has endured from his day to our own. Baudelaire confronted the reality like the hero he strove to be ; he had the courage both of his attitude and his art, and the result of his unremitting exercise of will in transforming his keen emotions is a poetic achievement that makes a single and profound impression upon our minds. Baudelaire, true to the practice of the great poet, had crystallized his experience; he had accumulated a weight of conviction to endorse his emotions. ' Dans certains états de l'âme presque surnaturels' (he wrote), la profondeur de la vie se révèle tout entière dans le spectacle, si ordinaire qu'il soit, qu'on a sous les yeux. Il en devient le symbole.' We have tried to elucidate the quality which Baudelaire discerned in 'the depth of life' and to disentangle some of the methods by which he sought to convey it to posterity. He was indeed the poet of rebellion ; but the resolution of his defiance was subtly modulated by doubts and dreams which he would entertain and cherish for a while and dismiss with an ironical contempt for his own unworthy weakness. Underneath his steely surface lay an infinity of sensitive responses. We could have deduced it ; deep resentments are born only of deep wounds, and the solidity of permanent poetry is the work only of the most delicate fingers. But the finest

179

artist seldom permits the precise quality of his personal response to appear. He makes his sacrifice to his own universality. It is for us to detect where most the man shows through the texture of his work ; and we may decide that Baudelaire reveals himself nowhere more plainly than in these last two stanzas of *l'Irréparable*:

> J'ai vu parfois au fond d'un théâtre banal
> Qu'enflammait l'orchestre sonore,
> Une fée allumer dans un ciel infernal
> Une miraculeuse aurore ;
> J'ai vu parfois au fond d'une théâtre banal
>
> Un être, qui n'était que lumière, or et gaze,
> Terrasser l'énorme Satan ;
> Mais mon cœur, que jamais ne visite l'extase,
> Est un théâtre où l'on attenêd
> Toujours, toujours en vain, l'Etre aux ailes de gaze.

[MARCH, 1921]

THE CREATION OF FALSTAFF

When we are confronted with the work of a great writer our first impulse is one to complete acceptance and surrender. We accept the miraculous gift which the author in his bounty places in our hands; we surrender ourselves utterly into his keeping. It is as though we stood before the gate, and he spoke the Open Sesame. The doors swing wide, and we enter a strange new-minted world, shining bright or sombre gleaming, of which the great writer is the sole emperor, through which he alone can guide us, in which we can only wonder and rejoice. We may be sad, we may be happy, while we wander behind him, but our sadness and our happiness are not of this world; for we are, when the door closes upon us once again, sad that we could have been so happy, and happy that we could have been so sad.

And this suffices many. Indeed it is sufficient. This, and nothing other, is what the writer has to give: he makes us free of a new kingdom of the soul. We accept his gift and rejoice.

But, in very truth, a miracle has been worked upon us. We cannot help it; we ponder this thing in our hearts. We begin to see that this kingdom of the soul which has been opened to us, must be also a kingdom of our own souls, otherwise we should never have recognised it or known it for what it was. The great writer vindicates our right to our own forgotten majesty and disturbs us with memories of the splendours of our own deep-buried past. He puts before us something far greater, far meaner, far darker, far brighter, than we ourselves are, and we accept it. We accept it, because we know—more than know—because we *feel* it is true. This character, so different from our waking selves, so infinitely more heroic, or more earthy, than we (it seems) ever have been or can ever be, is approved by us. Long silent voices arise from within us and salute it: 'This is true!'

How do we know, in virtue of what faculty do we feel, that 'This is true?' And the answer is, I believe, that we are in fact far greater than we know, and far more mysterious than, in this strange life in which we have encased and imprisoned ourselves, we can suffer to admit ourselves to be. Our roots strike deeper into the darkness, and our flowers rise more splendid into the light than we dare to acknowledge. Darkness is not more terrible than light; the extreme uplifting of which the human soul is capable terrifies no less than the warm gloom of chaos whence it sprung and to which, in its mightiest moments, it must return. We turn away from the blinding poles. Does not light blind as well as darkness? But at moments we are visited by gleams and whispers which we acknowledge, not knowing what we do. Under the compulsion of a great writer chiefly, we confess what we are.

Then, in our pondering, comes the further question: What manner of man is this who works these spells upon us, who can turn our faces to the darkness from which we rose and to which we must descend, and to the light towards which we soar and from which we must fall, who brings down gleams and calls up whispers which are new and old and familiar and strange, so that, having heard them, we are like the wakened lovers of John Donne, who return from the darkness wherein they have plunged to the limbo-light in which we live, the twilight-mist in which we seek our safety, the dim draping with which we envelop the world in order to call it real. Like Donne's lovers, we say:

> And now, good-morrow to our waking souls
> Which watch not one another out of fear.

Fear of the deeps, fear of the heights, between which human life is perilously swung; fear of the great downward thrust of the root, fear of the great upward surge of the bursting flower. Fear, and a secret thrill of the triumph we glimpse but never shall achieve; fear, and a secret pulse of expectation we shall never justify. What manner of man is this who works this magic, black magic and white, upon our souls?

> What is your substance, whereof are you made
> That millions of strange shadows on you tend?

And the answer is: Of what the great writer makes us aware, of that he is. As he, in the strange rediscovery of life which is his mission and his privilege, plunges down and rises up, renewed in darkness and renewed in light, we are down-plunged and uplifted with him. The more we know of where he has

182

taken *us*, the more we know of where *he* himself has been; the more we are aware, by his mysterious potency, of what we are, the more we are aware of what he is.

The writer creates out of his deepest experience. Deep, deep it *must* go, if his work is to outlast the ages, for by his power of reawakening deep experience in us, alone he lives. The bounds of the twilight world, we call the real, change with the centuries, even with the years, but the depths below and the heights above remain for ever. And the height a man can compass depends upon the depth to which he can descend.

It is no use blinking the fact of Shakespeare. If we know, as we do, in our bones and bowels, that he was great, then we must know him, and in order to know him we must submit ourselves to him. We must accept him wholly; we must not smile on this part and turn away from that If we try to accept the light and refuse the darkness, we shall end by not even understanding the light, for it is conditioned and made possible and given its own peculiar quality by the darkness.

Before we can approach the problem of the creation of Falstaff, we must have a notion of the process in which the problem has its place, in order to understand what Falstaff meant for Shakespeare, we must have some sense of the motion of his mind and being. Not that we can ever regard Shakespeare as it were an abstract potency swinging free of all human limitation. What he was, was severely and strictly conditioned. Nevertheless, he was what he was: and that was something more than a member and a shareholder of a company of Elizabethan actors, and a maker of stage plays for his fellows. He was one of the greatest souls in human history. We know nothing about him—for practical purposes, nothing. When he was born—and that not certainly—when he died, a few traditions. For my own part, I neither expect nor desire to know more. What he could and would tell the world, he told. There are his works: there is the man.

A man, then, born with great and glorious gifts of speech and fancy: overbrimming with them. abounding, luxuriant and rich; finding life as generous as himself, enchanted by the wonder of living and writing and being, splendidly sensuous, delicately understanding. It seems that no man was ever so gloriously fitted for the life into which he was born as Shakespeare. He needed to deny nothing: in his eyes everything had its own indefeasible right to existence, bore its own unique and authentic bloom. He could do nothing wrong, because nothing was wrong: it was, therefore it was good. A tragedy? Why, yes, of course he could write tragedy: he could write anything. But *Romeo and Juliet* is not a tragedy after all: it is only a magical love lyric, more substantial and more real than any in our language save only Chaucer's *Troilus and Cressida.* And *Richard II*? That is sad, but sad only with the sadness of its most beautiful line:

And tell sad stories of the death of kings.

Nothing to grind the heart or stab the soul. At worst something for a wry smile or a tear that is a pleasant relief from happiness.

No, truly, it was a golden world into which Shakespeare was born, a golden man to delight in it. There was a soft and steady sunshine upon everything.

Then, something happened. What it was, we do not know. At least, in the manner of our speech, we say we do not know. But by that we mean only that we do not know the event, the outward visible happening that would make a headline in the newspapers or a nine days' scandal for the gossips of the town. But what in heaven's name, does it matter whether we know this or not? Could we, by knowing it, know one single jot or tittle more about the living soul of the man who suffered the discomfiture? They write books about Shakespeare the man, they hunt out for him hypothetical mistresses, they claim to tell us what the Sonnets mean in terms of outward events—as if by this blind raking in obscurity they could discover something. They scarcely pause to remember that, the greater a man is, the more completely is an event merged in his inward reaction to the event. Not what happens to, but what happens *in* him, is the subject for our care: not what he suffers, but what he becomes. We cannot help our human curiosity; it is not a bad thing. It has its root in common human sympathy and flowers in the desire to make the great man as familiar as our neigh-

184

bour. But these trivial searches so easily lead us to forget that the road of knowledge lies elsewhere and is as open as the day. Any one who cares to may know far more about Shakespeare than he can about his nearest and dearest friend. He can know the very notion of Shakespeare's mind, the very pulse of his being.

Something may or may not have happened *to* Shakespeare; but something happened *in* him. Suddenly the world that was rich and single and golden became bitter and double and dark. It was rent asunder. On the one hand, darkness and loathing, on the other, a blinding light and an anguished longing. Ineffable darkness and ineffable light. Read Claudio's speech to Isabella in *Measure for Measure*.

> Aye, but to die and go we know not where;
> To lie in cold obstruction and to rot;
> This sensible warm motion to become
> A kneaded clod, and the delighted spirit
> To bathe in fiery floods, or to reside
> In thrilling region of thick-ribbed ice;
> To be imprisoned in the viewless winds
> And blown with restless violence round about
> The pendent world; or to be worse than worst
> Of those that lawless and incertain thought
> Imagines howling: 'Tis too horrible.

And read beside it *The Phœnix and the Turtle*, the most miraculous poem of unearthly love we have,—the voice of the consummation when spirit has winged its way free of all the mud of earth, and passion has become virginal once more.

On the other hand the whole atmosphere of *Measure for Measure* is heavy with disgusted sensuality, and the same oppression (or the same obsession) is in *Hamlet*. Yet these are all the works of a single period. Disruption has come, and out of what was single, the spiritual and the animal have resolved themselves—the incessant strife of the ideal and the actual has begun, the struggle which was to carry Shakespeare through *Macbeth* and *Lear* to *Antony and Cleopatra*, and, if not to a final serenity, to the mysterious alliance between a belief that life is illusion and a dreaming faith in a generation yet unborn for whom this vision and this conflict should no longer be. For *The Tempest* is, as it were, a crystal in which Shakespeare shows us a universe ordered anew—another harmony, another whole-ness, a reuniting of the divided parts. In the words of Virgil's Messianic eclogue:

Magnus ab integro saeclorum nascitur ordo;
Jam nova progenies caelo demittitur alto.

The movement of Shakespeare's mind to this conclusion, the incessant forward-swinging from ideal to real, from darkness to light and back again, including ever more of the totality of human experience in its ambit, and at last the brightness of the light become dazzling by virtue of the depth of darkness to which it is opposed—the story of this movement is one upon which I cannot enter here. What I have said is nothing more than the roughest sketch of the curve of Shakespeare's progress, in order to make clear the position which this question of Falstaff holds in the whole problem of Shakespeare.

Falstaff is the greatest creation of the yet undivided being of Shakespeare. He is the creature of Shakespeare's golden prime, of his first maturity; he is, in a sense, the symbol of Shakespeare's natural attitude, the spontaneous fruit of his uninterrupted growth. Or rather, I should say he is this in essence and by intention: actually, as I shall try to show, he is something differ-ent. He is conditioned and maimed and stunted.

I cannot *prove* my contention; I may hope to convince you of it, but that is all. The facts in an inquiry such as this are not of an order that admits of proof. They are not, and cannot be made, objects for scientific scrutiny. The facts are four plays: the two parts of *Henry IV*, *The Merry Wives* of *Windsor* and *Henry V*. There is, no doubt, a sense in which these can be made objects for scientific scrutiny. You can measure the lines, compute the number of weak endings and of strong, establish the proportion of prose to verse; or you can examine them as though they were logical demonstrations, find out the missing steps, the inconsistencies, the non-sequiturs; or you can calculate how much actual time is consumed by the action or pre-supposed by it. All these things have been done, and they will probably be done over again, many times. They

186

are nearly all irrelevant. For, in this order of things—this pre-eminently spiritual order—the fact of a play is not so many lines of printed words, but our reaction to them.

Once granted that the facts with which we have to deal are our reactions, the next thing is to discriminate among our reactions. Our natural inclination is to regard Falstaff as a whole. He appears in the first part of *Henry IV*; he reappears in the second part; he reappears once more in *The Merry Wives*; and he dies in *Henry V*. Nothing could be simpler. Where is the problem, you may ask. And, indeed, if Falstaff is merely a name, nothing *could* be simpler, and the problem is not there. The name appears, re-appears, disappears. *Actum est.*

But Falstaff is far more than a name: he is a character, he is the embodiment of a vision of life. And if we look more closely into the quality of his appearances and reappearances, we can see that he is not a whole, and that there is a problem. It comes to us first in these terms: Falstaff is completely alive in *Henry IV*, Part I; he is far less alive in Part II; he is something altogether different in *The Merry Wives*; and in *Henry V* he is dead.

Falstaff is completely alive in *Henry IV*, Part I. But we can say more than that. In that play, Falstaff is *primus inter pares*; he is the first and greatest, but he is the first and greatest among equals. Hotspur, being a character of history, with his fate appointed in the authorities, has to die: but if he could have been spared, he might have become another Falstaff for posterity. Of course, there could not be another Falstaff; but there could have been a rival to Falstaff—a character animated by a like fundamental irresponsibility; the antithesis of Falstaff, but his complement also; as careless in his pursuit of honour as Falstaff in his pursuit of pleasure. It is a curious relation that holds between the man who thought—

> It were an easy leap
> To pluck bright honour from the pale-faced moon,

and the other who said:

'Can honour set to a leg. No. Or an arm? No. Honour hath no skill in surgery, then? No. What is honour? A word. What is that word honour? What is that honour?

187

Air. A trim reckoning! Who hath it! He that died o'
Wednesday. Doth he feel it? No. Doth he hear it? No. 'Tis
insensible then? Yes, to the dead. But will it live with the
living? No. Why? Detraction will not suffer it. Therefore,
I'll none of it. Honour is a mere scutcheon; and so ends my
catechism.'

But though it is a strange one, the relation between these two
exists. It is not a relation that would have been recognised by
either of them in daily life. Hotspur would have despised
Falstaff; and Falstaff, when safely out of reach of his sword,
would have laughed at Hotspur. It is a relation of another kind.

For Hotspur, like Falstaff, is a character of the first order;
in sheer imaginative reality he runs the fat knight very close.
His scene with Lady Percy, his scene with Glendower, belong
to the very highest manifestations of Shakespeare's creative
power in his first unbroken period, when he seems to have been
simply a force of nature in a sense in which perhaps only Homer
and Tolstoy and Dickens have been forces of nature expressing
themselves through the written word. We feel that the first
part of *Henry IV* is naturally balanced and harmonious. It plays
within a single world of Shakespeare's imagination. Falstaff is
one denizen of it, Hotspur another; they breathe the same air,
the same sunlight shines upon them, and we feel that if our
vision were delicate enough we could see how the one creation
implied the other, for we have a sense of them as necessary
projections of the same moment in the same mood of the same
genius. And what is true of these two heroes of the play holds
good of the play altogether. There is an astonishing interde-
pendence of the parts: they are irradiated by a shining
atmosphere which unites them all, but which it would need
much labour to define, for it is by nature almost beyond definition. But the word to describe it is 'lambent'; tongues of
smiling flame play over everything. A point at which we can
nearly capture the essence in a few lines is, perhaps, Prince
Henry's casual remark:

'I am not yet of Percy's mind, the Hotspur of the North;
he that kills me some six or seven dozen Scots at a breakfast,
washes his hands, and says to his wife, "Fie upon this quiet

188

life! I want work." "Oh, my sweet Harry," says she, "how many hast thou killed to-day?" "Give my roan horse a drench," says he, and answers, "Some fourteen," an hour after. "A trifle, a trifle." '

Intrinsically, it is perhaps not funnier than a dozen of the things that Falstaff says; but its effect in its place, following immediately upon the marvellous scene between Hotspur and his wife, is prodigious. This slant and smiling sunbeam, we feel, can be thrown upon anything. Hotspur throws it on the gentleman who came to demand his prisoners and on Glendower, Prince Harry on Hotspur, Falstaff on Prince Harry, and Shakespeare himself on the world.

But in the second part this magical condition—this champagne atmosphere—exists no longer. The second part contains, of course, many wonderful things, but this radiant naturalness is intermittent. Instead of being a play in which Falstaff is only a triumphant particular crystallisation of the general element, there is no general element at all—neither unity, nor atmosphere of unity. Against an irrelevant background of unsavoury history, Falstaff performs, and as often as not he has no heart at all in the performance. He is as often merely mechanical as he is inspired. This falling-off has been recognised by many; and condoned or excused or explained. It has been said, for instance, that between writing the first and the second parts of *Henry IV*, Shakespeare had come under the influence of Ben Jonson's inferior and mechanical conception of comedy. It is not likely on general grounds that a commanding genius, conscious of its powers, should be warped by the theories of a talent. To be influenced is one thing, to be inhibited is quite another. And as a matter of fact, it is precisely where the comedy of *Henry IV*, Part II, is in setting and externals most Jonsonian, that Shakespeare first becomes himself again. The tavern scene, where Falstaff dines with Mistress Quickly and Doll Tearsheet—a trick of name Shakespeare may very well have taken from Jonson—may offend our modern pretences of refinement; it is nevertheless superb—quite how superb we can only realise at the end, when it is plain that Shakespeare has achieved the miracle of carrying a thread of true sentiment clean

189

through the scene without even a momentary discord.

And Falstaff is himself again in the scenes in which he is engaged in monstrously misusing the King's Press in Gloucestershire. It is when he is alone, with no other comic characters to bear him up, that it is most evident that the virtue has departed from him. His opening scene with the Lord Chief-Justice is a queer affair. Falstaff says some good things in the course of it: if it were taken away we should never know that 'he was born about three o'clock in the afternoon, with a white head and something a round belly'; and, certainly, we should never have guessed that he had lost his voice 'with hollaing and singing of anthems.' But for the most part the richness is departed. The fat knight's wit has become thin and verbal and boring: the stage-play is effective, but the substance of the talk is not. And when Falstaff plays the old, old comic trick of pretending not to hear the Lord Chief-Justice, we know that Shakespeare is getting through an uncongenial task by relying on his knowledge of stage technique. Falstaff never had to depend for his being upon such props before; nor did he ever descend so low as in his reply to the Lord Chief-Justice's rebuke:

    CH.-JUST.: There is not a white hair on your face but should have his effect of gravity.

    FALS.: His effect of gravy, gravy, gravy.

Let us hope that that is a gag of the Elizabethan clown which has found its way into the text. There is nothing quite so imbecile as that in the scene.

On the whole, it is not too much to say that in this second part of *Henry IV* Falstaff is rather carried on than re-created. There is his great monologue on the virtues of sherris-sack; there are a few scattered sentences, of which the most famous perhaps is: ' I am not only witty in myself, but the cause that wit is in other men.' But in this play the wit in himself is conspicuous chiefly by its absence; the wit in other men of which he is the cause becomes only the more striking. For it is, to say the least, very peculiar that in his three most admirable scenes —the scene of his arrest for debt, the tavern scene with Quickly and Tearsheet and Pistol, and the recruiting scene in Gloucestershire, the only scenes in the play which are bathed in the true

Falstaffian quality—Falstaff himself has little or nothing to say. In the first it is Mistress Quickly, in the second, Mistress Quickly and Pistol, in the third, Justice Shallow, who set the pace and give the tone. Sir John's presence is rather felt than manifested: the company is fit for him, we know that he is among it, and our imagination does the rest. Partly through the transferred vitality of his companions, partly in virtue of the radiant afterglow which persists from the first part and appears at the mention of his name, we incline to see him as the same Jack Falstaff, wrapped in the same rich clouds of glory. But he is not. He has his moments of indubitable inspiration; but he is in a decline. He is being kept alive, as it were, only by a transfusion of blood. He has become, in fact, something of a vampire, whose veins can be filled only by the sacrifice of fresh children of Shakespeare's creative imagination.

The disease and the heroic remedy point to a single conclusion. Shakespeare had begun to tire of Falstaff. He is no longer interested in him; he is, indeed, interested in anybody rather than him. To enable himself to go on writing comic scenes in which Falstaff can be kept afloat, in which an illusion of Falstaff's presence can be plausibly maintained, he has either to expand characters that existed in outline only, or to invent new ones. Thus in the tavern scene it is the richly-matured Mistress Quickly—first mother of that great succession of comic Cockney landladies and charwomen which touches the zenith again in Mrs. Gamp and descends into Samuel Butler's Mrs. Jupp in *The Way of All Flesh*—and Pistol (why, oh, why, is Pistol so funny, seeing that nine-tenths of his jokes are unintelligible?)—it is these two who carry the thing through. And even in Gloucestershire it is Shallow and Silence and the rich procession of Mouldies, Warts, Feebles, and Bullcalves who bear Sir John's banner high. Falstaff is no longer the executant, but the impresario. We remember his past triumphs and are content, and when he comes forward to the front of the stage to take his benefit with a monologue on the dangers of thin potations, we are ready for a moment to swear he is as good a man as ever he was. But our heart misgives us; we have a premonition that the end is near.

191

Now I think that from this evidence alone it is clear that, for some reason or other, Shakespeare's heart was no longer wholly in his creation of Falstaff. The situation is that he is perfectly ready to create new comic characters—he had apparently at this moment an inexhaustible store of them, waiting to be born —but he is not willing to go on creating Falstaff. About the whole of the play hangs an air of lassitude, except in certain of the comic scenes. They are masterly, in so far as they are independent of the fat knight. A particular inhibition in his regard was apparently at work. So much we could deduce from a mere comparison of the second with the first part of *Henry IV*. We might even look for the cause of Shakespeare's disinclination. We might, if we have a turn for the imputation of ideal motives, suggest that it was because Shakespeare realised that Falstaff, in obedience to history, had to be disgraced and rebuffed by Prince Harry. It was not an end which Falstaff had deserved; it was not an end which could be truly assigned to him: for Falstaff belongs to an ethereal world in which such tragic issues are discordant. Shakespeare had to make a creature who had nothing whatever to do with history obey the laws of history. He was faced with a problem impossible of solution; he knew the impossibility, and lost interest. That would be, in itself, a fairly convincing explanation. I myself believe it counted for something in the final destiny of Falstaff.

Fortunately for the argument, there is other evidence, and evidence which is, to me, quite conclusive. The second part of *Henry IV* winds up very exceptionally with an Epilogue. Naturally a great deal has been made of this Epilogue, but not altogether, it seems to me, in the right way. No doubt it is interesting, and in some degree important, to know by its evidence that Sir John Falstaff was originally Sir John Oldcastle and that Shakespeare was compelled to change the name owing to protests from the family. But there are surely more important things about it—this paragraph, for instance:

> Be it known to you—as it is very well—I was lately here in the end of a displeasing play, to pray your patience for it and to promise you a better. I did mean indeed to pay you with this; which, if like an ill venture it come unluckily home,

I break—and you, my gentle creditors, lose. Here I promised you I would be, and here I commit my body to your mercies.

In the first place, we have to remember, it is the Epilogue (or the Dancer) who speaks, and not Shakespeare, and he speaks not on Shakespeare's behalf, but on that of the company, though Shakespeare wrote his words for him. There is, therefore, no means of knowing whether the play which fell flat was one of Shakespeare's own or not. It *may* have been *As You Like It*, which not only has an Epilogue that is own brother to this one, but also belongs to this period (1597-1599) and does not seem to have been very popular. But that is another question. The point of importance for our present purposes is that it is clear that the regular audience of Shakespeare's company had been displeased, and in order to send them contented home, the Epilogue had been put forward to promise them another play with Falstaff in it. The first part of *Henry IV* had been a roaring success; Falstaff had taken the town, or the play-going part of it, by storm. What was the unfortunate company to do, faced with a hissing audience, but promise it some more 'fat meat'?

So Shakespeare had to put his back into it. More Falstaff, and quickly, too, was, in both senses, the *mot d'ordre*. Perhaps he had a rough outline of the second part in his head. At a pinch, we might interpret 'I did mean, indeed, to pay you with this one' as referring to the time when the play was promised, and it is perhaps only reasonable to suppose that Shakespeare, confronted with the success of Falstaff, realised, both as playwright and as shareholder in the company, that he would very soon have to produce some more of him. He may have grown tired of English history, and turned to *As You Like It* in order to put off the evil day. There is no means of knowing. But what we do know—is it not written as large as life all over the Epilogue?—is that, in the event, more Falstaff had to be produced against time. 'Be it known to you—*as it is very well*' has an unmistakably ominous ring. Probably there had been calls for the new Falstaff every night for the last few weeks.

A man of genius can undoubtedly do very marvellous things to order and against time. What he cannot do in such circumstances is the same thing over again. If he has done one thing superlatively he can do another thing superlatively, but he cannot do the same thing superlatively. Simply because he is a creative genius, some profound inhibition is at work to prevent him from repeating himself. And self-repetition was precisely what was required of Shakespeare. The audience was not asking for another Shakespeare play, not even for another comic Shakespeare play, either of which might have been supplied without danger; but it was asking for more Falstaff, according to sample. It was asking the impossible precisely because it asked. Shakespeare, good man of business as he was, would doubtless have gone to any length to supply it; but he was prevented by something more urgent and essential than his business mind. His genius, his dæmon, had a word to say: several words, in fact, and they spelt Quickly, Pistol, Shallow, Silence. But it hardly got beyond the first syllable of Falstaff.

And at the end he had to promise still more:

One word more I beseech you. (*We know the gesture*: *hand uplifted to stem the applause and make a silence*.) If you be not too much cloyed with fat meat (*roars of ironical laughter*); our humble author will continue the story, with Sir John in it, and make you merry with fair *Katherine of France*: where, for anything I know, Falstaff shall die of a sweat (*pause*)—unless already a' been killed with your hard opinions (*more roars of ironical laughter*); for Oldcastle died a martyr and this is not the man.

But there is, in *Henry V*, no Sir John. 'His heart is fracted and corroborate' before the play begins. No doubt 'his sweet boy's' behaviour at the end of *Henry IV*, Part II, had dealt it something of a blow, but not a very bad one. His heart was sufficiently tough to put up with 'being very well provided for' until his conversation should 'appear more wise and modest to the world.' Of course, if we remember that Falstaff' is a created character and not a human being, we must indeed say that this necessity to mend his ways is a death sentence on the knight, and anticipate Pistol in condoling him. A reformed Falstaff is not Falstaff. Still, Shakespeare had obviously left the door open for his return, and the Epilogue leaves no doubt that he

194

was intended to perform some more exploits (perhaps at Agin-court) before his nose became as sharp as a pen. Yet he was killed. Why?

Because, in the meanwhile, another burden had been laid upon Shakespeare. The Queen had commanded that the fat knight should be shown in love, and she had fixed a day for the exhibition. It allowed Shakespeare a fortnight for the writing of his play. That is the tradition. It is one of the oldest Shakes-peare traditions we possess. It is plausible in itself, for we need to find some explanation why Falstaff should suddenly rush through a couple of centuries to make his appearance in a play of contemporary life, and of contemporary life at Windsor; and, when we come to look more closely into the destiny of Falstaff as we have been doing, we can see that if the tradition did not exist it would have been necessary to invent it. For, between the finishing of *Henry IV*, Part II, and the writing of *Henry V*, Shakespeare's plans with regard to Falstaff changed once more. In the Epilogue he had been ready to promise more of him in *Henry V* on condition that he was allowed to give him his quietus at the end of the play. Instead, he killed him before the beginning of it. So it is obvious that, if Shakespeare was sick of Falstaff by the end of *Henry IV*, Part II, he was sick to death of him by the beginning of *Henry V*. The bare facts are enough to show that there was some intervening circumstance to intens-ify Shakespeare's weariness with his own creation. Without the tradition, we should have guessed the intervening circum-stance was *The Merry Wives*: with the tradition, the explanation is complete.

A Falstaff play to be finished in a fortnight, and at the Royal Command! Authors and actors take Royal Commands ser-iously enough now; even in this twentieth century they cause them sleepless nights. How much more should Shakespeare have been troubled in the sixteenth century when Royalty was a good deal more regal than it is now—Shakespeare who had something of a weakness for blue blood! The marvel is that he should have done so well; for in spite of the superior attitude towards the farce of *The Merry Wives* which is frequent in English criticism, it is a most excellent play. It has to be

195

regarded in and for itself as the separate object that it is. It is no good objecting to it that it is a play of a different kind from the other Falstaff plays. No man, not even the most consummate genius, can command at will the spirit that irradiates the first part of *Henry IV*. Shakespeare had a peculiar problem to solve: to construct an amusing play—a play to amuse a particular person whose taste in laughter was not of the highest —in a record time.[1] He went about it in the way a playwright, faced with the same problem, would go about it to-day. He looked for a strong and sturdy farce-plot on which to build, so that if his invention failed, as it most likely would fail, under pressure, the strength of the mere situation would carry him through: he wanted a plot on whose scaffolding he could depend. Now, it was no use to trust to his imagination to invent incomparable speeches for Falstaff: they might never come: such things were not to be squeezed out, even of Shakespeare's head.

Whether Shakespeare himself invented the plot of *The Merry Wives* we cannot say. But we can say, knowing his own habit elsewhere, and knowing what a playwright in a like situation would do to-day, that it is improbable. The modern writer would try to get a plot from somewhere, skim through the latest French farces, ask his friends if they knew of anything, hunt up the comedies that held the stage years ago. Not otherwise do we imagine Shakespeare. And when his latest Cambridge editors, with remarkable detective skill, extract from *The Merry Wives* itself fairly convincing evidence that it is a remodelling of a comedy of intrigue set in the contemporary life of Elizabethan London, we are admiring but not surprised. It is what we should have expected.

What we could not have expected, however high we place Shakespeare's genius, is that under such circumstances he should have brought off the miracle. *The Merry Wives* is farce, farce of what they call nowadays the 'slap-stick' kind, but the play is sweet as a good apple. The unsavoury smell of the dirty linen in the buck-basket is quite blown away by the country air which pours in from every side. We feel that the

---

[1] Molière's *L'Amour Médecin* was written and played in *five* days: but it has not the real substance of more than a single act of *The Merry Wives*.

stage does not run off at the wings to pasteboard scenery, but to country lanes and hedgerows; it backs not on to a curtain, but on to the rushy margin of the Thames. The play is redolent of early summer—the air is full of May or June. And if Falstaff is no longer the pure ethereal essence of comedy that he has been, but a rather disreputable adventurer on his beam-ends in a country town—well, we cannot have everything in a fortnight. And, even in this fortnight of slavery—slavery is certainly a mild word for the conditions necessary for the achievement— Shakespeare's pure creativeness would out. His dæmon would *not* be denied. Not only is there the incomparable 'materpiece of nonentity,' Slender, who, one guesses, belonged to rather too rarefied an order of creation to appeal to his royal audience— the true and only original of the man 'who could not say Bo to a goose' would hardly have struck Elizabeth as funny at all— but there is a really comic Welshman. He may be crude, but he *is* comic. And he plainly went down. Not only was he the chief attraction (after Falstaff himself) on the title page of the pirated Quarto, under the mistaken style and title of 'Sir Hugh, the Welch knight,' but he was obviously the precursor of Fluellen in *Henry V*. In the manner of Sir Hugh's reception, Shakespeare saw an opening to cover his deliberate murder of Sir John. On that he was determined.

He could take no more risk of command performances, whether at the summons of the Queen or of the London groundlings. Falstaff had to die without delay, even though his newly acquired trick of moving on a time-machine through the centuries might make the *coup de grâce* more difficult to give. But Shakespeare was resolute. Falstaff was never suffered to be seen, or even his rich voice to be heard on the stage of *Henry V*. We can say, beyond any reasonable doubt, that no other of Shakespeare's created characters led his creator such a life as Sir John Falstaff. Shakespeare himself was probably the only human being who was 'cloyed with too much fat meat,' and perhaps it would not be merely fanciful to say that half Shakespeare's other comic characters represent the attempts of his genius to escape from the incubus it had conjured out of nothingness.

This, in rough outline, is the story of Falstaff's creation as I find it written in the plays themselves: first, a magnificent play with a comic character who takes the town by storm—remember that the evidence is that Falstaff was by far the most popular character of Shakespeare's in his own day; then, at the end of the run, the company produces a play which falls flat, the manager goes to Shakespeare while the audience is still booing and hissing, there is a hurried colloquy behind the scenes, Shakespeare (who is a shareholder as well as a playwright) agrees, and the angry audience is sent away contented by the promise of another play 'with Sir John in it'; then, the second part is written against time, with the immediate success that was inevitable—the audience by this time was in the condition of a modern audience at the beginning of a film by Charlie Chaplin: the fat knight had only to appear for the house to rock with laughter—and Shakespeare, foreseeing a life of slavery if he does not take action, declares in the Epilogue that the next play will be the last in which Falstaff will appear; but he is not quick enough, the news of the latest Falstaff success has reached the Queen, she probably has the second part played at court before her, and at the end commands that Sir John be shown in love. 'When is my first free evening ' she asks the Lord High something or other, who keeps the Royal engagement-book. 'Monday fortnight, Your Majesty.' 'Very well, on Monday fortnight.' If it had been Monday week, no doubt Shakespeare would have had to 'deliver the goods.' He did his work; though he produced not Falstaff but another person of the same name and appearance. But that was the last straw. Instead of keeping his promise to the London audience that his new play should also have 'Sir John in it'—the first mention of him is the news that he is on his death-bed already.

It may be said that all this is theory. In one sense it is; but in that sense all criticism is theory. My little story is a deduction from the facts; I believe it satisfies and accounts for the facts: only I would remind you again that the facts in such an enquiry as this, and in all literary criticism worthy the name, are not the measurable and quantitative facts of science, but more volatile and intangible reactions—intuitions and impressions. But, in their kind, the facts with which I have dealt are admitted: that

198

the Falstaff of the second part is inferior to the Falstaff of the first, and that the play itself is an inferior play; that *The Merry Wives* is of a quite different order from the other Falstaff plays: these judgments are the commonplaces of Shakespeare criticism. But the conclusions drawn from these judgments, when conclusions are drawn from them, are very different from mine. There are traditional conclusions, as there are traditional judgments. I feel I should be dealing unfairly if I did not examine them.

It is generally said that the degeneration of Falstaff in the second part is due to a deliberate dramatic intention on Shakespeare's part. Falstaff had to be shown in his true colours in order that the fate which awaited him at Prince Harry's hands should be seen to be deserved. So Falstaff is represented as 'in a progressive moral decline.' It is an argument which seems at first sight almost plausible. Then we begin to look at the facts. If we start out by considering Shakespeare wholly superhuman, a demi-god who could by nature make no mistakes, never feel tired, never get bored—well, we shall never be able to see the facts, we shall never be able even to *smell* them through the odour of sanctity. But if we keep our eyes clear, we shall, I think, admit quite freely that the second part of *Henry IV* as compared with the first is a very poor play. The comic scenes have no particular relation to the main dramatic action, and the main dramatic action can be given that name only by an effort of charity. The play, in fact, is slung together rather than designed. The chance that Shakespeare was following a deliberate plan in exhibiting Falstaff in a moral decline are exceedingly poor, to begin with.

But the real question is: Whether Falstaff *is* in a moral decline? Very likely it is true that we, the readers and the audience, are more conscious of his dubious morality in the second part and in *The Merry Wives*. But that is precisely what would happen if Shakespeare's creative power were weakening and he were failing to maintain his comic hero in the imaginative world in which alone he could truly live. For, in fact, neither in the second part nor in *The Merry Wives* are Falstaff's acts and sentiments by the smallest degree, by one single fraction of a commandment, less moral than they are in the first part. How could they be? We have only to listen to the description with which he was ushered into the world, to read the label tied round his neck when he was dropped from the creative heaven on to the boards of the Blackfriars Theatre, to know that moral degeneration is strictly inconceivable for Sir John.

'Thou art so fat-witted with drinking of old sack, and unbuttoning thee after supper, and sleeping on benches after noon, that thou hast forgotten to demand that truly which thou wouldst truly know. What a devil hast thou to do with the time of the day? Unless hours were cups of sack, and minutes capons, and clocks the tongues of bawds, and dials the signs of leaping-houses, and the blessed sun himself a fair hot wench in flame-coloured taffeta, I see no reason why thou shouldst be so superfluous as to demand the time of the day.'

And Falstaff does not deny it: it would be preposterous if he did. Even though he is notoriously reluctant to admit any imperfection in himself, he is forced to confess that his character has suffered by his keeping company with Prince Harry.

'Thou has done much harm upon me, Hal: God forgive thee for it! Before I knew thee, Hal, I knew nothing; and now am I, if a man should speak truly, little better than one of the wicked. I must give over this life, and I will give it over; by the Lord, an I do not, I am a villain: I'll be damned for never a king's son in Christendom.'

Falstaff was intelligent enough for a hundred, but it would have passed even his wit to find the way to degenerate from the moral altitude on which he is first presented to us.

The fact is that a truly comic character cannot degenerate morally, for he moves completely outside the kingdom of moral law. He can decline creatively, and quite frequently a creative decline is accompanied by a moral advance. Gogol's Tchichikov is a good case in point. And altogether, as Charles Lamb quite properly argued, the application of the moral judgment to comic heroes is merely a way of blinding ourselves to their real significance. So we are on our guard against the arguments of those who would interpret the fact that we begin to be conscious

200

of Falstaff's moral weakness as meaning that he is less moral than he was; it means simply that Shakespeare is failing to create him. A recent critic, in his desire to show that what Shakespeare did to Falstaff was deliberately done, has gone so far as to try to whitewash the Falstaff of the first part.

'The Falstaff of Part I,' he says, 'is a humorist pure and simple, against whom little that is really reprehensible can be urged. He takes part, it is true, in a highway robbery, but such an offence committed by high-spirited youths was venial, in the eyes of Shakespeare's contemporaries at least. Otherwise there is little evidence on which to impeach Falstaff, except such as he himself furnishes against himself; and that evidence may generally be allowed to pass as the product of a fertile imagination and humorous invention. In the second part, on the contrary, the character of Falstaff is presented unsympathetically and in a uniformly unfavourable light. . . . .'

The explanation of the phenomenon, as I have tried to show, is simple. The only light which falls on Falstaff is the light of Shakespeare's creativeness; when it begins to fail and flicker, we begin to be aware of him as a rather disreputable adventurer. He always was that, if we chose to regard him as a real man: but Shakespeare neither intended nor allowed us so to regard him.

In a lower social, but an equal artistic order Charles Dickens's Sarah Gamp is the object of the same sort of alchemy. If we were to consider that comic heroine realistically, she would appal us—as a kind of horrible and evil caricature of all that a nurse, a sister of Mercy, should be. But it is impossible to do this; or rather, we can do this only by taking her right out of the imaginative realm in which she has her being. In that realm she is not merely the creation of a rich fantasy, like Falstaff, but also like Falstaff (as George Gissing observed) she is herself endowed with the same sort of creative fantasy. Her Mrs. Harris is of the same stuff as Sir John's men in buckram at Gadshill. (And what a strange coincidence it is, by the bye, that this scene of Falstaff's imaginary and imaginative triumph should be so intimately associated with the genius of Dickens!

201

One is liable to the fancy that in this case Shakespeare's imagination, by giving airy nothing a local habitation and a name, had endowed Gadshill with a comic numen, a peculiar *genius loci*, which could be evoked again only by an imaginative power of the same order.) In both Falstaff and Mrs. Gamp the subtle magic of the alchemy resides in a bewildering richness or fecundity of language. For example when after the madly magnificent quarrel with Betsey Prig, in which Betsey declared of Mrs. Harris: "I don't believe there's no sich person," Mrs. Gamp gives utterance.

"If she had abuzed me, bein' in liquor, which I thought I smelt her when she come, but could not believe not bein' used myself, I could have bore it with a thankful art. But the words she spoke of Mrs. Harris, lambs could not forgive. No, Betsey!" said Mrs. Gamp, in a violent burst of feeling, "nor worms forget."

"Nor worms forget"—it is a supreme comic benediction, an uncovenanted mercy, poured out of the creative cornucopia. Before it comes, it is unimaginable. When it is come it is inevitable.

We know more about Dickens's creative methods than we do about Shakespeare's. Dickens said that he saw his creatures before him and only copied down what they said. We may, we must, believe him. One cannot imagine that extraordinary lingo of Mrs. Gamp's being set down by any other means: and it is reasonably certain that Shakespeare created Falstaff in the same way. The crux of the business therefore would appear to lie in the ability to "see"—in the mind's eye, Horatio—such characters. This capacity, one would suppose, could not be drawn upon at will. The appearance of Falstaff or Mrs. Gamp was as much the effect of a visitation as of a conjuration; and it was not really within the author's power to prolong the vital existence of the figure beyond the imaginative occasion—the original complex of imagined circumstances—which gave him birth.

Dickens lived in touch with his public to a degree surpassed perhaps only by Shakespeare. But he was master of the situation in a way that Shakespeare never was. At no period of his life can one imagine Dickens saying bitterly:

> "Alas, tis true, I have gone here and there
> And made myself a motley to the view,
> Gored mine own thoughts, sold cheap what is most
>   dear. . . ."

Partly because Dickens's sensibility was not quite so fine as Shakespeare's; but more because he had achieved a freedom with regard to the public which Shakespeare never enjoyed. If his readers had demanded more of Mrs. Gamp, he was in a position to ignore the clamour, confident that a new constellation of characters would be equally delightful to them. If Queen Victoria herself—*per impossibile*—had asked for more of Sairey and Betsey, Dickens would have been politely firm in refusing. So greatly had society and the status of the writer changed in 250 years.

Such affectionate mastery of the public as Dickens enjoyed, was never Shakespeare's. He *had* to produce more Falstaff, when the Queen or the mob called for it: and most probably, the Falstaff whom they demanded was quite as much a particular and favourite comic actor as the creature of Shakespeare's imagination. That made it easier for Shakespeare to comply. Very likely he could and did leave it partly to the comedian to make his own gags. Nothing for example will induce me to believe that Shakespeare himself *wrote* down: "His effect of gravy, gravy, gravy". I am not suggesting that Shakespeare did not intend to write Henry IV, Part II, or that he did not intend that Falstaff should be prominent in it. But the evidence, internal and external, is that he had to hurry over it more than he wanted. And because of this compulsion Shakespeare's imagination flagged. He had to force Falstaff before his mind's eye, rather than wait for him to appear. In consequence the cloud of comic glory by which he is enveloped and transfigured wears at times rather thin. We are more conscious of the disreputable "reality" than we ought to be; and the illusion is produced on some who should know better that Falstaff is in a moral decline—or even, on the assumption that Shakespeare is infallible and does everything with a definite artistic purpose, that Shakespeare deliberately represented him as a sordid knave in order to justify the Prince's repudiation of him.

But the details themselves do not for one moment bear out this theory of moral degeneration. As a matter of fact, if we consider them realistically, and imagine Falstaff brought before a police magistrate, it is clear that Falstaff's crimes are less serious in the second part then they are in the first. If in the first they are venial, then they are less than venial in the second. He equally misused the King's Press in both plays. To get yet another ten pounds out of Mistress Quickly—was that a crime when the lady herself condoned it? To borrow a thousand pounds of Justice Shallow, of which the lender would never see even five hundred back again—if Sir John had nothing worse than this on his conscience, Mistress Quickly was right in saying, 'Nay, sure, he is in Arthur's bosom.' And so far from being presented in a uniformly unfavourable light, he is represented as having gained, and somehow as having deserved, the loyalty both of Doll Tearsheet and Mistress Quickly. You may, if you choose, regard Mistress Quickly's parting words merely as the evidence that she, after the reputed habit of her sex, insists on being gulled:

> 'Well, fare thee well; I have known thee these twenty-nine
> years come peascod-time, but an honester, truer-hearted man
> —well, fare thee well.'

But the effect of them on most well-ordered sensibilities is quite simple. Mistress Quickly means what she says, and Falstaff, not for what he does but for what he is, deserves that it should be said of him. And up till now no one who was not engaged in making a case has ever thought Bardolph a fool for wanting to be with him wherever he was, or Mistress Quickly a dupe for being certain he was not in hell.

No, it would be truer to our impressions to say not merely that Shakespeare was not engaged in Part II in presenting Falstaff in a uniformly unfavourable light, but that he was trying at moments to make amends for the creative injustice he knew he was doing to the creature of his imagination. The injustices were two: first, Falstaff had to be produced again when Shakespeare was not in the mood for him; second, and more important, Shakespeare had involved him in a catastrophe that was inevitable. A being who belonged to the ether of pure comedy had to be brought back into the world of fact and history. He was bound to languish and die. What conceivable action of King Harry's could have mitigated his fate? The only thing that could have been done was that Shakespeare should transfigure the traditional history of England into the same creative world as he had done in Part I. Sooner or later, in such an enterprise, the facts became adamant. Harry the warrior-king was a fact not to be trifled with, any more than Lord Roberts or Lord Kitchener could be trifled with by a popular playwright nowadays. The audience knew quite well what he ought to be, and eventually Shakespeare had to vamp up a very moderate play—with some patches of dazzling rhetoric—to provide them with what they wanted. But we can imagine him with a consciousness of guilt towards the creature he had been forced to betray.

The Falstaff whom the King of England was bound to repudiate was not the Falstaff whom Shakespeare had created. One was a common ne'er-do-well; the other was an incarnation of the very spirit of comedy. Shakespeare had to pretend that they were the same person; he had to drag his hero down to an earth where he was never meant to live, and inflict upon him a disgrace which he could not possibly have deserved. No one can doubt that Falstaff at his birth was beloved of his begetter. Since his penultimate sufferings were not to be avoided, Shakespeare, who was tired of the labours he had been forced to undergo for Falstaff's sake, would pull himself together and try to ensure that the creature of his brain should make a good end. Once more Shakespeare achieved the miracle. Nothing Falstaff ever said is more magical than the talk of Mistress Quickly and Bardolph and the page about his death: nothing is more truly his own than these words he did not speak, by which he is uplifted once more into that ethereal kingdom from which his creator had been forced to force him to descend, in order that the king should 'kill his heart.'

BARD.: Would I were with him, wheresome'er he is, either in heaven or in hell!

HOST.: Nay, sure he's not in hell; he's in Arthur's bosom.

A'made a finer end and went away an it had been any christom child; a' parted even just between twelve and one, even at the turning o' the tide: for after I saw him fumble with the sheets and play with flowers and smile upon his fingers' ends, I knew there was but one way; for his nose was as sharp as a pen, and a' babbled of green fields. 'How now, Sir John.' quoth I. 'What man. Be of good cheer.' So a' cried out: 'God, God, God.' three or four times. Now I, to comfort him, bid him a' should not think of God, I hoped there was no need to trouble himself with any such thoughts yet. So a' bade me lay more clothes on his feet: I put my hand into the bed and felt them, and they were as cold as any stone; then I felt to his knees, and so upward, and all was as cold as any stone.

Every time I read it, that extraordinary passage works the same magic upon me. It seems to me that never was a more sovereign portion of Shakespeare's surpassing genius crammed into a bare two hundred words. Their beauty is as great as their simplicity. Yet what a miracle is accomplished in them! These three creatures, of the earth earthy and it might seem of the very commonest clay, are transfigured in our sight, by the divine compulsion of two hundred simple words. Not one is recondite; everyone belongs to the everyday speech of the common folk: yet for concentrated loveliness of sound and sense, they stand at the very pinnacle of poetic achievement.

The words laugh and cry, they smile and are solemn. As the sun a mist, they scatter the foolish imaginations of petty men. The love that utters itself in them sweeps triumphantly over the conceits of religion. Bardolph—he of the glowing nose—in fourteen words sets his master and himself in a place where the gates of Hell cannot prevail against them. Dame Quickly, in bidding Sir John a should not think of God, covers him in the radiance of that love which is alone divine. She gathers him under her wing like a nestling; sees in him the innocence which, if God condemns, He ceases to be God; and lifts him straight into the Heaven whose reality none can deny.

O battered and blessed and radiant trinity, created by the imagination of an Englishman, engendered by the love he cherished towards these creatures of his invention, whom he had been forced to betray into the toils of fact and history! O magnificent redemption! O incredible translucent mystery of love and loyalty in Shakespeare's heart, and of genius in his mind, to utter in such a fashion, the absolute of simplicity, the absolute of beauty and the absolute of truth!

THE END OF HERMAN MELVILLE

In 1851 Herman Melville published *Moby Dick*; in the next five years *Pierre*, which was received with cold hostility, *Israel Potter* and the *Piazza Tales*. Then, to all intents and purposes, there was silence until his death, which did not come till thirty-five years later, in 1891.

The silence of a great writer needs to be listened to. If he has proved his genius, then his silence is an utterance, and one of hardly less moment than his speech. It is easy to talk of flagging creative energy ; but men are not given the power of the word by some capricious daemon who touches their lips now to leave them dumb hereafter. The silence of a writer who has the vision that Melville revealed in *Moby Dick* and *Pierre* is not an accident without adequate cause : and our feeling that silence was the only appropriate epilogue to Melville's masterpiece is the form of our instinctive recognition that the adequate cause was there. After *Moby Dick* there was, in a sense, nothing to be said, just as after *King Lear* there seemed nothing for Shakespeare to say. Shakespeare, who was greater than Melville, did find another utterance in *Antony and Cleopatra*: then he too was silent. For, whatever names we may give to the 'romantic' plays of his final period, and however high the praises we sincerely heap upon them, they belong to another order and have a significance of another kind than the great tragedies. They are, essentially, the work of a man who has nothing more to *say*, but who is artist and genius enough at last to contrive a method of saying even that.

Herman Melville could not do that, but then nobody save Shakespeare has been able to work that miracle. Probably Melville knew exactly what Shakespeare had achieved in the faint, far reflection of *The Tempest*, for in the *Battle-pieces and other Poems* (1866) with which he made scarce so much as a ripple in his own silence, is this strangely irrelevant verse on Shakespeare :

> No utter surprise can come to him
> Who reaches Shakespeare's core ;

    That which we seek and shun is there—
    Man's final lore.

That is the highest claim ever made for Shakespeare, and the truest. It was made by one who had a right to speak, *en connaissance de cause* : for *Moby Dick* belongs to the same order as *Macbeth* and *King Lear* ; it is inspired by the same knowledge and disturbed by the same tremors ; it is, as they are, superhuman. It contains, as they do, the terrible and tremendous discovery made by a man big enough to take the risks and pay the price for ' man's final lore.' Melville knew where Shakespeare had been : no doubt he also knew where Shakespeare at last arrived, but he could not communicate those mysterious faint echoes of a certitude—that certitude 'which we seek and shun'—which are gathered together into *The Tempest*.

    Yet Melville was trying to say more during his long silence. How much he struggled with his dumbness we cannot say : perhaps during most of those thirty-five years he acquiesced in it. But something was at the back of his mind, haunting him, and this is something he could not utter. If we handle the clues carefully we may reach a point from which we too may catch a glimpse of it ; but then, by the nature of things, we shall be unable to utter what we see. We can only indicate the clues. They are to be found, one at the beginning and one at the end of the silence. *Pierre* is at the beginning. It is, judged by the standards which are traditional in estimating a ' work of art,' a complete failure. The story is naïve, amateur-ish, melodramatic, wildly improbable, altogether unreal. Let those who are persuaded that a novel is a good story and nothing more avoid *Pierre*. But those who feel that the greatest novels are something quite different from a good story should seek it out: to them it will be strange and fascinating, and they will understand why its outward semblance is clumsy and puerile. Melville is trying to reveal a mystery : he is trying to show that the completely good man is doomed to complete disaster on earth, and he is trying to show at the same time that this must be so, and that it ought to be so. The necessity of that 'ought to be so' can be interpreted in two ways : as Melville calls them, horologically or chronometrically. Horologically, that is, estimated by our local and earthly time-pieces, the disaster of the good ought to be so, because there is no room for unearthly perfection on earth: chronometrically, that is, estimated by the unvarying recorder of the absolute, it ought to be so because it is a working out, a manifestation, of the absolute, though hidden, harmony of the ideal and the real. In other words, Melville was trying to reveal anew the central mystery of the Christian religion.

He did not succeed. How could he succeed? Nobody understood *Pierre*, apparently nobody had even a glimmering understanding of it. And the thirty-five years of silence began. At the extreme end of them, moved perhaps by a premonition of coming death, Melville wrote another 'story.' *Billy Budd* is carefully dated : it was begun on November 16, 1888, the re-writing began on March 2, 1889, and it was finished on April 19, 1891. In the following September Melville was dead. With the mere fact of the long silence in our minds we cannot help regarding *Billy Budd* as the last will and spiritual testament of a man of genius. We could not help expecting this, if we have any imaginative understanding. Of course, if we are content to dismiss, in our minds if not in our words, the man of genius as mad, there is no need to trouble. Someone is sure to have told us that *Billy Budd*, like *Pierre*, is a tissue of *naïveté* and extravagance : that will be enough. And, truly, *Billy Budd is* like *Pierre*, startlingly, terribly like. Once more Melville is telling the story of the inevitable and utter disaster of the good and trying to convey to us that this must be so and ought to be so—chronometrically and horologically. He is trying, as it were with his final breath, to reveal the knowledge that has been haunting him—that these things must be so and not otherwise.

Billy Budd is a foretopman, pressed out of the merchant service into the King's Navy in the year of the Nore mutiny. He is completely good, not with the sickly goodness of self-conscious morality, but as one born into earthly paradise—strong, young, manly, loyal, brave, unsuspecting, admired by his officers and adored by his shipmates. And he is hated by the master-at-arms, the policeman of the lower deck. Claggart hates him, simply because he is Billy Budd, with the instinctive and ineffaceable hatred of the evil for the good. Melville is careful to explain that there is no reason whatever for his hatred, he puts it deliberately before us as naked and elemental —the clash of absolutes. Claggart is subtle and cool, he works quietly, and he is a man of courage. He involves Billy Budd in the thin semblance of revolutionary mutiny. No more is possible, Billy Budd being what he is, and the semblance is almost transparent: Claggart knows the risk he is taking in denouncing the foretopman to Captain Vere, who has remarked and admired him. The master-at-arms deliberately risks his own life in order to destroy his enemy's. He risks it, and loses it, for in the privacy of his own cabin the captain confronts the accuser with his victim and in a flash of anger Budd strikes the master-at-arms dead. The moment in the story is unearthly.

But Billy Budd is doomed : he has killed his officer in time of war. The captain who understands and loves him presides over the court-martial, and Budd is condemned to be hanged at dawn. Before dawn the crew is piped to quarters.

Billy stood facing aft. At the penultimate moment, his words, his only ones, words wholly unobstructed in the utterance were these — 'God bless Captain Vere!' Syllables so unanticipated coming from one with the ignominious hemp about his neck—a conventional felon's benediction directed aft towards the quarters of honour ; syllables, too, delivered in the clear melody of a singing bird on the point of launching from the twig, had a phenomenal effect, not unenhanced by the rare personal beauty of the young sailor, spiritualised now through late experiences so poignantly profound.

Without volition, as it were, as if indeed the ship's populace were the vehicles of some vocal current electric, with one voice, from alow and aloft, came a resonant echo— 'God bless Captain Vere.' And yet at that instant Billy alone must have been in their hearts, even as he was in their eyes.

At the pronounced words and the spontaneous echo that

211

voluminously rebounded them, Captain Vere, either through stoic self-control or a sort of momentary paralysis induced by emotional shock, stood erectly rigid as a musket in the ship-armourer's rack.

The hull, deliberately recovering from the periodic roll to leeward, was just regaining an even keel, when the last signal, the preconcerted dumb one, was given. At the same moment it chanced that the vapoury fleece hanging low in the east was shot through with a soft glory as of the fleece of the Lamb of God seen in the mystical vision, and simultaneously therewith, watched by the wedged mass of upturned faces, Billy ascended ; and ascending, took the full rose of the dawn.

In the pinioned figure, arrived at the yard end, to the wonder of all, no motion was apparent save that created by the slow roll of the hull, in moderate weather so majestic in a great ship heavy-cannoned.

That is the story, told with a strange combination of naïve simplicity and majestic serenity—the revelation of a mystery. It was Melville's final word, worthy of him, indisputably a passing beyond the tremendous nihilism of *Moby Dick*, to what may seem to some simple and childish, but to others will be wonderful and divine.

[1927]

THE DIVINE PLAIN FACE

In the National Portrait Gallery, among the portraits of female Victorian celebrities, from George Eliot to Harriet Martineau, is a pencil drawing of a lovely face—a wild woodland gleam amid the rigours of high seriousness. You look and look; looking is enough, but it brings no word. For there is singularly little to be *said* about that face. Its charm lies in some exquisite perfection of ordinariness, which belies the emphasis of adjectives. This loveliness is immune from the caprice of fashion, unruffled by the breath of any *Zeitgeist*. Were it met to-morrow, or a hundred years hence, it would be recognized straightway for what it was; as some one met it more than a hundred years ago, and fell in love, and found the perfect phrase.

For this is Charles Lamb's Fanny Kelly, of Drury Lane, and 'the divine plain face'; and this is, as near as may be, the face as it was when its glimpses haunted him at his desk in East India House. There is nothing on the drawing to tell you that it is veritably she; in her company of female celebrities she has taken on a protective colouring and become Frances Maria Kelly (1790-1882). The drawing was taken in 1822, when she was thirty-two. Three years before, Charles Lamb had proposed to her and been rejected. She lived to be ninety-two, and never married.

The story is no secret; yet not so familiar that it will not bear retelling. It contains, I fancy, more of the elusive essence of Charles Lamb that any other single episode of that well-mastered life.

When Charles Lamb's admiration of Fanny Kelly first began there is no saying. She was on the stage of Drury Lane at seven years old; at eleven she was playing Prince Arthur to Mrs. Siddon's Constance, and feeling the great actress's tears (real tears!) drop warm upon her neck. The first sign made by Charles Lamb was in 1813, in the first dramatic criticism he wrote for a newspaper, Leigh Hunt's *Examiner*. In his article he contrasted the old acting and the new, of course to the advantage of the old. The new school was tainted with the vice of playing to the audience, not the play: but there was one bright exception :

> I am sure that the very absence of this fault in Miss Kelly and her judicious attention to her part, with little or no reference to the spectators, is one cause why her varied excellencies, though they are beginning to be perceived, have yet found their way more slowly to the approbation of the public than they have deserved.

Probably at this time—when Fanny was twenty-three and Lamb thirty-eight—was written the poetic version of the same sentiment which appeared in the *Works* of 1818 as a sonnet :

TO MISS KELLY.

You are not, Kelly, of the common strain,
That stoop their pride and female honour down
To please that many-headed beast, *the town*,
And vend their lavish smiles and tricks for gain;
By fortune thrown amid the actor's train
You keep your native dignity of thought;
The plaudits that attend you come unsought,
As tributes due unto your natural vein.
Your tears have passion in them, and a grace
Of genuine freshness, which our hearts avow;
Your smiles are winds whose ways we cannot trace,
That vanish and return we know not how—
And please the better from a pensive face
And thoughtful eye, and a reflecting brow.

Soon after 1813, I imagine, they became acquainted. For, though it is not till October, 1817, that her name appears in his letters, the habit of talking to her in the green-room was by that time of old standing. 'Have you' (he writes to the Kenneys in France) any play and green-rooms, and Fanny Kellys to chat to?' A little later (in February, 1818) he writes to Wordsworth as though his admiration for Fanny Kelly were familiar to his friends, with a confession of 'the darling thoughts all his own' that might occupy his mind at his ledgers, were it not for the interruptions of 'a set of amateurs of the Belles Lettres— a faint memory of some passage in a Book—or the tone of an absent friend's voice—a snatch of Miss Burrell's singing—a

214

gleam of Fanny Kelly's divine plain face.'

In December, 1818, he published an anonymous note in the *Examiner* complaining that Miss Kelly was not in the new comedy at Drury Lane: he had seen her sitting among the spectators. What was the reason? Was there a cabal against her among the managers? I fancy that this little note was inspired,' and that it was with Charles Lamb that Fanny Kelly was sitting in the theatre. Next month, January, 1819, he published the following unsigned comparison of Fanny Kelly with her famous predecessor:

Mrs. Jordan's was the carelessness of a child . . . she seemed one whom care could not come near. . . . . Hence, if we had more unmixed pleasure from her performances, we had perhaps less sympathy with them than with those of her successor. The latter lady's is the joy of a freed spirit, escaping from care, as a bird that has been limed: her smiles, if I may use the expression, seem saved out of the fire, relics which a good and innocent heart had snatched up as most portable; her contents are visitors, not inmates; she can lay them by altogether, and when she does so I am not sure that she is not greatest. . . .

I do not know whether I am not speaking it to her honour, that she does not succeed in what are called fine lady parts. Our friend C. once observed that no man of genius ever figured as a gentleman.

In this the *personal* preoccupation is manifest. Lamb is not merely considering Fanny Kelly as an actress; but he is evidently bent on separating the woman from the actress to the uttermost, driving, indeed, with all his delicate strength, a wedge between them. Fanny Kelly's function, for him, is to be herself. When her part permits it he is satisfied; when it does not he is malcontent.

By July he is still further advanced in admiration, and goes one further in his criticism. He writes on Fanny Kelly's appearance in Brome's *Jovial Crew*.

The Princess of Mumpers was *she* that played Rachel. Her gabbling, lachrymose petitions; her tones such as we have heard by the side of old woods when an irresistible face has come

215

peeping on one on a sudden: with the full black locks, and a *voice*—how shall we describe it?—a voice that was by nature meant to convey nothing but truth and goodness, but warped by circumstance into an assurance that she is telling us a lie . . . her jeers, which we had rather stand, than be caressed by other ladies' compliments, a summer's day long—her face, with a wild out-of-doors grace upon it. . . . No less than the "Beggar Maid" whom "King Cophetua wooed."

' "What a lass that were," said a stranger who sate beside us, speaking of Miss Kelly as *Rachel*, "to go a gipseying through the world with!"

Charles Lamb's stranger, without a doubt, bore the same name as he. Nothing more nearly resembling a proposal of marriage ever did, or ever will, masquerade as a dramatic criticism. As far as man could he had prepared the way: it remained only for him to take the plunge *in propria persona*. Another fortnight, and it was done. On July 20th he wrote to Fanny Kelly:

'Dear Miss Kelly,—We had the pleasure, *pain* I might better call it, of seeing you last night in the new Play. It was a most consummate piece of Acting but what a task for you to undergo! at a time when your heart is sore from real sorrow! It has given rise to a train of thinking, which I cannot suppress.

'Would to God you were released from this way of life; that you could bring your mind to consent to share your lot with us, and throw off for ever the whole burden of your Profession. I neither expect nor wish you to take notice of this which I am writing in your present over-occupied and hurried state.—But to think of it at your leisure. I have quite income enough, if that were all, to justify for me making such a proposal, with what I may call even a handsome provision for my survivor. What you possess of your own would naturally be appropriated to those, for whose sakes chiefly you have made such sacrifices. I am not so foolish as not to know that I am a most unworthy match for such a one as you, but you have for years been a principal object in my mind. In many a sweet assumed character I have learned to love you, but simply as F. M. Kelly I love you better than them all. Can you quit these shadows of existence, and

216

come and be a reality to us   Can you leave off harassing your-self to please a thankless multitude, who know nothing of you, and begin at last to live to yourself and your friends.

'As plainly and frankly as I have seen you give or refuse assent in some feigned scene, so frankly do me the justice to answer me. It is impossible I should feel injured or aggrieved by your telling me at once, that the proposal does not suit you. It is impossible that I should ever think of molesting you with idle importunity and persecution after your mind once fairly spoken—but happier, far happier, could I have leave to hope a time might come, when our friends might be your friends, our interests, yours; our book-knowledge, if in that inconsiderable particular we have any advantage, might impart something to you, which you would every day have it in your power ten thousand fold to repay by the added cheerfulness and joy which you could not fail to bring as a dowry into whatever family should have the honour and happiness of receiving *you*, the most welcome accession that could be made to it.

'In haste, but with entire respect and deepest affection, I subscribe myself.

'C. LAMB.'

Prompt indeed came the reply:

'Henrietta St., July 20, 1819.

'An early and deeply-rooted attachment has fixed my heart on one from whom no worldly prospect can well induce me to withdraw it, but while I thus *frankly* and decidedly decline your proposal, believe me, I am not insensible to the high honour which the preference of such a mind as yours confers upon me —let me, however, hope that all thought upon this subject will end with this letter, and that you will henceforth encourage no sentiment towards me than esteem in my private character and a continuance of that approbation of my humble talents which you have already expressed so much and so often to my advant-age and gratification.

'Believe me I feel proud to acknowledge myself

'Your obliged friend

'F. M. KELLY.'

217

It is almost a model of the common form of the period: 'How to decline an offer of Marriage,' I wonder whether the myriad lovely ladies who made use of it—'Let me, however, hope that all thought upon this subject will end, etc.' really expected, or really desired, that their commands should be obeyed. If they did, women have changed in a hundred years; for I am told, on excellent authority, that the women of to-day find no small pleasure in the knowledge that they are the objects of a fruitless passion.

Lamb, however, played the game according to the rules; and characteristically went one better. Still on the same day, July 20th, he replied:

'Dear Miss Kelly,—*Your injunctions shall be obeyed to a tittle.* I feel myself in a lackadaisical no-how-ish kind of a humour. I believe it is the rain, or something. I had thought to have written seriously, but I fancy I succeed best in epistles of mere fun; puns and *that* nonsense. You will be good friends with us, will you not? let what has past 'break no bones' between us.[1] You will not refuse us them next time we send for them.

'Yours very truly,

' C. L.'

'Do you observe the delicacy of not signing my full name? 'N.B.—Do not paste that last letter of mine into your Book.'

I would give much to know precisely how Fanny Kelly felt on receiving that. Was she hurt? Or sad? Or did she merely feel that there was no accounting for Charles Lamb. And what did she feel when, a fortnight later, she read the epilogue to this little love-story in print in the *Examiner*? Charles Lamb wrote of her performance in *The Hypocrite*:

Miss Kelly is not quite at home in *Charlotte*; she is too good for such parts. Her cue is to be natural; she cannot put on the modes of artificial life, and play the coquet as it is expected to be played. There is a frankness in her tones which defeats her purposes. . . . . She is in truth not framed to tease or torment even in jest, but to utter a hearty *Yes* or *No*; to yield or refuse

---

[1] The "bones" here were the tokens which served as passes into the theatre.

218

assent with a noble sincerity. We have not the pleasure of being acquainted with her, but we have been told she carres the same cordial manners into private life.

That was the end of Lamb's brief career as a dramatic critic. Since every one of his newspaper criticisms was concerned with Fanny Kelly, and since they end promptly with his proposal and rejection, we may conclude not only that he originally embraced the career for the sole purpose of singing Fanny Kelly's praises, but that, perhaps unconsciously, it was to him a means of preparing the way to his offer of marriage. In fact, it was Charles Lamb's peculiar method of courtship. Once he was refused the courtship ceased.

But it is not easy to get a real glimpse of Fanny Kelly through Charles Lamb's rose-coloured spectacles. One feels that here for once his good-humoured and whimsical faculty for seeing things as they are had failed him a little. There is that in the tone of a part of his truly charming letter of proposal which makes me suspect that he had misconceived the situation, by imputing to Fanny Kelly herself his own sense that the theatre was a bondage (and a little even of a degradation) to her. That was what Lamb felt; the feeling peeps out plainly in his criticisms, And, no doubt, Fanny Kelly herself in conversation lent substance to Lamb's eager imagination. Artists of all kinds are prone to talk to the admiring and sympathetic listener of the burden of their lives; but it does not mean they want to change them. Lamb would have understood this well enough of any other person; but of Fanny Kelly he was only too willing to believe that she felt herself as a caged bird behind the footlights—a fine spirit, like Ariel, waiting for the word of freedom.

How Lamb was inclined to romanticize Fanny Kelly appears plainly from his story of 'Barbara S—' which was avowedly based on an incident of Fanny's childhood. In that story, you may remember, the little actress Barbara, aged eleven, goes to draw her weekly half-guinea, on which her family wholly depended. By mistake the Treasurer pops into her hand a whole guinea. Not till she reaches the first landing of the stairs does she notice it; the struggle in her mind whether to return

219

or no carries her to the second. Then virtue triumphs, and she returns. In her old age Fanny Kelly told the true story, and told it extraordinary well—better, I think, than Lamb had done. At least, I find nothing in Lamb's story so moving and so real as the anxious question put to little Fanny as she returns from the paybox by a grown woman of the company: 'Is it full pay, my dear.' That is the real accent of behind the scenes in the old days.

The true story, as Fanny Kelly told it in 1875, was of a mistake between a one-pound and a two-pound note. The two-pound note, given her by mistake, had been torn and joined again with a thick strip of gummed paper

Now observe (she wrote) in what small matters Fanny and Barbara were to a marked degree different characters. Barbara, at eleven years of age, was some time before she felt the different size of a guinea to a half-guinea, *held tight in her hand*. I, at nine years old, was not so untaught, or innocent. I was a woman of the world. I took *nothing* for granted. I had a deep respect for Mr. Peake, but the join might have disfigured the note—destroyed its currency; and it was my business to see all safe. So I carefully opened it.'

There is surely a sub-acid flavour in the comment: 'I was a woman of the world.' Probably, all through her friendship with Charles Lamb she was a little more of the woman of the world than he wanted to, or did, believe. In her later life she confessed that the reason why she did not accept his proposal was her fear of the strain of madness in the family. Perhaps, also, £600 a year was rather less in her eyes than it was in his: for when she retired from the stage in 1835, she retired with a competence of £13,000. To be sure, she lost it not long after, by building a small theatre, where she opened an academy of dramatic art, which failed. The theatre is now the Royalty in Dean Street.

Fanny Kelly was assuredly none the worse for being 'a woman of the world': it was her business to be. In her face one discovers a sense of realities; it is a frank and open face, but not a dreamer's; the charm is open and above-board, the charm of a charming friend. And a friend of the Lambs she

220

remained. The next year Mary Lamb was teaching her Latin; and it was then, I imagine, that little Mary Novello, who was also being taught Latin by Mary Lamb in Lamb's rooms in Russell Street, saw a lady come in who appeared to her strikingly intellectual looking, and still young: she was surprised, therefore, to hear the lady say, in the course of conversation, 'Oh, as for me, my dear Miss Lamb, I'm nothing now but a stocking-mending old woman.' It was Fanny Kelly. Mary Novello records having seen her twice again—once, elegantly dressed, drinking porter out of a tankard with Charles and Mary Lamb on a bench before an inn near Enfield, and, for the last time, when the Lambs were dead and gone, during the rehearsals of the famous performance of 'The Merry Wives' which Dickens arranged in 1848. Fanny Kelly was coaching the company of amateurs, Mary Novello—then Mary Cowden Clarke—among them. 'Keep your eyes on the people in the upper row of boxes, my dear,' said Fanny. 'Then your under eyelids will save you from the glare of the footlights.' Good, sound professional advice, no doubt; but Charles Lamb's shade may have winced a little to hear it.

[1925]

CORIOLANUS

Criticism is oddly undecided about *Coriolanus*. Is it because *Coriolanus* is the most neglected of Shakespeare's greater plays? Or is the play neglected because of the indecision it provokes? The divergence of opinion about it is extraordinary. Mr. Lytton Strachey, for instance, declared that 'rhetoric, enormously magnificent and extraordinarily elaborate, is the beginning and the middle and the end of *Coriolanus*. The hero is not a human being at all.' Mr Bernard Shaw, on the other hands, puts Coriolanus with Faulconbridge as 'admirable descriptions of instinctive temperaments,' and says, with intelligible paradox, that 'the play of *Coriolanus* is the greatest of Shakespeare's comedies.' Mr. T. S. Eliot has maintained that *Coriolanus* is Shakespeare's 'most perfect work of art.'

Divergence of this kind does not in the least resemble a recent controversy as to whether *Hamlet* is an æsthetic success or an æsthetic failure. All the world, and not least the particular disputants, is agreed that *Hamlet* is a mighty work; its precise degree of perfection alone is in debate: its greatness is admitted. Quite otherwise with *Coriolanus*. Nobody seems quite certain if it is a great play or not. and it is so seldom performed that there is no consensus of popular opinion as to its dramatic merits. The reason why it is so seldom performed is that the theme is unsympathetic to the ordinary man, who cannot accept as a tragic hero one whose ungovernable pride forces him to become a renegade. It is to this instinctive sentiment that Mr Shaw gives paradoxical expression when he says that *Coriolanus* is the greatest of Shakespeare's comedies. Coriolanus is human enough, but he is so human that we are angry with him for not behaving more sensibly; we do not feel that his conduct is inevitable, like Othello's; we prefer to say that it is life-like. By one burst of temper he exiles himself from Rome, by a second he kills himself. Nothing is changed in him—as he was at the beginning of the play so he is at the end. Whereas a tragic hero *deserves* to die. Coriolanus does not. A hero of great Shakesperian tragedy deserves to die because we cannot conceive him continuing to live. But the death of Coriolanus is a shock to us; we are not surprised that Shakespeare scamped it and, by making Aufidius repent it on the instant, turned it into an accident. To put the matter irreverently, Coriolanus is a big schoolboy; Molière might have disposed of him better than Shakespeare.

Still, not even Molière could have made him live as Shakespeare has. To say, as Mr. Strachey says, that he is not a human being at all, is indeed astonishing. He is, of course. a human being of a quite different kind from the heroes of the great tragedies; but he is more of the mere human being than they Compared with Antony, it is true, he is almost thin-blooded; but who is not thin and unsubstantial compared to that King of men? In his own play and his own setting, Coriolanus is absolutely convincing. He is not so complete a man as Antony; he inhabits a sphere of more primitive development, but within that sphere he is fixed as solid as a rock. Coriolanus is Shakespeare's Homeric hero; and it is largely because of the completeness with which he is presented that his tragic end becomes perfunctory. That such a man should meet with a violent end is too natural to be inevitable; his death is a physical rather than a spiritual consummation. To give it a spiritual significance Shakespeare needed to employ another Iago, to arrange the toils into which the instinctive man must fall. But there was no Iago in the story. It is true he might have made Aufidius into one. At the beginning, indeed, he seems to have intended to. Aufidius's speech at the end of the first act:

> Mine emulation
> Hath not that honour in't it had, for where
> I thought to crush him in an equal force,
> True sword to sword. I'll potch at him some way
> Or wrath or craft may get him—

begins to put an Iago before us; but Shakespeare could not hold him to his task. Aufidius also, at the critical moment becomes the instinctive Homeric hero. When Coriolanus appeals to him at Antium, he reveals himself as Coriolanus's blood-brother, incapable of treasons, stratagems, or spoils; and

there he is so fully presented that the faint-hearted indications
of his subsequent designs have no power to change the figure
before us. We feel that he acts in a rage of sudden jealousy,
in a burst of temper, like Coriolanus himself. 'My rage is
gone', he says, 'and I am struck with sorrow.' That is true
of the Aufidius Shakespeare has actually given us; it is not
true of the Aufidius he began by giving us. Aufidius-Iago
might have made Coriolanus's death inevitable; the Aufidius
we have makes it an accident.

Aufidius is the weak point of the play. Dramatically, his
function was to play in the second part of the drama the *rôle*
held by Sicinius and Brutus, the Tribunes, in the first, but to
play it with more steadiness of hatred even than they, because
Aufidius has to compass Coriolanus's death, while the Tribunes
need only his exile. But whereas the Tribunes play their part
to the life, and we know and follow and comprehend their
every move in entangling Coriolanus in his own weakness,
Aufidius is as impulsive as Coriolanus himself, and as evidently
incapable of plotting as he. Instead of being plainer to us
than Sicinius and Brutus, he becomes more shadowy.

But Coriolanus is magnificent, and in so far as he is the
play, the play is magnificent also. He is Plato's man of impulse to the life. When his wounds are mentioned we see the
schoolboy blush, with more of vanity than true modesty in it,
come to his face. He cannot remember the name of the man
of Corioli for whose freedom he begs. 'Marcius, his name?'
asks Lartius.

> By Jupiter, forgot!
> I am weary; yea, my memory is tired.
> Have we no wine here?

Thus swiftly is the physical man presented? Coriolanus knows
nothing of himself. His consciousness, his memory, his purpose
—these are all in the keeping of his mother Volumnia, or
Menenius. His mind is sharp and his eye clear only on the
battlefield. When he turns away from it, he is bewildered and
lost in a strange country. He cannot notice things or people;
he barely recognises the wife whom he loves. The idea that
he should behave in the city with the same circumspection

224

with which he orders a battle or takes in a town is quite incomprehensible to him; when his mother suggests it, he cannot understand. It is Volumnia, not he, who has the Consulship in mind when he returns victorious; his mind is in abeyance for plans beyond the battlefield. He does what he is told, like a reluctant child, and, after the fatal outburst of his anger against the citizens, he is hopeless and pathetic; he feels his mother has deserted him.

> I muse my mother
> Does not approve me further, who was wont
> To call them woollen vassals.

And he returns, after much persuasion, to make amends like a child, repeating the key-word of his conduct in case he should forget it. 'The word is mildly.' Past and future have no existence for him. He remembers only what he feels, the burning glow of an insult that has not been revenged, and not till he sees his mother and his wife before him has he an inkling that he is committing an act of shame in threatening his own city, Rome, with fire and sword. Till that moment Rome is no more than the source of his insult. At the last, with one of those amazing strokes of whose sheer simplicity lesser writers are afraid, Shakespeare makes him turn on Aufidius.

> AUF.: Name not the God, thou boy of tears!
> COR.: Ha!
> AUF.: No more.
> COR.: Measureless liar, thou hast made my heart
> Too great for what contains it. Boy! O slave!
> Pardon me, lords, 'tis the first time that ever
> I was forced to scold.

The first time! It is hopeless. Coriolanus is lost in life.

Seeing how marvellously Coriolanus is put before us, it is hard to understand the difficulty which has been felt by many critics concerning Coriolanus's conduct in advancing against his native city. It is apparently felt that his renegade act needs more explanation than Shakespeare has given. These are Mr.A. C. Bradley's words:

As I have remarked, Shakespeare does not exhibit to us

225

the change of mind which issues in this frightful purpose; but from what we see and hear, we can tell now he imagined it and the key lies in that idea of *burning* Rome. As time passes, and no suggestion of recall reaches Coriolanus, and he learns what it is to be a solitary, homeless exile, his heart hardens, his pride swells to a mountainous bulk, and the wound in it becomes a fire. The fellow patricians from whom he parted lovingly now appear to him ingrates and dastards, scarcely better than the loathsome mob. Somehow, he knows not how, even his mother and wife have deserted him. He has become nothing to Rome, and Rome shall hear nothing from him. Here in solitude he can find no relief in a storm of words; but gradually the blind intolerable chaos of resentment conceives and gives birth to a vision, not merely of battle and indiscriminate slaughter, but of the whole city one tower of flame. To see that with his bodily eye would satisfy his soul; and the way to the sight is through the Volscians. . . . This is Shakespeare's idea, not Plutarch's. In Plutarch there is not a syllable about the burning of Rome.

Yet, with all deference to so great an authority, we cannot help feeling that this is Mr. Bradley's idea, not Shakespeare's. Certainly, there is a good deal of talk about the burning of Rome. The Tribunes and Menenius take it for granted; Cominius reports that Coriolanus's eye is 'red as he would burn Rome.' But our impression is not that it is particularly insisted on: it recurs merely, and we also, like the Tribunes and Menenius, take it for granted. Coriolanus intends revenge.

Mr. Bradley is trying to circumvent the difficulty of Coriolanus's monstrous purpose. He does not leave Rome vowing revenge; he seems to agree with Cominius that he may be recalled; 'I shall be loved,' he says, 'when I am lacked.' Yet, when he reappears, he reappears as the renegade whose fixed purpose is the destruction of Rome. All this is true. But what of it? Shakespeare's Coriolanus sees neither before nor after. He is ignorant of his own nature as a savage. How should the man who cried at the last moment of his life: ''Tis the first time that ever I was forced to scold,' know the hidden workings

226

of his own heart? His purposes loom on him only when they are being accomplished. And surely Shakespeare has taken care that we shall understand him, without our being compelled to invent processes of mind for him; surely, the crucial words are the last which Coriolanus speaks to his mother, wife, and friends when he leaves the gates of Rome.

> While I remain above the ground you shall
> Hear from me still, and never of me aught
> But what is like me formerly.

Is not that tragic irony of the finest? The monstrous thing that Coriolanus is to do is 'like him formerly.' He who knows nothing of himself may mean it as Menenius understood it, 'That's worthily'; but we, who have watched his blind, angry blundering bring to nothing the considered purposes his friends have fixed upon him, know that the former self, like which he will remain, is a thing of impulse only, of pride and anger and resentment and courage. The Tribunes provoked him and he tried to kill them; Rome has provoked him and he will try to kill it. We know; he does not, and he is far more surprised than we are to find himself entering Antium. His brief soliloquy—his only one in the play—gives us the exact measure and quality of his surprise. 'O world, thy slippery turns!' It seems to him odd and strange that he should be seeking out Aufidius.

> So, fellest foes
> Whose passions and whose plots have broke their sleep
> To take the one the other, by some chance,
> Some trick not worth an egg, shall grow dear friends
> And interjoin their issues.

The incredible change in his actions is to him just the result of 'some trick not worth an egg.' He cannot understand it; he can see no more of himself than his actions; and when, confronted with Aufidius, he finds that his action needs some explanation, he instinctively reshapes the immediate past to his purpose. The friends who have tried to protect him and to prevent his suicide, who have offered to share his exile, suddenly become 'the dastard nobles who have all forsook me.' True, that is in Plutarch. But what Shakespeare has done is what

Plutarch could never do—to put before us the living man whose thoughts and words have always been the servants of his impulses alone. Shakespeare has omitted all that Plutarch says about Coriolanus's calculations and plans.

> Whereupon, he thought it his best waye, first to stirre up the Volsces against them (the Romans) knowing they were yet able enough in strength and riches to encounter them, notwithstanding their former losses they had receyved not long before and that their power was not so much impaired, as their malice and desire was increased, to be revenged of the Romaines.

Shakespeare takes all such calculation away from Coriolanus. Instinct sends him to Aufidius: in that he is 'like himself formerly.' 'Like himself formerly,' he suddenly yields to his mother and wife; 'like himself formerly,' he dies.

Coriolanus is the drama, and since he is perfectly presented, the drama is all but perfect. But the weakness of Aufidius remains, and we cannot help speculating how Shakespeare came to fumble with him. Perhaps we may suggest a reason. In Plutarch's story, Aufidius appears on the scene only after Coriolanus has been exiled. We imagine that when Shakespeare first read through the story in North and shaped it as a drama in his mind, he had a clear conception of the part Aufidius was to play as the man of hate and conspiracy. When he came to write the play, with his eyes fixed even more closely upon North's book than they had been during the writing of *Antony and Cleopatra* a year before, he followed his own conception of Aufidius during the first act. There was nothing in North to change it; Aufidius simply did not appear. But when he reached Coriolanus's exile, and Aufidius made his entry into North, he found a different Aufidius from the one he had conceived. Instead of a man poisoned by jealousy, he found a chivalrous enemy—'a man of great minde.' Plutarch's Aufidius is said, indeed, to hate Coriolanus; but it is the hate of one enemy for another; and there is something sportsmanlike, schoolboyish even in their rivalry. 'Many times in battels where they met, they were ever at the encounter one against another, like lusty coragious youths, striving in all emulation of honour.

To this suggestion Shakespeare unconsciously succumbed, at a moment when he was following North's language more closely than ever. He forgot the Aufidius he had presented two long acts ago, the Aufidius who had declared his nature thus:

> My valour's poison'd
> With only suffering stain by him . . .
> Where I find him, were it
> At home, upon my brother's guard, even there,
> Against the hospitable canon, would I
> Wash my fierce hand in's heart. . . .

Instead of this, Aufidius now becomes Coriolanus's impulsive counterpart. Shakespeare gives him a magnificent speech:

> Know thou first
> I loved the maid I married; never man
> Sigh'd truer breath; but that I see thee here
> Thou noble thing? more dances my rapt heart
> Than when I first my wedded mistress saw
> Bestride my threshold.

There is no hint of Aufidius's wonderful words in North. But Shakespeare could not resist North's suggestion of 'the emulation of honour.' The noble rivalry still exists. And yet, when he first presented Aufidius, he had used that very phrase to show that Aufidius's nobility was a thing of the past. 'Mine emulation hath not that honour in't it had.' But the temptation was too great. Back comes all the honour to Aufidius's emulation. We are given a moving and magnificent scene. But the two Aufidiuses can never now be reconciled. The poisoned plotter has to carry on the action of the play to its tragic end; but it is the generous opponent who lives in our minds, the man who could no more have suborned assassins to murder Coriolanus than he could have resisted Coriolanus's swift appeal: 'Pray you, Stand to me in this cause!' All through the fifth act we feel that Shakespeare does not know what to do with Aufidius, and in the final scene the conflict of the two characters who bear one name is manifest and unresolved. Aufidius has deliberately plotted Coriolanus's murder, and played even more cold-bloodedly than the Tribunes upon his temper to sting him to an outburst. Suddenly he changes parts again. He becomes the chivalrous enemy.

> My rage is gone,
> And I am struck with sorrow.

Perhaps this attempted analysis of the actual working of Shakespeare's mind in the construction of *Coriolanus* from the material of North's story may appear fanciful; but I believe it gives a coherent psychological explanation of the radical duality in the conception of Aufidius, which has been noticed by many critics before me. As Mr. R. H. Case puts it.

> On the whole, Aufidius can be understood as well as des· pised; but the delineation of the character does not satisfy, and leaves the impression of an unpleasing task, accomplished with as little trouble as possible. It is in contrast with the careful presentation of the Tribunes.

But it is difficult to leave it at that. At one moment, at least, Shakespeare spent all the force of his poetic genius on putting an heroic Aufidius before us, in his speech to Coriolanus; and Shakespeare was not in the habit of shrinking from 'unpleasant tasks' (in Mr. Case's sense of 'unpleasant,' anyhow): he did not flinch from Iago. When we remember that two acts and a half intervene between the first presentation of Aufidius's character and his reappearance; that at the time of his reappearance Shakespeare was working with his eyes glued to the book; and that the phrase 'emulation of honour' had been as it were a key-word that stuck in his brain from his first reading of North—then, we believe, it becomes probable that under the immediate influence of North, Shakespeare reverted to a conception of Aufidius which had really been dismissed to the past by Aufidius's speech in Act I, sc. 10, and which was inconsistent with his original idea of that dramatic action of the play. Then, perhaps, we may value Aufidius's speech in Act IV, sc. 5, as something more than the most splendid piece of poetry in a play full of splendid poetry—as an indication of when and how and for what cause Shakespeare's human instincts triumphed over his artistic purposes.

Of the other characters besides Virgilia, to whom we will

return, there is little that is new to be said. But there is a correspondence in the play which seems to have escaped attention, though it reveals the subtlety of Shakespeare's characterisation. At the very beginning of the first scene he suggests the peculiar relation between Coriolanus and his mother. 'Though soft-conscienced men,' says the First Citizen, 'can be content to say it was for his country, *he did it to please his mother* and to be partly proud.' We call this nowadays the Œdipus complex. But what is amazing is the way Shakespeare conveys that Coriolanus and Volumnia together are one being—Volumnia the mind and purpose, Coriolanus the body and strength. Hence the subtlety of his creation of Virgilia. There is really no place for her in the play; if she is to be given at all, she must be given in a hundred words. But Virgilia is a being apart. The real and binding unity is that between mother and son. At a like moment Shakespeare even makes them use the same phrase. When Coriolanus has been banished, Volumnia in a frenzy of rage waylays the Tribunes, and cries:

> I would my son
> Were in Arabia and thy tribe before him,
> His good sword in his hand!

When Coriolanus is at bay in Antium in the final scene he also cries:

> O that I had him
> With six Aufidiuses and more, his tribe,
> To use my lawful sword!

Whether the repetition was deliberate, calculated art, who can tell? It does not matter, for if it was involuntary, it is another proof of Shakespeare's instinctive feeling of the blood-bond of temper between mother and son.

§

We can see clearly enough why *Coriolanus* should be that among Shakespeare's greater plays which is most neglected by the public, and therefore the least familiar to the stage. It is not so easy to undersand why it should have been so neglected by the critics, unless perhaps they are not quite so immune from the effects of instinctive sympathy as in theory they ought to be. By the critics I mean the true literary critics, not the textual 'philologers'. These have been busy enough, sometimes to good effect, as with the whole line which they have neatly restored from North's Plutarch, but at least as often in a spirit perhaps best described as one of slight impatience with poetry. This is, however, not the occasion to catalogue the things they have done which they ought not to have done; but only to try to show that they have also left undone a few things that they ought to have done. I have no desire to shiver a lance in open battle with the editors; I only ask their leave to ride to the rescue of an all but vanished lady to whom they have had no time to stretch out a helping hand.

All that needs to be premised is the simple fact that *Coriolanus* was first printed in the Folio of 1623, and that we have no other authority for the text. On the whole we may say that the Folio text is careless enough, although I believe that— obvious misprints apart—it is at least as near to Shakespeare's original as most modern recensions, which take us much farther away by some of their readings as they bring us nearer to it by others. The most persistent weakness of the Folio *Coriolanus* is the haphazard distribution of lines among the speakers. One of the most palpable of these blunders has been rectified by common consent. In Act III (Sc. i, l. 237) when Menenius is trying hard to persuade Coriolanus to moderate his contemptuous language towards the plebs, the Folio gives him these impossible words:

I would they were barbarians, as they are,
Though in Rome litter'd: not Romans, as they are not,
Though calved i' th' porch o' th' Capitol:

It is as certain that Menenius did not speak them as it is certain that Coriolanus did. They have been properly restored to the hero. The Folio *Coriolanus* then, although the true and authentic original, is far from impeccable.

So much by way of preamble to the attempt at rescue.

Of all the characters in *Coriolanus* one alone can be said to be truly congenial; and she is the least substantial of them all. Virgilia. Coriolanus's wife, though she is present throughout the whole of four scenes, speaks barely a hundred words. But a sudden, direct light is cast upon her by a lovely phrase when Coriolanus welcomes her on his triumphant return from Corioli as 'My gracious silence!' Magical words! They give substance to our fleeting, fading glimpses of a vision which seems to tremble away from the clash of arms and pride that reverberates through the play. Behind the haughty warrior and his Amazonian mother, behind the vehement speech of this double Lucifer, the exquisite, timid spirit of Virgilia shrinks out of sight into the haven of her quiet home. One can almost hear the faint click of the door behind her as it shuts her from the noise of brawling tongues. Yet at moments in her presence, and in the memory of her presence, Coriolanus becomes another and a different being. It is true we may listen in vain for other words so tender as 'My gracious silence!' from his lips. But in the heat of victorious battle, when Coriolanus would clasp Cominius in his arms for joy, he discovers in himself another splendid phrase to remember his happiness with Virgilia.

> Oh! let me clip ye
> In arms as sound as when I woo'd, in heart
> As merry, as when our nuptial day was done
> And tapers burned to bedward.

And even in the anguish of the final struggle between his honour and his heart, when his wife comes with his mother to intercede for Rome, it is in the very accents of passionate devotion that he cries to Virgilia,

> Best of my flesh!
> Forgive my tyranny; but do not say,
> 'For that forgive our Romans.' Oh! a kiss
> Long as my exile, sweet as my revenge!
> Now, by the jealous queen of heaven, that kiss
> I carried from thee, dear, and my true lip
> Hath virgin'd it e'er since.

In the proud, unrelenting man of arms these sudden softenings are wonderful. They conjure up the picture of a more reticent and self-suppressed Othello, and we feel that, to strike to the heart through Coriolanus's coat of mail, it needed an unfamiliar beauty of soul, a woman whose delicate nature stood apart, untouched by the broils and furies of her lord's incessant battling with the Roman people and the enemies of Rome.

In the play Virgilia speaks barely a hundred words. But they are truly the speech of a 'gracious silence', as precious and revealing as they are rare. She appears first (Act I, Sc. 3) in her own house, sitting silent at her sewing. Coriolanus has gone to the wars. Volumnia tries to kindle her with something of her own Amazonian ecstasy at the thought of men in battle. 'I tell thee, daughter, I sprang not more in joy at first hearing he was a man child than now in first seeing he had proved himself a man.' Virgilia's reply, the first words she speaks in the play, touch to the quick of the reality of war and her own unquiet mind.

But had he died in the business, madam; how then?

The thoughts of her silence thus revealed, she says no more until chattering Valeria, for all the world like one of the fashionable ladies in Colonel Repington's diary, is announced. She has come to drag her out to pay calls. Virgilia tries to withdraw. Volumnia will not let her, and even while the maid is in the room waiting to know whether she may show Valeria in, she bursts into another ecstatic vision of her son in the midst of battle, 'his bloody brow with his mailed hand then wiping.' Again Virgilia reveals herself.

His bloody brow? O Jupiter, no blood!

Valeria enters on a wave of small talk. She has seen Virgilia's little boy playing. The very image of his father; 'has such a confirmed countenance'. She had watched him chase a butterfly, catching it and letting it go, again and again. 'He did so set his teeth and tear it. Oh I warrant how he mammocked it!"

Volum. One on's father's moods.

Val. Indeed, la, 'tis a noble child.

Virg. A crack, madam.

'An *imp*, madam!' The meaning leaps out of the half-contemptuous word. Don't call him a noble child for his childish brutality. It pains, not rejoices Virgilia. Nor, for all the persuasions of Volumnia and Valeria, will she stir out of the

234

house. She does not want society; she cannot visit 'the good lady that lies in'. She is as firm as she is gentle.

'Tis not to save labour, nor that I want love.

Simply that she is anxious and preoccupied. She will not 'turn her solemness out o' door'; she cannot. Coriolanus is at the wars.

So, in two dozen words and a world of unspoken contrast Virgilia is given to us: her horror of brutality and bloodshed, her anxiety for her husband, her reticence, her firmness. She is not a bundle of nerves, but she is full of the aching fears of love. Truly, 'a gracious silence'.

She next appears when the news is come that Coriolanus has triumphed (Act II, Sc. 1). Volumnia and Valeria are talking with Menenius. She stands aside listening. He is sure to be wounded, says Menenius; he always is. She breaks out: 'Oh, no, no, no!' She retires into her silence again while Volumnia and Menenius talk proudly on. 'In troth, there's wondrous things spoken of him,' says chattering Valeria. Virgilia murmurs: 'The gods grant them true!' 'True! Pow, wow!' says Volumnia, in hateful scorn: one can see her sudden turn, hear her rasping voice. Virgilia is not one of the true breed of Roman wives and mothers. And indeed she is not. She is thinking of wounds, not as glorious marks of bravery, but as the mutilated body of the man she adores. Wounds, wounds! They talk of nothing but wounds. Virgilia suffers in silence. Coriolanus is wounded. That to her is a wounded world.

Coriolanus enters, crowned with the oaken garland and swathed in bandages, unrecognizable. He kneels before his mother. Then he sees Virgilia, standing apart, weeping silently. These are the words of the Folio text. Only the spelling has been modernized; the punctuation has been left untouched.

Corio. My gracious silence, hail:
    Would'st thou have laugh'd, had I come coffin'd home,
    That weep'st to see me triumph? Ah my dear,
    Such eyes the widows in Corioli wear
    And mothers that lack sons.
Mene. Now the Gods crown thee.

Com. And live you yet? Oh my sweet Lady, pardon.
Volum. I know not where to turn.

Oh welcome home: and welcome General,
And y'are welcome all.

The first two of these speeches and their speakers contain no difficulty. But, obviously, 'And live you yet? Oh, my sweet Lady, pardon,' does not belong to Cominius. On his lips it is nonsense. The editors have resolved the problem by giving the line to Coriolanus, and the following speech of Volumnia to Valeria. Coriolanus is supposed to say to Menenius, 'And live you yet!' then, suddenly catching sight of Valeria, to beg her pardon for not having seen her before.

We have a free hand in disposing of the line. There is no objection to Volumnia's speech being given to Valeria, whose effusive manner it suits better. But to make Coriolanus surprised that Menenius is still alive is pointless; he had no reason to suppose that the armchair hero was dead. Moreover, to make him turn to Valeria, and say, 'Oh, my sweet Lady, pardon,' is to give the great warrior the manners of a carpet knight.

Now think of the relation between Virgilia and Coriolanus; remember how her imagination has been preoccupied by his wounds; see her in imagination weeping at the pitiful sight of her wounded husband—and read the lines through without regard to the speakers. It will, I believe, occur to any one with an instinct for psychology that 'And live you yet?' may take up Coriolanus' previous words. 'Ah, my dear,' he has said, 'it is the women who have no husbands who weep as you do.' Then, and not till then, Virgilia breaks silence. 'And live you yet!' And are you really my husband? Is this thing of bandages the lord of my heart? At her sudden, passionate words, Coriolanus understands her tears. He has a glimpse of the anguish of her love. He has been an unimaginative fool. 'Oh, my sweet Lady, pardon!' This, I suggest, is the way the passage should be read:

Corio.   Ah my dear,
Such eyes the widows in Corioli wear
And mothers that lack sons.
Mene. Now the gods crown thee!

236

Virg. And live you yet?
Corio. Oh, my sweet lady, pardon . . .
Val. I know not where to turn.

Virgilia appears again in the scene following Coriolanus'
banishment (Act IV, Sc. 2) Here the alterations necessary are
self-evident, and it is difficult to understand why they have not
been made before. Again the test of reading through the short
scene with an imaginative realization of Virgilia must be
applied. Again her exquisite timidity of speech must be contrasted, as Shakespeare deliberately contrasted it, with Volumnia's headstrong and contemptuous anger. It will then, I
believe, be plain that of Volumnia's final words,

Anger's my meat; I sup upon my self
And so shall starve with feeding. Come, let's go.
Leave this faint puling and lament as I do,
In anger, Juno-like. Come, come, come,

the last two lines are addressed to Virgilia alone. Besides
Volumnia herself only Menenius is there. The lines cannot be
spoken to him. Only Virgilia remains. She is not angry, but
sad, at Coriolanus' banishment, just as in his triumph she was
sad, not joyful; and just as then, Volumnia scorns her for her
weakness.

Now read again the Folio text, which is that of the modern
editions, of lines 11-28. Volumnia meets the two tribunes who
have been the prime movers in her son's banishment:

Volum. Oh y'are well met:
   Th' hoarded plague a' th' gods requite your love.   (10)
Mene. Peace, peace, be not so loud.
Volum. If that I could for weeping, you should hear,
   Nay, and you shall heare some. Will you be gone?
Virg. You shall stay too: I would I had the power
   To say so to my husband.   (15)
Sicin. Are you mankind?
Volum. Aye, fool, is that a shame. Note but this, fool,
   Was not a man my father? Had'st thou foxship
   To banish him that struck more blows for Rome
   Than thou hast spoken words.

Sicin. Oh blessed Heavens!   (20)

Volum. More noble blows than ever thou wise words.
  And for Rome's good, I'll tell thee what: yet go:
  Nay, but thou shalt stay too: I would my son
  Were in Arabia, and thy tribe before him,
  His good sword in his hand.   (25)

Sicin. What then?

Virg. What then? He'ld make an end of thy posterity

Volum. Bastards, and all.
  Good man, the wounds that he does bear for Rome!

It is obvious that the peremptory 'You shall stay too!' (1. 14) is not spoken by Virgilia. It is as completely discordant with her character, and with Volumnia's description of her behaviour during the scene ('this faint puling') as it is accordant with the character of Volumnia. Volumnia forces first one, then the other tribune to stay; we can see her clutch them by the sleeve, one in either of her nervous hands. At her words Virgilia interposes a sighing aside, 'I would I had the power to say so to my husband!'

It is equally clear that Virgilia cannot possibly have indulged in the imagination of line 27. 'What then? He'd make an end of thy posterity.' There is no stop at the end of the line in the Folio; it runs on to the next half line; and the whole line and a half undoubtedly belong to Volumnia. A simple transposition of the rubrics is all that is needed.

Volum.   What then?
  He'ld make an end of thy posterity,
  Bastards and all.

Virg. Good man, the wounds that he does bear for Rome!

It is another sighing aside and another indication that Virgilia is haunted by the memory of those wounds she could not bear to see. Unless these asides are restored to her, and the brutal words taken away, quite apart from the violation of her character, Volumnia's final sneer at her 'faint puling' is ridiculous.

Virgilia appears for the last time as the silent participant in Volumnia's embassy of intercession. For the first time and only time a bodily vision of her beauty is given to us, when Coriolanus cries:

> What is that curt'sy worth? Or those dove's eyes
> Which can make gods forsworn? I melt, and am not
> Of stronger earth than others.

She has no need of words to make her appeal; her eyes speak for her. She says simply:

> My lord and husband!
>
> *Corio.* These eyes are not the same I wore in Rome.
> *Virg.* The sorrow that delivers us thus changed
>   Makes you think so.
> *Corio.*   Like a dull actor now,
> I have forgot my part, and I am out,
> Even to a full disgrace. Best of my flesh,
> Forgive my tyranny: but do not say,
> 'For that forgive our Romans.' Oh! a kiss
> Long as my exile, sweet as my revenge!
> Now, by the jealous queen of heaven, that kiss
> I carried from thee, dear; and my true lip
> Hath virgin'd it e'er since.

After this Virgilia speaks but a single sentence more. Volumnia ends her pleading with an impassioned adjuration to her son:

>   For myself son,
> I purpose not to wait on Fortune, till
> These wars determine: if I cannot persuade thee
> Rather to show a noble grace to both parts
> Than seek the end of one, thou shalt no sooner
> March to assault thy country, than to tread—
> Trust to't, thou shalt not—on thy mother's womb
> That brought thee to this world.
> *Virg.*   Ay, and mine
> That brought you forth this boy, to keep your name
> Living to time.

Virgilia's words contain much in little space. They, her last words in the play, are the first in which she shows herself at one with her husband's mother. Always before, Volumnia has been angry, impatient, and contemptuous towards Virgilia;

239

and Virgilia had held her peace without yielding an inch of
ground to Volumnia's vehemence. We have felt throughout
that they are the embodiments of two opposed spirits—of pride
and love. Not that Volumnia's pride has now changed to love;
it is the same pride of race that moves her, the fear of disgrace
to a noble name:

> The end of war's uncertain; but this is certain,
> That, if thou conquer Rome, the benefit
> Which thou shalt thereby reap is such a name
> Whose repetition will be dogged with curses,
> Whose chronicle thus writ: 'The man was noble
> But with his last attempt he wip'd it out,
> Destroy'd his country, and his name remains
> To the ensuing age abhorr'd.'

But now these spirits of love and pride are reconciled; for
once they make the same demand. Volumnia pleads that her
son shall remember honour, Virgilia that her husband shall
remember mercy. The double appeal is too strong. Coriolanus
yields to it, and pays the penalty.

Not one of the readjustments suggested in this essay calls
for the alteration of a single word in the text of the Folio. They
consist solely in a redistribution of words among the speakers,
and in the most complicated instance a redistribution of some
kind has long since been seen to be necessary and long since
been made. I venture to think that together they will help to
disengage the true outline of one of Shakespeare's most delicate
minor heroines. There was no place for a Desdemona in the
story of Coriolanus; but in a few firm touches Shakespeare has
given us a woman whose silence we can feel to be the unspoken
judgment on the pride of arms and the pride of race which are
the theme of the play.

For it is surely not against the democratic idea that
Coriolanus is tried and found wanting. In spite of Signor
Croce's assurance to the contrary, it is impossible to believe
that the contempt for the city mob with which the play is
penetrated was not partly shared by Shakespeare himself.
The greatest writers strive to be impersonal, and on the whole
they achieve impersonality; but, though they carve out an image

that is not wholly like themselves, they cannot work wholly against the grain of their own convictions. Prejudice will out. And the aversion from the city mob which is continually expressed in Shakespeare' work and comes to a head in *Coriolanus* was indubitably his own. It is indeed less plausible to deny this than it would be to argue that at a time when his genius was seizing on themes of a greater tragic scope it was his sympathy with the antiplebeian colour of the Coriolanus story that led Shakespeare to choose it for his play.

This is not a question of Shakespeare's political views. We do not know what they were, and we do no more than guess at them. Signor Croce is thus far right. But when he goes on to assure us that it is a wild goose chase to look to discover where Shakespeare's sympathies lay in the world in which he lived, we can point to the knowledge we actually have of every great writer. We do know their sympathies. It may be an illegitimate knowledge, but the laws it violates are laws of Signor Croce's own devising. It is his own logical fiat that holds the kingdoms of aesthetic and the practical asunder. In fact, there is no dividing line between them. A writer's predispositions in practical life do constantly colour his aesthetic creation, and every great writer who has been conscious of his activity has either confessed the fact or gloried in it.

We know that Shakespeare disliked the city mob. If we care to know why we have only to exercise a little imagination and picture to ourselves the finest creative spirit in the world acting in his own plays before a pitful of uncomprehending, base mechanicals.

Alas, 'tis true, I have gone here and there
And made myself a motley to the view,
Gored mine own thoughts, sold cheap what is most dear

The man who used that terrible phrase, who 'gored his own thoughts' to wring shillings from the pockets of the greasy, grinning crowd in front of him, has no cause to love them: and Shakespeare did not. He was an aristocrat, not in the political sense, but as every man of fine nerves who shrinks from contact with the coarse-nerved is an aristocrat, as Anton Tchehov was an aristocrat when he wrote, 'Alas, I shall never

241

be a Tolstoyan. In women I love beauty above all things, and in the history of mankind, culture expressed in carpets, spring carriages, and keenness of wit.'

Shakespeare could not therefore measure Coriolanus against the democratic idea in which he did not believe; nor could he pit the patriotic idea against him, for Coriolanus was immune from a weakness for his country. It is domestic love that pierces his armour and inflicts the mortal wound. And perhaps in Shakespeare's mind the power of that love was manifested less in the speech of the vehement and eloquent Volumnia than in the silence of the more delicate woman to whom I have attempted to restore a few of her precious words.

§

Finally, there are one or two points of textural criticism upon which I have suggestions to make. In Act I, Sc. 4, l. 40, the Folio text runs thus:

> Come on,
> If you'l stand fast, we'l beat them to their wives
> As they us to our trenches followes
>> *Another alarum and Marcius follows them to gates,*
>> *and is shut in.*

It is important to note that this stage-direction is altered in the modern editions, where it appears as *Another alarum. The fight is renewed. The Volsces retire into Corioles, and Marcius follows them to the gates.* Whether the new direction is better is of no moment; the point is that it is different. The real question at issue is whether Shakespeare wrote 'As they us to our trenches followes.' The rhythm is wretched in itself, and doubly wretched as the conclusion to a soldier's desperate appeal in battle. Nor is it improved, save in a purely mechanical sense, by reading 'followed.' The dramatic force is frittered away by the rhythmical debility. The same incident is referred to a little further on by a Messenger ('I saw our party to their trenches *driven*'), and by Cominius ('Where is that slave which told me they had *beat* you to your trenches?'). Nothing so weak as 'followes' there. Is it conceivable that Shakespeare should have made the prime actor in the heat of battle use the flabby word in the flabby line?   At all events, no one will deny that—

> Come on,
> If you'l stand fast, we'l beat them to their wives
> As they us to our trenches!

is better poetry, better Shakespeare, and better drama.   Have we the right to improve the Folio?   If we take the Folio stage-direction, we find the suspect word in it.   If we count spaces as letters, the distance from 'As' to 'followes' in the text is twenty-seven letters; while the distance from 'Another' to 'followes' in the stage-direction is also twenty-seven letters. Surely the conclusion is that in the copy from which the play was set up 'followes' came immediately after 'trenches,' but in the line below.   The change of the stage-direction has concealed the process of the corruption.

When Cominius is celebrating Coriolanus's exploits in the Senate, he makes this stirring speech:

> His sword, death's stamp,
> Where it did marke, it took from face to foot:
> He was a thing of blood, whose every motion
> Was timed with dying cries; alone he entered
> The mortal gate of the city which he painted
> With shunless destiny; aidless came off,
> And with a sudden reinforcement struck
> Corioles like a planet.

That is, at least, what the Folio makes him say.   But Tyrwhitt conjectured that the first two lines should read:

> His sword, death's stamp,
>
> Where it did marke, it took: from face to foot:
> He was a thing of blood.

Since then, all the editors have followed Tyrwhitt.   It may seem that the change in punctuation is trivial.   But here the meaning of the passage is changed by it, and changed, I think, for the worse.   For the crucial passage to elucidate this elaborate metaphor is Hamlet I, i. 162.   'The nights are wholesome; then no planets strike, No fairy takes.'   'Takes' is in its good Elizabethan sense of 'infects.'   'Struck Corioles like a planet' shows that the metaphor is continued to the end. Coriolanus's sword infects 'from face to foot.' He is 'a thing of blood,' not in the sense that he was covered with blood, but like the Avenging Angel. The 'shunless destiny' with which 'he paints the mortal gate of the city' is a reminiscence of the plague-mark on the door of an infected house. And finally he 'struck Corioles like a planet', because 'planet-stricken' was the name for sudden death to which the doctors could assign no cause. The metaphor is splendidly sustained, and it is simply because Tyrwhitt did not recognise that 'takes' bore the still familiar sense of vaccination 'taking' that he altered the punctuation of the passage, and made it difficult for us to understand it.

With less conviction, I offer a suggestion for the famous crux:

Fortunes blows
When most struck home, being gentle wounded, craves
A noble cunning.

Dr. Johnson explained it ingeniously. 'The sense is: When Fortune strikes her hardest blows, to be wounded and yet continue calm requires a generous policy.' Apart from the intolerably awkward syntax, the use of 'gentle' is unparalleled; and, after the straightforward lines that precede, the sudden tangle brings us up with an unpleasant jar. When Shakespeare overrides syntax, he usually makes his sense clear. Moreover, Coriolanus is quoting his mother's proverbs. The three before have the simplicity of proverbs; this one is a riddle. I cannot believe that Shakespeare wrote the lines as they stand. The natural sense in the context is, 'Fortune blows when most struck home, being . . . , crave a noble cunning.' The three words beginning with 'being' represent a phrase in apposition to, and explanatory of, 'Fortune's blows when most struck home.' We suggest, diffidently, that behind the meaningless 'gentle' is concealed the adjective 'tentles' (tentless, i.e. impossible to probe), and that the line originally read:

When most struck home, being tentless wounds do crave
A noble cunning.

They are wounds beyond the skill of the ordinary surgeon.

Shakespeare in this martial play was particularly fond of

using the word 'to tent' metaphorically, *see* i., 9, 31, and in particular iii., 1, 235. "'Tis a sore upon us you cannot tent yourself.'

Of minor importance textually, but of some significance for the psychology of Coriolanus, are two changes from the Folio made by all the editors. In iii., 1, 91 Coriolanus breaks out at Sicinius's word 'shall remain.'

COR.:   Shall remain!
Hear you this Triton of the minnows? Mark you
His absolute 'shall'?
    COM.:   'Twas from the canon.
    COR.:   'Shall!'
O God! but most unwise patricians: why
You grave but reckless senators. . . .

Theobald's change of 'O God!' to 'O good, most unwise . . .' has been universally followed. The original sounds to me rather more like Coriolanus. Further in ii, 2, 74, Coriolanus says to Brutus, the Tribune:

You sooth'd not, therefore hurt not; but your people
I love them as they weigh—
    MENENIUS: Pray, now, sit down!

For some inscrutable reason the dash of the Folio has been replaced by a full stop. Dashes to mark interruption are not so plentiful in the Folio that we can afford to throw them away. Menenius, as ever, tries to stop Coriolanus from his furious outburst. We could supply Coriolanus's unspoken words from this very play. Probably they were: 'That's lesser than a little!'

[1921-22]

THE MORTAL MOON

Lately Dr. Leslie Hotson as put forward the novel and astonishing theory that Shakespeare's famous Sonnet 107 containing the cryptic line

The mortal Moone hath her eclipse indur'de

should be dated in 1588 or very soon after, because "the mortal Moone" refers to the crescent formation of the Spanish Armada.

The theory is surprising in itself, for this sonnet is certainly one of Shakespeare's latest, and the consequence of accepting the theory would be that we should also accept that the bulk of Shakespeare's sonnets were written before 1588—that is to say, when Shakespeare was twenty-four, which is incredible to me. What is even more surprising is that the theory has encountered very little serious objection. The case against it is in danger of going by default.

If Sonnet 107 was written in 1588 or thereabouts it is possible that the phrase "the mortal Moone" might have been taken as referring to the Spanish Armada. Even if the sonnet had been written then, I do not believe the identification would have been anything like so natural and inevitable as Dr. Hotson claims. But to make this questionable identification the ground for asserting that the sonnet was written in 1588 seems to me quite extravagant.

Hitherto the general consensus of Shakespeare criticism has assigned the sonnet, rather hesitatingly, to 1603, on the ground that it contains a specific reference on the death of Queen Elizabeth and to the liberation from prison of the Earl of Southampton, which occurred on the accession of King James.

I do not agree with this: but still less do I agree with Dr. Hotson's proposed interpretation and dating. I think the general consensus is right in taking the natural meaning of "the mortal Moone" to an Elizabethan mind as Queen Elizabeth; but I think it is mistaken in assuming that there is any reference in the sonnet to Shakespeare's friend being liberated from prison. It is immaterial for the purposes of this argument whether Shakespeare's friend was the Earl of Southampton, though I believe he was.

246

What is neglected, equally by Dr. Hotson and the critics before him, is the plain and important fact that the sonnet is not isolated, and cannot be interpreted in isolation. It is squarely and firmly set among a sequence of sonnets (100-112) which are obviously connected. So that if the sonnet is dated as early as 1588 or as late as 1603, we must either date these adjoining sonnets equally early or equally late—which involves us in insuperable difficulties—or conclude, against the evidence of our senses, that this group of sonnets is a mere jumble arranged in no coherent order at all.

It is necessary to examine Sonnet 107 carefully in its context of Sonnets 100 to 112. The first four sonnets of the group have all a similar burden. Sonnet 100 begins:

> Where art thou, Muse, that thou forgetst so long
> To speak of that which gives thee all thy might?

And it, and the following three, are all apologies for a long period of silence. Shakespeare's excuses are various and fanciful. In Sonnet 104 he tells how his love for his friend has lasted now three full years. In Sonnet 105 he defends himself for sticking always to the one theme: the beauty, the kindness and the loyalty of his friend: which comes, very naturally, at a moment when he is trying to rouse his muse again. In Sonnet 106 he declares that all beauties praised by the poets of old did but prefigure the beauty of his friend; while he who has the prefigured beauty before him lacks a tongue to praise it duly. The order of these seven sonnets is eminently natural. as will be evident to any one who reads them with care and responsiveness.

Then comes the disputed Sonnet 107:

> Not mine owne feares, nor the prophetick soule
> Of the wide world. dreaming on things to come,
> Can yet the lease of my true love controule,
> Supposed as forfeit to a confin'd doome.
> The mortall Moone hath her eclipse indur'de,
> And the sad Augurs mock their own presage,
> Incertainties now crowne them-selves assur'd,
> And peace proclaims olives of endless age,

> Now with the drops of this most balmie time,
> My love lookes fresh, and death to me subscribes,
> Since spight of him I'll live in this poore rime,
> While he insults ore dull and speechlesse tribes.
>> And thou in this shalt find thy monument.
>> When tyrants crests and tombs of brasse are spent.

I will postpone considering its meaning for the moment, for the primary concern is to grasp the context in which it is set

Sonnet 108 asks. 'Is there anything more he *can* write to express either his own love, or his friend's deserts?' Yet he must go on repeating his song like the Lord's Prayer. Their love, though old, is young. Where one would have expected it to die, it lives on undiminished.

Sonnet 109 opens a new theme. Shakespeare replies to definite reproaches of his friend for neglecting him—a neglect which naturally seems to be that for which Shakespeare excused himself in Sonnets 100-103. He now confesses that absence did seem 'to qualify his flame', but denies that he was disloyal at heart. 110-112, famous sonnets all of them, confess that he had, during this absence, 'made old offences of affections new', that 'public means' had bred in him 'public manners', and he sighs 'to be renewed'. But he cares not what men say, now that 'the love and pity' of his friend fill the impression

> Which vulgar scandal stamped upon my brow.

At this point a well-defined and extremely important group of sonnets ends. This group of sonnets is quite coherent. The sequence is natural, the psychological process revealed convincing. First, an acknowledgement that his poetry in praise of his friend had dropped off; then a backward look over the three years of their friendship; then, a certain embarrassment at beginning his sonnets again; then, Sonnet 107; then a delighted but slightly wondering recognition that their love had lasted, though length of time and appearances would point against it; then an embarrassed confession of disloyalty in absence, and of scandal which his friend's love has forgiven. The story is clear enough. An absence, a neglect to write poetry about his friend, a fear that his friend would not forgive, a meeting, a delighted discovery that his friend was still fond of him, and an awkward—but moving—defence of himself for his apparent defection. In this story Sonnet 107 appears at a crucial point. Does it belong to it, or not? It seems evident that it does.

But first let us observe a detail of vocabulary. The word 'confined' appears in three sonnets of this little group and nowhere else in the whole of the sonnets. The detail is of some importance. It not only points to the sonnets having been composed at the same time; but it gives a hint towards the interpretation of the word in Sonnet 107, where its meaning is much disputed. "Confined" in Sonnet 105: 'my verse to constancy confined', and in Sonnet 110: 'A God in love, to whom I am confined'—clearly means 'limited'. There is no sense of irksomeness in the limitation, no hint of imprisonment.

With this preparation we may undertake the interpretation of the first four lines of Sonnet 107:

> Not mine owne feares, nor the prophetick soule
> Of the wide world, dreaming on things to come,
> Can yet the lease of my true love controule,
> Supposed as forfeit to a confined doome.

Naturally, indeed obviously if we have regard to Shakespeare's fondness for legal phrases, it is 'the lease of my true love' and not 'my true love' which has been 'supposed as forfeit'. We may compare, among many other parallels, (1) 'This bond is forfeit'; (2) 'My bonds in thee are all determinate'; (3) 'So should that beauty which you hold in lease Find no determination'. A lease is not subject to imprisonment, but it is always subject to determination; and 'determination' is precisely the meaning here of 'a confined doom', i.e. a sentence of limitation. To imagine that ll. 3-4 mean that Shakespeare's friend has been supposed condemned to imprisonment for life is to show ignorance of the language of the sonnets and a complete neglect of the context of this one in particular. Shakespeare's fears have already been amply explained by the preceding sonnets: he feared, and had good reason for fearing, that the love between him and his friend was at an end. He had indeed supposed it as forfeit to a confined doom. The words are exactly paraphrased by the concluding couplet of the next Sonnet, 108.

> Finding the first conceit of love there bred

249

Where time and outward form would show it dead.

Thus the meaning of the first four lines seems certain. Neither my own apprehensions of its decease, nor even the prophetic dreams of the world-soul itself, can yet set a term to the lease of my true love, which has been supposed to be at an end.'

The 'mortall Moone' of the next four lines has been generally supposed to be Queen Elizabeth. It needs to be emphasized that, if the 'mortall Moone' is the Queen, the natural meaning of

The mortall Moone hath her eclipse indur'de

is not: 'The Queen is dead', but 'The Queen has recovered'. The normal meaning of 'endure' in Shakespeare is 'to suffer and survive'. You endure torments in Shakespeare's language; you do not endure death. The natural meaning of the line, leaving aside the probable reference to Elizabeth, is: 'The mortal Moon has been obscured and now shines as bright as ever', and that meaning is confirmed by the next line:

And the sad Augurs mock their own presage.

Why, unless the moon had recovered from eclipse, should the augurs *mock* their own presage? Otherwise we must suppose they had prophesied prosperity, and were now despondently jeering at their own mistake. Such an interpretation hopelessly conflicts with the following two lines:

Incertainties now crowne them-selves assur'de
And peace proclaims olives of endless age.

The conclusion is that if (as is probable) the reference is to the Queen, it is to her happy recovery, not her death.

The next lines:

Now with the drops of this most balmie time
My love lookes fresh.

mean, simply, 'this time of happiness is like the elixir of youth to my passion';

and death to me subscribes
Since spight of him I'll live in this poore rime
While he insults ore dull and speachlesse tribes.

As my love has triumphed over a threatened death, 'so I have

250

also my own particular triumph over him, in the immortality of my poems'.

> And thou in this shalt find thy monument
> When tyrants' crests and tombs of brasse are spent.

'So, too, my friend triumphs over death in this verse of mine.'

The sonnet thus appears perfectly coherent in itself, and perfectly appropriate in its context. Indeed, the best commentary on it is contained in the surrounding sonnets. The substance of it can be reduced to 'Our love which threatened to die has survived, and no one dares to set a term to it. Just as the Queen herself has recovered from the death which was prophesied for her, and the uncertainties of the greater world are resolved in peace, so our love has recovered and has renewed its youth. Just as our love has survived the threat by death, so we, the two lovers, have each our separate victory over death. I as the writer. he as the hero, of these poems.'

If, thus interpreted, it is read in its place in the sequence of Sonnets 100-112, it seems not difficult to read the story.

It is now three years since Shakespeare met his friend. Shakespeare has been absent a long while; in his absence he has made new friendships, encountered infatuations even, and his flow of sonnets in praise of his friend and their love has been slackened. The friend reminds him of this loss of ardour; and Shakespeare, with an embarrassed conscience, begins again. He feels at once guilty and grateful; guilty, that he has deserved the reminder, and grateful for the proof of his friend's constancy that it gives. They meet again, and to Shakespeare's surprise and joy all is as it was between them: the golden years return. But, when the first joy of meeting is over, Shakespeare has to submit to the just reproaches of his friend, for his behaviour during absence: he excuses himself by saying —with deadly seriousness—that his behaviour is due to his discredited and discreditable profession.

I have been concerned to establish a positive and a negative case. The positive case is that the sonnet fits with perfect appropriateness in its context. The negative case is twofold, namely, that it is unnatural. and does violence to Shakespeare's language to interpret (1) ll. 3-4 as meaning: 'it has been supposed that my friend would die in gaol' and (2) 1. 5 as meaning 'Queen Elizabeth is dead'.

The positive and negative issues are interdependent: for if it could be established that 1. 5 means 'The Queen is dead', it follows that the date of the sonnet is 1603 and the period of just over three years given to the friendship begins in 1599 —to me a nonsensical date.

If we suppose that the friend is Southampton, as I do, the beginning of the friendship was probably in 1593—the year of the dedication of *Venus and Adonis*. That would give, if my interpretation of the sonnet is correct, about 1596 for the date of it. On grounds of style, that date is convincing to me.

On the purely internal evidence which is set out above, I had reached the conclusion that Sonnet 107 was probably written in or about 1596, when Mr. G. B. Harrison showed, in a letter to *The Times Literary Supplement*, that in the year 1596 Queen Elizabeth fell ill and that her illness caused great alarm in England; further that peace was established in France. The complete agreement of Mr. Harrison's purely historical argument with my own internal one I have hitherto held to be as conclusive as such things can be.

Against this weight of evidence Dr. Leslie Hotson's theory seems to me singularly unsubstantial and inconvincing, and I must confess to a mild astonishment that it should have been taken seriously at all. Its consequences are quite intolerable. It would require us to believe that when he was twenty-four, *five* years before the dedication of *Venus and Adonis*, Shakespeare's love for his friend had already lasted three years. Yet the group of sonnets to which Sonnet 107 belongs was manifestly written by a much older man to a younger one. And that psychological impossibility is matched by the stylistic impossibility. If one can believe that Shakespeare wrote Sonnet 107 five years before he wrote *Venus and Adonis*, one can believe anything about Shakespeare.

[1931-1950]